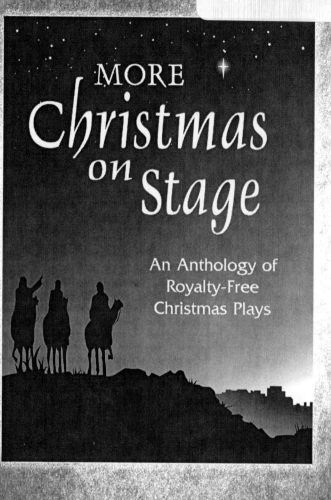

MORE
Christmas
on *Stage*

An Anthology of Royalty-Free Christmas Plays

Edited by Rhonda Wray

MERIWETHER PUBLISHING L[
Colorado Springs, Colorado

Meriwether Publishing Ltd., Publisher
PO Box 7710
Colorado Springs, CO 80933-7710

www.meriwether.com

Editor: Rhonda Wray
Cover design: Jan Melvin

Library of Congress Cataloging-in-Publication Data

More Chrismas on stage : an anthology of royalty-free Christmas plays / edited by Rhonda Wray. — 1st ed.
    p. cm.
ISBN 978-1-56608-151-1
1. Christmas plays, American. 2. Children's plays, American. 3. Young adult drama, American. I. Wray, Rhonda, 1962-
PS627.C57M67 2008
812.008'0334--dc22

                        2008044739

1   2   3   08   09   10

This book is dedicated to Arthur L. Zapel, whose vision, creativity, work ethic and determination launched Meriwether Publishing Ltd and Contemporary Drama Service over forty years ago. I marvel at the steps that took you from writing that first play on the train in Chicago as an advertising executive to creating and overseeing a publishing company in Colorado Springs. Your life inspires and influences us all. Thank you.

Contents

Preface

Christmas play performances are right up there with card-sending, cookie-making, and shopping for gifts as cherished holiday traditions. That you want to do *something* at your church or school is a given — but what? Recognizing the needs that vary from group to group in terms of audience expectations, available talent, and style preferences, we've included a Christmas potluck of choices in this collection of some of our finest Christmas scripts.

Each of these scripts has had its moment on the stage in churches and schools across the country. They all found wide and grateful audiences, so it's our privilege to share them with you here. Their royalty-free status makes them easy on your budget — especially because Christmas programming is an ongoing annual need. This resource book can help you for many years to come. Full of drama? Indeed.

Our talented authors have written scripts for the whole season, from Advent to Epiphany. Their plays encompass many situations and performers in these specific areas:

Casting Requirements

We've included a variety of scripts to fit your personnel, from children to adults, from casts as small as one to a whole Sunday school department or school class, and those from a variety of cultures to explore the richness and diversity of our Christmas celebrations.

Style

This book features the secular and the sacred. It encompasses all denominations and worship style preferences, from contemporary and informal to traditional and elegant. There's a fair share of humor added as well.

Specific Types

Some examples of what you'll find in these pages include dinner theatre and plays inspired by Christmas carols, stories behind the customs of Christmas, and a nod to *The Nutcracker*. There are plays from the perspective of the stable animals, some inquisitive angels, and even trees. And there's our first play ever published, *And the Child Was Born*.

Production Notes at the beginning of each script will tell you, the director, everything you need to know in order to perform the script effectively. All are user-friendly, with minimal rehearsal and staging requirements — because we know the Christmas season is packed full of activities and commitments demanding your time. What is so inspiring is that you will take the printed words herein and turn them into a production uniquely your own, infusing them with your own actors, staging area, costumes, and props.

The movie *Home Alone* refers to Christmas as "the season of perpetual hope." And so it is. When the lights are dimmed and the players take the stage, may you create a respite of reflection and hope in the midst of the to-do lists and busyness of the season to celebrate this birth announcement of the best kind. "Glory to God in the highest, and peace to those on whom his favor rests!"

Advent Sketches

Getting Ready for Christmas
By Paul Neale Lessard

Four contemporary sketches for the Advent Wreath

Production Notes

The four Sundays of Advent are a time of preparation to celebrate both the first and second coming of Jesus Christ. Advent is a time of making ready our hearts and reassessing our lives of faith as we come to the conclusion of yet another year.

The four sketches contained in this playkit are designed to be used in conjunction with the lighting of the Advent Candles. They are written to introduce the theme of each Sunday in Advent. At the beginning of each sketch, the candles on the Advent wreath should be unlit. The lighting of the candle(s) accompanies the reading of the Narrator's part. The actors should be ready to start the sketch as quickly as possible once the candles are lit. The Narrator will give a cue line to effect the transition.

I Can't Wait!
(First Sunday of Advent)

Theme
Waiting, expectation — the Candle of Prophecy.

Synopsis
A family is preparing to spend Christmas with the grandparents. Their child is having a hard time waiting for them to leave, even though the parents have promised that they will be going soon.

Characters
Brian — husband, rather irritable.

Janet — wife, good-humored.

Isaac/Chelsea — son/daughter about four or five. (The gender is not critical to the role. The child is never seen, so this role could be played by an older child with a young voice.)

Narrator

Props
Suitcases, clothes to pack, microwave oven (unplugged) on rolling cart, mug.

1	*(Scene opens with BRIAN and JANET packing the suitcases. One*
2	*could be folding clothes and the other packing. Or an ironing*
3	*board could be set up with one ironing while the other packs. Some*
4	*of the clothes should be piled by the microwave. BRIAN and*
5	*JANET should be packing throughout their entire dialogue. The*
6	*child is Off-stage, in his bedroom, and is never seen, only*
7	*heard — the reverse of how it should be in real life. An adult can*
8	*be backstage with the child to prompt the lines.)*
9	**BRIAN:** *(Putting a mug in the microwave and pantomiming turning it*
10	*on)* **Do you want any tea, Janet?**
11	**JANET: No thanks.**
12	**BRIAN: I think Isaac must have finally fallen asleep.**
13	**ISAAC:** *(Off-stage in a loud, pleading voice)* **I can't** *waaaiiit!*
14	**BRIAN:** *(Yelling, with an edge to his voice)* **Isaac! No more talking!**
15	**JANET:** *(More gentle than her husband)* **Go to sleep now, honey.**
16	**ISAAC: I want to go to Grandma and Grandpa's** *now!*
17	**BRIAN: I told you we will leave in two days.**

1   ISAAC: But that's too long!

2   BRIAN: *(To himself)* No, that's not "too long." "Too long" is the

3   amount of time we will be *staying* at your grandparents' place.

4   *(Dirty look from JANET)*

5   ISAAC: I can't *waaaiiit* ...

6   BRIAN: *(Cutting ISAAC off)* Not another word, or I'll have to come

7   into your room. *You won't like that.* *(Silence from the room)*

8   That's better. I don't know what his trouble is — he knows

9   that we aren't leaving until Tuesday. *(Shakes his head.)*

10   JANET: Be easy on him. He is just so excited about going.

11   BRIAN: Why can't he be more patient when he knows how long it

12   will be?

13   JANET: Isaac is still too young to really understand the concept of

14   time, so it's very hard for him to wait.

15   BRIAN: But I promised him that we would go to Grandma and

16   Grandpa's. Doesn't he believe me when I say we'll leave in

17   two days?

18   JANET: *(Stopping her work for a second)* Brian, he has no idea how

19   long two days is. That's like a lifetime for him. It's hard to be

20   patient when you live each moment at full speed like he does.

21   ISAAC: *(Loudly)* I want to go now!

22   BRIAN: *(Getting up quickly)* That's it!

23   ISAAC: *(In a panic)* I'm sleeping, Dad, I'm sleeping.

24   BRIAN: *(Sitting back down, to ISAAC)* Not another word! *(To*

25   *JANET)* But I made a promise that we would go there for

26   Christmas. It seems like he should be old enough to trust us.

27   JANET: Oh, Isaac trusts us. But he can't understand waiting

28   longer than ten minutes for anything. When we make a

29   promise and it isn't fulfilled within his understanding of how

30   long things should take, he thinks that we have changed our

31   minds.

32   BRIAN: But I haven't changed my mind. My promise still stands.

33   JANET: Of course it does, and he will find that out on Tuesday

34   when we get into the car and leave for Mom and Dad's.

35   BRIAN: Well, the sooner he understands time the way I do, the

1   **easier life will be around here. I'm tempted not to go just to**
2   **teach him a lesson.**
3   **JANET:** *(Seriously)* **Whoa, it sounds like he's not the only one who**
4   **needs to have a little patience.**
5   **BRIAN:** *(Looks quickly at her, about to say something but pauses.)*
6   **Yeah, maybe you're right. I guess I can't blame him for not**
7   **understanding something that is so foreign to him. He will just**
8   **have to trust me, though. I will come through on my promise.**
9   **JANET: He'll see that. Can you hand me those shirts by the**
10   **microwave?**
11   **BRIAN: Sure.** *(When he goes to get the shirts, he stops at the*
12   *microwave, opens the door, and takes a sip from the mug. Irritable*
13   *again)* **What's the deal with this microwave? It takes forever**
14   **to get a hot cup of water!** *(Turns to JANET with the cup in his*
15   *hand.)* **I sure get tired of waiting on this thing.** *(Freeze)*
16   **NARRATOR: Just like Isaac didn't understand time the way his**
17   **parents did, so we often do not understand time as God does.**
18   **God had said he would send the Messiah, Emmanuel, many**
19   **years before the promise was realized. As Isaiah the prophet**
20   **predicted:**
21   **"The people walking in darkness have seen a great light; on**
22   **those living in the land of the shadow of death a light has**
23   **dawned"** (Isaiah 9:2).
24   **"For to us a child is born, to us a son is given, and the**
25   **government will be on his shoulders. And he will be called**
26   **Wonderful Counselor, Mighty God, Everlasting Father,**
27   **Prince of Peace"** (Isaiah 9:6).
28   **"The Lord himself will give you a sign: the virgin will be**
29   **with child and will give birth to a son, and will call him**
30   **Immanuel"** (Isaiah 7:14).
31   **We, too, live with a promise that is almost two thousand years**
32   **old — the promise that Jesus will come back again. The**
33   **promise is still good, and we wait with patience and**
34   **anticipation for that day.** *(Lights one candle.)* **I light the Candle**
35   **of Prophecy.**

House Cleaning
(Second Sunday of Advent)

Theme
Making our hearts and homes ready for the Christ child — the Candle of Bethlehem.

Synopsis
While Esther (Grandma) and Joe (Grandpa) are preparing the guest room for the arrival of their grandchildren at Christmas, their mix-up in communication tells us how we should prepare ourselves for the celebration of Jesus' birth.

Characters
Joe (Grandpa) — this character is quite enthusiastic and demonstrative by the end of the sketch. Make sure that the seeds of these emotions are seen in the character from the beginning.
Esther (Grandma) — good-natured.
Narrator

Set
Two play areas divided by a pulpit, piano, or something of substance to create the illusion of two different rooms. One room is the guest room. This setting may be established quite easily by placing a pillow and a bedspread on a bench for a "bed." Add a chair with some sheets hanging over the back, a wastebasket, and some newspapers scattered about, and the guest room is ready for Grandma's clean-up job!

Props
Telephone (could be mimed), telephone book or church directory, sheets, blankets, a bedspread, two pillows, broom, newspapers, wastebasket.

1 NARRATOR: **On the first Sunday of Advent we lit the Candle of**
2 **Prophecy, which symbolized the time of waiting for the light that**
3 **broke over the world that first Christmas.** *(Lights one candle.)*
4 **On this, the second Sunday of Advent, we light the Candle of**
5 **Bethlehem.** *(Lights a second candle.)* **It symbolizes the making of**
6 **our hearts and homes ready for the Christ child. It also reminds**
7 **us of the impending birth of Jesus.**
8 **"But you, Bethlehem Ephrathah, though you are small among**

1 the clans of Judah, out of you will come for me one who will be
2 ruler over Israel, whose origins are from of old, from ancient
3 times" (Micah 5:2).
4 The preparation of our hearts for Christmas is not unlike the
5 woman who was preparing her home for company.
6 *(Scene opens with ESTHER tidying up the guest room. She should*
7 *be working the whole time she is talking. There should be sheets*
8 *hanging over the back of a chair, a wastebasket, newspapers*
9 *scattered about, and miscellaneous homey touches to create the*
10 *illusion of a guest room. The "bed" should be unmade. JOE is on the*
11 *phone in the other area. He is holding one of the pillows. He looks*
12 *up a number in the telephone book and dials as ESTHER begins to*
13 *speak.)*
14 ESTHER: *(To herself, shaking out a pillow)* My, my! Everything is
15 pretty dusty in here. This place will need a thorough cleaning if
16 it's going to be ready for the kids. I want to get the house in tip-
17 top shape today.
18 JOE: *(On the phone)* Hi, Curt? Yeah, Joe Campbell here. Esther said
19 that you had called.
20 ESTHER: *(To herself)* If I put Patty in here, I can put Janet in her old
21 room. That way there will be enough space for Isaac's cot.
22 JOE: *(On the phone)* That's *this* Tuesday already? Wow, I didn't
23 realize it was coming up so soon.
24 ESTHER: *(To herself, brushing her hair out of her face, looking around*
25 *the room)* I keep this house as clean as I can, but whenever we
26 have company coming, it seems I see this place in a new light.
27 *(Notices the "bed.")* I'll need to change that bedspread too.
28 *(Starts to make the bed.)*
29 JOE: *(On the phone)* Sure. I'll be there. Thanks for reminding me.
30 *(Hangs up the phone. To himself)* This Tuesday is Christmas
31 caroling at the jail. I forgot that I'm supposed to talk about how
32 we prepare our hearts to celebrate Jesus' birth. *(Starts to think*
33 *about what he is going to do.)*
34 ESTHER: *(To herself, looking around)* Now, where is that other
35 pillow? Oh, Joe went to get it. I wonder if he's ready to help me

1   yet. *(Yells.)* **Joe, are you ready?**
2   **JOE:** *(Responds.)* **No, I'm not ready. I completely forgot about it.**
3   **ESTHER: When do you think you'll be ready?**
4   **JOE: Well, I still have two days.**
5   **ESTHER: Two days!** *(To herself)* **I want to get this house done today.**
6   **We'll have a house full of company in two days.** *(To JOE)* **Joe, we**
7   **have to get prepared.**
8   **JOE: I know. That's what I'm thinking about.**
9   **ESTHER:** *(Straightens up, to herself)* ***That's what I'm thinking about?***
10   **While he's *thinking* about getting this house prepared, *I'm doing***
11   ***it*. Maybe I'll just *think* about making dinner tonight.** *(Begins to*
12   *pick up some newspapers off the floor and puts them into the*
13   *wastebasket.)*
14   **JOE:** *(To himself, thinking out loud)* **OK, if I prepare myself to**
15   **celebrate Jesus' birth, I must ... I must ...**
16   **ESTHER:** *(To JOE)* **We'll have to clean some of this stuff out.**
17   **JOE:** *(To ESTHER)* **Exactly!**
18   **ESTHER:** *(Dryly, to herself)* **He can sure be supportive when he's**
19   **trying to avoid work.**
20   **JOE:** *(To himself)* **Esther is right. We must clean out the clutter in our**
21   **lives and make room for Jesus again.** *(To ESTHER)* **What would**
22   **you do next, dear?**
23   **ESTHER:** *(Caustically)* **I'd remind you of what we are preparing for!**
24   *(The tempo of the lines should start to pick up here as JOE's*
25   *excitement builds.)*
26   **JOE:** *(To himself, blown away by her insight)* **Wow, remember what we**
27   **are preparing for — Christmas, Jesus' birth, the single most**
28   **important event in the history of the world. Esther is right — we**
29   **have to remember, and ... and ... *refocus* on the meaning in our**
30   **own lives.** *(The lightbulb comes on above his head.)*
31   **ESTHER:** *(Putting the finishing touches on the room and taking a look*
32   *around)* **This doesn't look bad at all.**
33   **JOE:** *(To himself, building enthusiasm, each phrase should be bigger*
34   *than the last)* **We take stock of our lives, throw out the garbage**
35   **that has accumulated, focus anew on the meaning of Jesus'**

1   **birth, and then, then ...** *(Big grin, mounting excitement but*
2   *searching for words, just an edge of panic)*
3   **ESTHER: My mother always said, "If the room was inviting, people**
4   **will want to be invited back"** *(To JOE)* **We need to be prepared**
5   **so that we can invite them back.**
6   **JOE:** *(With a rush of gratitude and, at the peak of excitement, very*
7   *emphatic)* **Yes, yes, we invite him back! We recommit! We sign up**
8   **for another year. We re-enlist! We re-up! Wow.** *(Overcome by his*
9   *own insight now)* **We focus anew on the meaning of his birth, and**
10   **then reaffirm our commitment by asking the Christ child to**
11   **once again make his home with us. Yes, that's it!** *(To ESTHER)*
12   **Thanks so much, honey. I'm prepared now.**
13   **ESTHER:** *(Sarcastically)* **No, thank you, Joe. Now, if you'll just bring**
14   **me the pillow, I'll be prepared too.** *(JOE looks down at the pillow*
15   *like he has never seen it before.)*
16   *(Freeze)*

Author's Note: Our response to Christ every Christmas should be that of giving ourselves back to him. I have made three suggestions as to how we can prepare ourselves for the celebration of Jesus' birth.

1. *Reassess* priorities, clean out your life and make space for Jesus. This may be especially hard to do in the business of this season.
2. *Remember* the significance of Jesus' birth and refocus on the meaning in your life of his birth.
3. *Recommit* yourself to the Christ child. Let him continue to live in your heart and be at the center of your life. *The above points may be included in the pastor's sermon to reinforce what was said in the sketch.*

A Lot of Work for a Birthday

(Third Sunday of Advent)

Theme

Sharing the good news of Jesus' birth with others — the Shepherds' Candle.

Synopsis

Two friends working in the inventory section of a doll manufacturing company discuss the importance of Jesus' birth.

Characters

Patty — early twenties.

Nicole — twenties or thirties, pragmatic, let's-get-the-job-done type, rather abrupt.

Narrator

Props

Clipboard, coat or jacket.

1   **NARRATOR: On the first Sunday of Advent, we lit the Candle of**
2   **Prophecy which symbolized the time of waiting for the light**
3   **that broke over the world that first Christmas.** (*Lights one*
4   *candle.*)
5   **Last Sunday we lit the Candle of Bethlehem.** (*Lights second*
6   *candle.*) **It symbolized our making ready to welcome the Christ**
7   **child into our hearts and homes.**
8   **On this, the third Sunday in Advent, we light the Shepherds'**
9   **Candle.** (*Lights the third candle.*)
10   **"And there were shepherds living out in the fields nearby,**
11   **keeping watch over their flocks at night. An angel of the Lord**
12   **appeared to them, and the glory of the Lord shone around**
13   **them, and they were terrified. But the angel said to them, 'Do**
14   **not be afraid. I bring you good news of great joy that will be**
15   **for all the people. Today in the town of David a Savior has been**
16   **born to you; he is Christ the Lord. This will be a sign to you:**
17   **You will find a baby wrapped in cloths and lying in a manger'"**
18   (Luke 2:8-12).
19   (*Scene opens with NICOLE holding the clipboard and counting the*

13

1   *people in the congregation. She is doing inventory in the company*
2   *warehouse and the people of the congregation are the dolls. For*
3   *most of the sketch NICOLE is silently counting and writing things*
4   *down.)*
5   NICOLE: **Seventy-seven, seventy-eight, seventy-nine, eighty ...**
6   *(Squints at someone in the middle of the congregation.)* **That doll**
7   **has got to be a "second," it doesn't seem to have all of its hair!**
8   *(Writes on her clipboard, squints at the person again, and*
9   *continues counting.)* **Eighty-one, eighty-two, eighty-three,**
10   **eighty-four, eighty-five ...** *(PATTY enters.)*
11   PATTY: **Hi, Nicole! Will you still be finished at three?**
12   NICOLE: **Eighty-six, eighty-seven, eighty-eight, eighty-nine,**
13   **ninety. There we go.** *(Writes on the clipboard again.)* **Hi, Patty.**
14   **What did you say?**
15   PATTY: **Do you think you'll be finished by three? If not, I need to**
16   **call my mom and dad and let them know I'll be home later**
17   **than I planned. My mom will worry.**
18   NICOLE: **It's only a three-hour drive.**
19   PATTY: **I know, but my sister and her family will be arriving**
20   **tomorrow, and Mom wants me to help finish cleaning the**
21   **house. She needs the house spotless so that my nephew Isaac**
22   **can mess everything up again.**
23   NICOLE: **Don't worry, Patty. I'm almost finished here so we**
24   **should be able to leave on time.** *(Begins to count dolls again.)*
25   **One, two, three, four, five, six, seven, eight, nine, ten ...**
26   PATTY: *(Looking around)* **I've never been in the warehouse before.**
27   NICOLE: *(Without missing a beat)* **Four, five, six, seven,**
28   **eight ...**
29   PATTY: **I never realized we manufactured so many dolls.**
30   NICOLE: **Yep, especially at this time of year. You know what they**
31   **say ...**
32   PATTY and NICOLE: *(Together)* **Delwood's delightful dolls, for all**
33   **your Christmas doll needs.**
34   PATTY: **It really is amazing how many dolls we sell at Christmas.**
35   *(Starts to count again.)*

1 NICOLE: It's amazing how much of *everything* is sold at
2 Christmas. *(Starts to count again.)*
3 PATTY: That's true. People do like to give at Christmas.
4 *(Thoughtfully)* And at this time of the year, it seems like people
5 work extra hard to be nice and caring.
6 NICOLE: *(Still counting, off-handedly)* Well, if you ask me, it seems
7 like a lot of work just to celebrate a birthday.
8 PATTY: *(Unclear)* I don't think I know what you mean, Nicole.
9 NICOLE: Christmas is really a birthday, right?
10 PATTY: Yes, I guess so, for Jesus.
11 NICOLE: So, really, Christmas is the birthday of a dead guy, and
12 everybody remembers this by going wild with gifts and
13 parties. It just seems like a lot of work.
14 PATTY: *(Hesitantly)* But he's not a dead guy. I believe that the little
15 baby Jesus who was born almost two thousand years ago is
16 still alive today. That's why I celebrate his birthday.
17 NICOLE: *(Stops counting and looks at PATTY.)* So then, is he coming
18 to your party?
19 PATTY: *(Uncomfortably)* Well, yes, I mean, he kind of is coming.
20 We've talked about this before Nicole: Jesus lives at the center
21 of my life, at the center of everyone who believes in him. He
22 doesn't have to walk around my Christmas tree with a glass
23 of eggnog in his hand to prove he's alive.
24 NICOLE: But Christmas is his birthday party.
25 PATTY: *(Unsure as to NICOLE's point)* Yes. There would be no
26 reason to celebrate if he hadn't been born.
27 NICOLE: *(Setting PATTY up)* OK, so what are you going to give him
28 for his birthday?
29 PATTY: *(Taken aback)* I don't understand, Nicole.
30 NICOLE: You said yourself that people like to give at this time of
31 the year. Everyone is buying presents for everyone else. But, if
32 it's Jesus' birthday and he really is alive, don't you think he'd
33 like something for his birthday? *(Pause)* So, what are you
34 going to give him?
35 *(Freeze)*

15

What We Give

(Fourth Sunday of Advent)

Theme
Caring, giving — the Candle of Love.

Synopsis
A family Christmas celebration is overshadowed by worry when one family member is late in arriving. When she finally arrives and tells her story, an important lesson about the gift of the Christ child is learned.

Characters
Brian — husband/son-in law, rather irritable.

Janet — wife/daughter, good-humored.

Isaac/Chelsea — son or daughter/grandchild, about four or five. (The gender is not critical to the role. The child is never seen, so this role could be played by an older child with a young-sounding voice.)

Joe — Grandpa.

Esther — Grandma.

Patty — early twenties, younger daughter.

Narrator

Props
Card table, two chairs, puzzle, a toy that requires assembly, the script calls for a remote-controlled monster truck; if not available, substitute another toy, Christmas tree, mugs, spoons, sugar and cream set, tray, wrapped packages.

1　**NARRATOR: On the first Sunday of Advent, we lit the Candle of**
2　**Prophecy which symbolized the time of waiting for Jesus'**
3　**birth.** *(Lights one candle.)* **The second Sunday we lit the Candle**
4　**of Bethlehem.** *(Lights second candle.)* **It symbolized our making**
5　**our hearts and homes ready for the Christ child. Last Sunday**
6　**we lit the Shepherds' Candle.** *(Lights third candle.)* **It**
7　**symbolized our sharing of Jesus' birth with others.**
8　　　**Today, the fourth Sunday of Advent, we light the Angels'**
9　**Candle, the Candle of Love.** *(Lights fourth candle.)* **It**
10　**symbolizes the glorious song of the angels over the hills of**

16

Bethlehem, proclaiming the birth of Jesus.

"The angels said to them, 'Do not be afraid. I bring you good news of great joy that will be for all the people. Today in the town of David a Savior has been born to you; he is Christ the Lord. This will be a sign to you: You will find a baby wrapped in cloths and lying in a manger.'"

"Suddenly a great company of the heavenly host appeared with the angel, praising God and saying, 'Glory to God in the highest, and on earth peace to men on whom his favor rests'" (Luke 2:10-14).

The angels announced the most incredible gift given to all people everywhere. The gift of Jesus Christ speaks of the powerful love of the Giver who is God. What do the gifts we give say about us?

(This sketch is set in the family room of grandparents JOE and ESTHER. The card table is set up off to one side with a couple of chairs around it. JANET is working on a puzzle. BRIAN is trying to put together some kind of a toy. ESTHER is standing and looking out a window. The window should be in the imaginary fourth wall. ISAAC is already in bed; he will be heard from Off- stage. Everyone looks just a little tense and on edge. A Christmas tree at the side of the set would be a nice touch.)

ESTHER: *(Worried)* **Where could she be?**

JOE: *(Reassuringly)* **Don't worry, Esther. She's on her way.**

JANET: Mom, Patty probably just left work later than she'd planned.

ESTHER: But she said that she would be here by seven, and now it's after nine ...

BRIAN: *(Shaking his head)* **Patty is always late, isn't she?** *(JANET gives him a dirty look.)*

ESTHER: No, Patty is always right on time. That's why I'm worried. I hope she's all right.

JOE: *(Comes up from behind and puts his hands on her shoulders. They both look out the window.)* **She's just running a little behind schedule, Esther.**

1   **ESTHER:** Oh, I hope so. The roads are so icy, anything could have
2   happened.
3   **BRIAN:** *(Reassuring tone of voice)* Listen, with a good set of winter
4   tires and cautious driving, these roads aren't bad at all. *(They*
5   *all stare at him.)*
6   **JOE:** She still has the summer tires on her car. I was going to put
7   the winter ones on while she was here.
8   **JANET:** And Patty is a terrible driver; everyone knows that.
9   *(JANET and BRIAN begin to look out the window as well.)*
10   **ISAAC:** *(Off-stage, in a loud, piercing voice)* Is it morning?
11   **ESTHER:** Not yet, sweetheart.
12   **JANET:** Go to sleep, honey. When you wake up, then we'll open
13   presents.
14   **BRIAN:** *(With despair)* It's like this *every* night. Just about the time
15   you relax and think he is sleeping, there is this shrill little voice
16   from the bedroom.
17   **JOE:** *(Not hearing, taking charge)* Well, standing here looking out
18   the window isn't going to change things at all. I'm sure she's
19   on her way. Would anybody care for some tea?
20   **BRIAN:** *(Sitting back down, goes back to assembling the toy.)* Sure,
21   I'll have a cup.
22   **JANET:** Me too, please. *(Goes back to her puzzle.)*
23   **JOE:** Esther?
24   **ESTHER:** *(Absently)* That would be nice, Joe. *(JOE exits.)*
25   **JANET:** Mom, come and help me with this puzzle.
26   **ESTHER:** *(Coming out of her thoughts)* Sure, I'll help you, Janet.
27   *(Brief pause, then JOE enters with a tray holding cups, sugar, and*
28   *creamer. The characters fix their "tea.")*
29   **EVERYONE:** *(Ad-lib as they take their cups.)* Thanks, Dad. Thanks,
30   Joe. *(Etc.)*
31   **JOE:** *(Sitting down)* So what's the big gift for Isaac this year?
32   **BRIAN:** I got him one of those remote-controlled monster trucks.
33   He's going to love it.
34   **ESTHER:** Isn't he a little young for that?
35   **BRIAN:** Well, maybe, but it's the kind of a toy that a boy can grow
36   into.

1 JANET: It sounds to me like the kind of a toy that a dad can grow
2   into as well.
3 BRIAN: *(Sheepishly)* You may be right. I can remember giving a
4   cap gun to my three-year-old sister when I was ten because I
5   was afraid that my parents weren't going to give me one.
6 ESTHER: *(Looking up from the puzzle)* What we give can say a lot
7   about what we want.
8 BRIAN: Pardon me?
9 ESTHER: Sometimes we give the things that we hope someone will
10   give to us, or we give them knowing that we'll be able to use
11   them ourselves.
12 JOE: Like Brian with the cap gun ...
13 ESTHER: Or Brian with the remote-controlled monster truck ...
14 JANET: Or Brian with the twenty-five-inch color TV for my
15   birthday. *(They all stare at him again.)*
16 BRIAN: *(Just a tad huffy)* Hey, isn't that like the Golden Rule? Give
17   unto others as you would have them give unto you?
18 JANET: *(Going over and giving him a hug)* Nice try, dear.
19 JOE: *(Reflectively)* What you give can say a lot about what you
20   want. I like that. *(PATTY enters with an armload of packages,*
21   *full of life and enthusiasm.)*
22 EVERYONE: *(Ad-libs)* Patty! Land sakes alive, girl! Where have
23   you been? *(Etc.)*
24 PATTY: Hi, Mom, hi, Dad, Brian and Janet. *(Miscellaneous hugs,*
25   *hellos, and "how are yas." PATTY sits down right in the center of*
26   *the action, and JOE brings her a cup of tea.)* Oh, it feels great to
27   finally be home!
28 JANET: What took you so long? We were getting pretty worried.
29 BRIAN: We were about to put your picture on a milk carton.
30   *(Another dirty look from JANET)*
31 PATTY: *(Apologetically)* I'm sorry. We left late, and then with all
32   that happened, I never had a chance to call.
33 ESTHER: What happened, Patty?
34 PATTY: Well, first of all, I had a pretty interesting discussion with
35   a friend from work who gave me a ride home. Her name is

1   Nicole, and she asked me what I was giving Jesus for his
2   birthday.
3   **BRIAN: What?**
4   **PATTY: She figured that if Christmas is Jesus' birthday, and if he**
5   **is still alive, 'cause I said that he was, and that if he was**
6   **coming to my place for Christmas, 'cause I said he would be,**
7   **then he would probably expect something for his birthday.**
8   **She thought Jesus might be rather put out that everyone will**
9   **get gifts on his birthday except him.**
10   **BRIAN:** *(With finality)* **That's stupid.**
11   **JOE: Actually, that makes a fair bit of sense.**
12   **PATTY: I thought so too, so as we were driving here, I tried to**
13   **think of what I could give Jesus for his birthday.**
14   **JANET:** *(Innocently)* **Did you consider a remote-controlled monster**
15   **truck?** *(BRIAN gives her a dirty look.)*
16   **PATTY:** *(Obviously not understanding)* **No, but I thought of the**
17   **obvious — you know, "I will give him my life," that kind of**
18   **stuff. But when I said that to Nicole, she told me that was too**
19   **easy. "Be practical," she said.**
20   **JANET: I'm glad I wasn't riding with her.**
21   **PATTY: What she said was good. It made me think. So, anyway, I**
22   **asked myself, "What would Jesus like for his birthday?" And**
23   **I thought that he would probably like a world that is full of**
24   **peace. Immediately I thought of God sending this little baby,**
25   **his Son, so that our world might have peace and love and joy.**
26   **God gave the Christ child because he wanted us to have those**
27   **things. Then it hit me that I haven't done anything to help**
28   **anyone experience that peace, love, and joy that God still**
29   **wants our world to have.**
30   **BRIAN:** *(Softly)* **So that's why you are late?**
31   **PATTY: Not completely. You see, after I realized all of this, and just**
32   **as we were coming into town, we saw a car broken down at the**
33   **side of the road.** *(Everyone kind of perks up and becomes very*
34   *focused on PATTY.)*
35   **ESTHER: Did you stop?**

1   PATTY: *(Thoughtfully)* **Yes, we did, Mom. In that car were four**
2   **screaming kids and one very stressed-out single mother. We**
3   **didn't know what was wrong with the car, but we got a tow**
4   **truck. They took the car into a station, and —** *(She pauses.)*
5   JANET: **And?**
6   PATTY: **I gave the mechanic my credit card and told him to fix the**
7   **car.**
8   JOE: *(To himself)* **I think I countersigned for that card.**
9   BRIAN: **Why?**
10   JOE: **Because she couldn't get it on her own. She didn't have a**
11   **credit history.**
12   BRIAN: **No, no. Patty, why did you give the mechanic your card to**
13   **pay for the car?**
14   PATTY: **It's part of my birthday present to Jesus. I want to help**
15   **others experience his peace, love, and joy.**
16   ESTHER: *(Crosses to PATTY and puts her arm around her daughter.)*
17   **What you are giving, Patty, says a lot about what you want.**
18   JANET: *(Somewhat impatiently)* **So, is that the whole story?**
19   PATTY: **Actually, there is one other small thing that I haven't**
20   **mentioned yet.**
21   JOE: **What's that?**
22   PATTY: **One very stressed-out single mother and four screaming**
23   **kids. They are out in Nicole's car right now, waiting for me to**
24   **bring them in.** *(Looks at her parents hopefully.)* **They need a**
25   **place to stay while their car gets fixed.**
26   ISAAC: *(Off-stage, very cheerfully)* **Daddy, I'm awake! Is it time to**
27   **open presents now?**
28   ESTHER: *(Looks at BRIAN, warmly.)* **He might as well get up. It**
29   **sounds like he's going to have some new friends to play with!**
30   *(To PATTY)* **Go out and invite them in. They're welcome to stay**
31   **with us.**
32   *(Freeze)*
33   NARRATOR: **What we give** *can* **say quite a bit about what we**
34   **want. So, what are you giving for Christmas?**

Multicultural
Drama

Christmas Around the World
By Karyl J. Garner

Production Notes

To make things easier, let each character and his/her mother be responsible for his/her costume and props. Request that each character use a shopping bag (clearly identified) to hold his/her costumes/props. This is a great help for the aides who will assist in dressing the cast. When you hand out the roles, include on the paper the dates and times of rehearsal and performance, as well as costume and prop requests and instructions. Do make a copy for yourself that can then be re-copied as cast members lose the originals — and they will.

Narrators

The narrators are identified in the script as A through M. This can be reduced, if preferred, to only two narrators: Man and Woman. The pageant has been written for the narrators to read in pairs (exception being M). They can share one lectern, or be divided, one on either side of the chancel. The narrator role is the perfect spot for many older participants. It also gives many the chance to participate. The more experienced should be chosen for the more difficult sections.

Lucia: (Nonspeaking)

Costume: White dress with red sash. Her crown can be fashioned of light cardboard, with greens glued or stapled around the base. Popsicle sticks can provide support if the candles need it. (See diagram.)
Props: One small tea set. Attach the serving pieces to the tray securely with double sided tape or glue.
Action: Does not join processional, but enters slowly from the back of the church during narration (or optional special music). During the proper narration, she wakens and serves family, decorates tree, and

circles it during song. At the end of the song, she helps clear set, then takes her seat.

Candle Snuffers: (2 to 6 optional, nonspeaking)
Costume: White shirts with dark trousers. Tuck the bottom of the pant legs into knee socks to resemble pages.
Prop: Each should carry a candle snuffer.
Action: Do not join processional, but accompany Lucia as she enters. Do not enter Center stage area, but stop before then. Remain until set is cleared, then be seated.

Swedish Family: (4 or 5, nonspeaking)
Costume: None, night stocking caps if desired.
Props: Perhaps a Christmas ornament for the tree.
Action: During congregational song, "O Come all Ye Faithful," sit on small chairs at Center Stage and pantomime sleep. They are awakened by Lucia, served breakfast; they set up tree, decorate with one ornament if desired, and circle tree during song. They should remove their own chairs during refrain to help clear set, then return to their seats.

Pilgrims: (Any number, 1 speaking)
These are good roles for the youngest participants since they only follow the speaking pilgrim in a procession. Use two older pilgrims to lead.
Costumes: Colorful! Boys can wear white shirts, wide sashes, serapes, sombreros, or straw hats (western style). Girls wear colorful skirts, peasant-type tops, ribbon choker with flower attached to it, flowers in their hair, colorful jewelry.
Props: The two leading pilgrims will need figures of Mary and Joseph to carry. If possible, puppets or small dolls attached to a stick (so they can be held up high) and dressed Mexican style. A small set of outdoor figures could also suffice. These should be placed on a tray to be carried.
Action: During traveling music, they form a procession, and move to the different houses as per narration. They enter the last house and sit on floor, one pilgrim to be selected to break the piñata. They then wave good-bye and exit to edge of Center Stage awaiting cue to surround manger and sing "Away in a Manger." During refrain, they return to seats.

Innkeepers: (3 speaking)
Costumes: Same as pilgrims.
Props: The third innkeeper needs a piñata, and a small stick for breaking the piñata. The piñata needs to hang from a long stick so it can be dangled over the heads of the children. (Piñata and stick should be placed near Center Stage prior to performance.)
Action: Assume proper place during the time that the pilgrims are forming their procession line. Third innkeeper joins in piñata breaking, then all should join the pilgrims during song, "Away in a Manger," and return to seats during refrain.

Befana: (Speaking)
Costume: Old lady dress, apron.
Props: Broom, small hand basket, small gifts such as wooden toy, fruit, handful of nuts. Optional: small candle lamp for cottage. (Props should be placed near Center Stage.)
Action: At proper time, Befana enters Center Stage and begins to sweep, following dialogue.

Magi: (3 speaking)
Costume: Rich-looking bathrobes or choir robes belted with gold, silver, or satin. Crowns fashioned from light cardboard and decorated with jewels.
Props: Each should carry a gift, such as a rich-looking box or urn.
Action: Enter as directed, following dialogue.

Shepherds: (2 or 3, 1 speaking)
Costume: Dark, drab bathrobe, belted. Dark towel or cloth on head, ends hanging down back, then a tie placed around head, knotted in back.
Props: Staff or long walking stick.
Action: Enter as directed, following dialogue. Also in final Nativity scene.

Mary: (nonspeaking)
Costume: Long, dark skirt and dark shawl to place over head.
Action: Final Nativity scene.
Joseph: (nonspeaking)

27

Costume: Similar to shepherds.
Action: Final Nativity scene.

Angels: (2 or 3, nonspeaking)

Costume: White robe (choir robe perhaps), small angel wings fashioned from cardboard and sprayed silver or covered with foil (see diagram). Use a length of silver tinsel made into a circle and laid on top of each angel head — attach with bobby pins.
Action: Final Nativity scene.

Non-cast but essential (2 or 3 aides)

These will be your right hands, so get solid commitments. You can use mothers who volunteer, or perhaps mature senior high students. Besides helping the cast to dress, they will assist in keeping order. They should sit with children during the performance and, using a script, can follow the action and jog a memory, if necessary.

Ushers

1. Cordon off pews reserved for cast.
2. Pass out programs and help with seating if necessary.
3. Alert cast when organist begins prelude.

Miscellaneous prop list

1. Step stool for narrators, if necessary.
2. Small Sunday school chairs that will be used as beds for Swedish family.
3. Small, portable Christmas tree.
4. Manger and baby.

 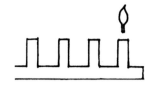

Costume Construction

Lucia's Crown: Fashion the crown from light cardboard. Make the flames of yellow, sturdy paper. Attach greens to the crown base with staples or glue. (The Magi crowns can be fashioned in the same manner with many variations. By having each magus do his/her own, they will all be different.)

Angel Wings: A good-sized cardboard box will do for the wings. Spray painting them silver, rather than using foil, is recommended. Punch holes at the dots and use cord (two pieces) threaded through holes, top/bottom. Knot each cord after leaving enough cord for the angel to put his or her arms through each loop (cape style). Safety pins at the shoulder seams of the robe will permit easy attachment of the cord to prevent them from falling off.

Rehearsals and Performance

Select your performance date, schedule the rehearsal(s), and reserve your location and organist or pianist. The accompanist can smooth over the performance more than any other person. With a script alongside the music, he/she can give the cast that extra minute to clear a set, or to get ready for the action.

Read the pageant and block out the action according to the physical characteristics of your own church. First decide where the narrators will read. Then, where will the main stage area be? Perhaps the most difficult to locate will be the first and second inns in Mexico (the last should be in the designated main stage area). Could the pilgrims walk all the way around the church? With the organ providing traveling music, why not? Think about the direction you want the Magi and shepherds to take. Once you have the action blocked out, assign the cast seats in the front pews, or pews closest to their action.

Casting

You can either have tryouts, or ask for volunteers from the Sunday school classes. The Sunday school teachers can probably help by recommending strong readers for the narrator roles. This is one of the most difficult phases of a Christmas pageant, for most children are eager to participate. It isn't easy to come up with something for everybody. For those with no desire to "ham it up," ushers and helpers are always welcome, and these functions give more children a chance to be part of the program. Optional suggestion: in case you need more slots for young cast members, make signs, each with Merry Christmas in a different language, for the youngsters to hold. They would stand beside the lectern during the narration, or during the songs that match the country they are representing; the country in which the songs originated could be listed in the program.

Music

If you are going to use the carols that have been suggested, how many verses of each will you use? Consult with your organist and fill him/her in on the action and your needs. Ask the Sunday school teachers if they would teach the children the words to "Jesus Loves the Little Children," "Away in a Manger," and "Silent Night." Pass out the script/costume/prop/schedule sheets to your cast in plenty of time.

Lighting

Unless you have access to a professional who won't bother you with details, forget it. Chancel lights off or on at strategic times might be all right if an adult or mature senior high student wants to give it a try. They will need a cue sheet and need to know exactly where and how the action is to take place. They need to be at rehearsal. Remember, if the church is too dark the congregation won't be able to read their hymnals.

Plan on the first part of rehearsal as strictly a walk-through. Seat the cast as per your assignment. Then, much like a movie in reverse, line the cast up, move them to the back of the church, and presto, you have a processional. (One of the aides should write down the order for use on performance night.) Have the cast run through the action several times, then add the music. If time permits, you could have more than one rehearsal, but this pageant has been performed successfully with benefit of only one rehearsal. It may appear that chaos reigns, but if your children know exactly what they are to do and when to do it, you'll be amazed on the night of performance how they "come through" like old hands.

Optional Ideas

Unless it is traditional for your church to have the children perform close to the 25th, you may want to consider a date earlier in December. This will eliminate added activity to an already hectic "week before Christmas rush." The children will not have left for vacation yet, and since Santa Claus makes his appearance in November, getting the children involved in a pageant early in December puts emphasis on the true meaning of Christmas at the very beginning.

It may be fun to coordinate this pageant with other church committee activities, such as an annual December potluck dinner or a social committee cookie and punch party. Although you should not get involved with details (you have enough already), those committees might enjoy planning something for the same evening.

You may want to use the youth choir for one of the musical selections.

— Karyl J. Garner

JESUS LOVES THE LITTLE CHILDREN

Anon.

George F. Root

Je-sus loves the lit-tle chil-dren, All the chil-dren of the world. Red and yel-low, black and white, they are pre-cious in His sight. Je-sus loves the lit-tle chil-dren of the world.

1   *(Swedish "beds" are in place. Organist plays a prelude.)*

2   READER: At the same time came the disciples unto Jesus, saying,

3   "Who is the greatest in the kingdom of heaven?" And Jesus

4   called a little child unto him, and set him in the midst of them,

5   and said, "Verily I say unto you, except ye be converted, and

6   become as little children, ye shall not enter into the kingdom

7   of heaven. Whosoever therefore shall humble himself as this

8   little child, the same is greatest in the kingdom of heaven. And

9   whoso shall receive one such little child in my name receiveth

10   me" (Matthew 18:1-5, King James Version).

11   NARRATOR B: Listen closely, world. Do you hear the children?

12   From all over the earth their voices blend. They are not

13   different, these children in God's world, they are the same.

14   They feel pain and they hunger. They laugh and they cry.

15   They sing and they dance. Together, these children teach us of

16   peace and love. *(Congregation sings* "Jesus Loves the Little

17   Children." *See note on page 41. Remain seated. Processional*

18   *during song, all except Lucia and Candle Snuffers.)*

19   NARRATOR A: The anticipation in a child's eyes, the sparkling

20   merriment from a child's heart, and the words of praise from

21   the child's sweet song, all emerge to proclaim the birth of the

22   Child, our Lord Jesus Christ.

23   NARRATOR B: Christmas celebrations and traditions of the

24   world's Christian children may differ, but the message

25   remains the same: Joy to the world, *our* Lord is come!

26   *(Congregation sings,* "Joy to the World." *Remain seated.*

27   *NARRATORS A and B return to seats during song, and*

28   *NARRATORS C and D advance to lectern.)*

29   NARRATOR C: The anniversary of the birth of Jesus is the

30   happiest celebration of the year. The Messiah's birthday and

31   the Good News of Easter are the most distinctive, solemn

32   events to occur for all mankind.

33   NARRATOR D: This holy anniversary is celebrated in Christian

34   nations all over the world. Tonight, in our magic aircraft,

35   we'll visit some of those countries. You will see just a few of

1   the many traditions that children eagerly look forward to.
2   And you will hear some of the traditional music that children
3   never get tired of singing. So polish off your imaginations and
4   "bon voyage!"
5 NARRATOR C: One word of caution: due to the speed of our
6   adventure, it is necessary that you hold onto your partner's
7   hand and stay with your tour guide. We do not want any
8   lost parents. The aircraft is ready, so welcome aboard.
9   *(Congregation sings "O Come All Ye Faithful." Remain seated.*
10   *During song, SWEDISH FAMILY take places and pantomimes*
11   *sleep on Center Stage. NARRATORS C and D return to seats, and*
12   *NARRATORS E and F advance to lectern.)*
13 NARRATOR E: This should be an interesting and exciting trip. I
14   enjoy learning about kids from other nations. Did you know
15   they celebrated Christmas differently?
16 NARRATOR F: No, I just figured that we all did it the same. I'll
17   tell you what — hook up your seat belt, hang onto your ticket,
18   and let's take off. Our first stop this evening is Sweden. It's
19   located in Northern Europe and is one of the Scandinavian
20   countries.
21 NARRATOR E: In Sweden, December thirteenth is the shortest
22   and darkest day of the year. The children begin the countdown
23   to Christmas by celebrating the traditional Festival of Light
24   on Lucia Day.
25 NARRATOR F: There is a story that tells of Lucia, a beautiful
26   Christian maiden. She was persecuted by the Roman
27   Emperor because she refused to give up her Christian faith.
28 NARRATOR E: Missionaries went to Sweden and told the story of
29   Lucia. To the Swedish people, it showed such great inner
30   strength and deep faith that they have kept the story as part
31   of their traditional Christmas time celebration. Legend tells
32   that St. Lucia gives gifts of food to the poor and needy during
33   this time of year. *(LUCIA carrying her tea set and CANDLE*
34   *SNUFFERS enter slowly from the back of the church during the*
35   *following narration or during the optional special music.)*

1   NARRATOR F: The villages and churches select a young lady to
2   be Lucia for their Festival of Light celebration. She wears a
3   long white dress with a red sash, and in her hair is a crown of
4   evergreens and lighted candles. Now since that could be
5   dangerous, Lucia is attended by several fellows with candle
6   snuffers. Everyone is delighted to get a glimpse of Lucia.
7   *(Optional special music if you happen to have a young soloist to*
8   *sing Lucia)*
9   NARRATOR E: Besides the large festivals, each Swedish family
10   also celebrates Lucia Day in their own home. They select a
11   daughter to portray Lucia.
12   NARRATOR F: What if there aren't any girls in the family?
13   NARRATOR E: In that case, the honor is given to the mother.
14   Anyway, at dawn on the twelfth day before Christmas, Lucia
15   begins to sing to wake up her family. Then she serves them a
16   breakfast of hot coffee and fresh, warm, homemade saffron
17   buns. *(LUCIA and FAMILY pantomime the wake up and serving*
18   *of food.)*
19   NARRATOR F: Hmmmm, I can almost smell them now. Sweden
20   also has a tradition for the Christmas tree. December twenty-
21   second is the special day to bring in the tree and set it in the
22   middle of the living room. Then on Christmas Eve, the family
23   joins hands in a circle around the tree and sings their favorite
24   Christmas carols. *(Congregation sings* "The First Noel," *or*
25   "Bring a Torch, Jeannette, Isabella," *or* "Angels We Have Heard
26   on High." *[All are French origin] Remain seated. LUCIA and*
27   *FAMILY set up the small tree, perhaps each can add an ornament,*
28   *then join hands and slowly circle tree during song. NARRATORS*
29   *E and F return to seats, NARRATORS G and H advance to*
30   *lectern. Organist can play a refrain for clean-up of scene. LUCIA*
31   *and FAMILY can be seated.)*
32   NARRATOR G: OK everybody, we're back on our aircraft for a
33   short jaunt to a country south of our own border.
34   NARRATOR H: That's right! Hang onto your sombreros, folks.
35   We're touching down in warm, sunny Mexico. Olé!

1   **NARRATOR G: On December sixteenth, the children of Mexico**
2   **begin to celebrate Christmas by acting out the journey of Mary**
3   **and Joseph to Bethlehem. The story is about their search for a**
4   *posada* **or lodging. Carrying figures of Mary and Joseph, the**
5   **procession of boys and girls, called pilgrims, winds through the**
6   **streets of their Mexican village. They approach a house ...** *(The*
7   *PILGRIMS leave their seats, form a procession, and move to the*
8   *first "house." The organ can provide traveling music most*
9   *effectively as the cast lines up and moves along. A softly played*
10   *"Mexican Hat Dance" tune can set a festive mood. Knock three*
11   *times)*
12   **INNKEEPER 1: Si, what do you want?**
13   **PILGRIM: Please, I ask for shelter. Mary is so tired and cannot**
14   **travel any longer.**
15   **INNKEEPER 1: Go away, go away. This is no inn. There is no**
16   **posada, no room here.**
17   **NARRATOR H: The pilgrims shake their heads sadly and move on**
18   **to the next house.** *(Organ provides same traveling music as*
19   *PILGRIMS advance to next house. Knock three times.)*
20   **INNKEEPER 2: Si, what do you want?**
21   **PILGRIM: Please, I ask for shelter. Mary is so tired and cannot**
22   **travel any longer.**
23   **INNKEEPER 2: Go away, go away. This is no inn. There is no**
24   **posada, no room here.**
25   **NARRATOR H: The pilgrims shake their heads sadly and move on**
26   **to the next house ...** *(Organ provides same traveling music as*
27   *PILGRIMS move to next house. Knock three times.)*
28   **INNKEEPER 3: Buenos dias. May I help you?**
29   **PILGRIM: Please, I ask for shelter. Mary is so tired and cannot**
30   **travel any longer.**
31   **INNKEEPER 3: Welcome, welcome to this humble dwelling.**
32   **NARRATOR G: The pilgrims enter the house to celebrate the**
33   **success of their search for a lodging. They can see the Nativity**
34   **in a place of honor, but the manger is empty.** *(PILGRIMS enter*
35   *house and sit on floor to pantomime excitement of piñata breaking.)*

1   NARRATOR H: Before ending this first evening of *Las Posadas*,
2   the children break the traditional piñata, which is filled with
3   candy and sweet treats. *(The INNKEEPER holds the piñata, and*
4   *a child is chosen to break the piñata — pretend to break the*
5   *piñata. PILGRIMS wave good-bye to INNKEEPER and exit to*
6   *edge of Center Stage. Accompanist plays traveling music during*
7   *the piñata pantomime.)*
8   NARRATOR G: In this manner, the celebration of *Las Posadas*
9   continues for nine days. Each night as they enter the last
10   dwelling, the manger is still empty.
11 NARRATOR H: But on *Noche Buena*, the Good Night of the
12   twenty-fourth of December, after meeting with failure at
13   several inns, the pilgrims are finally welcomed at a *posada*.
14   They enter the lodging and on this last night of *Las Posadas*,
15   there is a difference. The Nativity is now complete. The Christ
16   child is asleep in the manger. *(Music plays until PILGRIMS or*
17   *CHILDREN sit on steps in front of manger or surround manger*
18   *and two of the Mexican PILGRIMS lay the baby in the manger.*
19   *PILGRIMS [or small children] sing "Away in a Manger," one*
20   *verse. Accompanist plays refrain as set is cleared, PILGRIMS*
21   *return to seats, NARRATORS G and H return to seats and*
22   *NARRATORS I and J advance to lectern.)*
23 NARRATOR I: Adios, amigos. Thank you for showing us your
24   Christmas tradition!
25 NARRATOR J: Fasten up your seat belts, moms and dads. We're
26   heading across the Atlantic Ocean again.
27 NARRATOR I: What a fast trip this evening! If you look out your
28   window, you can see Italy below us already. The families of
29   Italy gather together on Christmas Eve and sit around the
30   fireplace and watch the yule log burn. After eating their
31   supper, they enjoy a dessert called *torrone*, (Pronounced: Tor
32   row nee) which is a mixture of honey and nuts. Then they all
33   attend church.
34 NARRATOR J: The children of Italy do not receive gifts on
35   Christmas Day, but rather January sixth, or Epiphany.

1   **Perhaps this makes sense, for Epiphany reminds us of the**
2   **three wise men who came to Bethlehem bearing gifts of gold,**
3   **frankincense, and myrrh.**
4   **NARRATOR I: There is a legend in Italy about the Magi and a**
5   **little old woman named Befana. It seems that Befana lived in**
6   **a small cottage by the road, where caravans of camels passed**
7   **by.** *(BEFANA takes her place and begins to sweep. The MAGI*
8   *enter and approach the cottage. The action can occur during the*
9   *narration, or during organ traveling music of* "We Three Kings"
10   *at this point.)*
11   **NARRATOR J: On the eve of January sixth, or Epiphany, three**
12   **richly dressed men knocked on her door. They told Befana of**
13   **the birth of Jesus in Bethlehem and of following a bright star.**
14   **MAGUS 1: We invite you to come with us.**
15   **BEFANA:** *(Thumping her broom)* **Can't you see that I am busy**
16   **sweeping?**
17   **MAGUS 2: Do come with us to see the infant Jesus.**
18   **MAGUS 3: We are taking gifts to him. Surely you have some little**
19   **gift for him?**
20   **BEFANA:** *(Shaking broom)* **When I finish sweeping, I must bring in**
21   **the wood.** *(The MAGI move along. Enter SHEPHERD)*
22   **NARRATOR I: So the Wise Men departed. Later, a shepherd**
23   **passed by and knocked on Befana's cottage door.**
24   **SHEPHERD: Come to Bethlehem with me and we will find the**
25   **Holy Babe and Mary and Joseph.**
26   **BEFANA:** *(Shaking head "no")* **I am cooking supper now. In the**
27   **morning maybe I will have time to go.**
28   **NARRATOR J: Later that night a great light shone in Befana's**
29   **window and she saw that the sky was filled with angels. It was**
30   **then that she realized that something very important had**
31   **happened at Bethlehem.** *(BEFANA pantomimes action of the*
32   *following narration, taking basket and broom when leaving*
33   *cottage.)*
34   **NARRATOR I: Determined to go, Befana packed a basket with a**
35   **few toys, blew out the lamp, and left her cottage. But in the**

1 dark, she became lost and come morning, no one could tell her
2 how to get to Bethlehem. She wandered and searched,
3 wandered and searched ...
4 **BEFANA:** I must find the Christ child. Oh please, can you help me
5 find Bethlehem? I must find the Baby Jesus. *(BEFANA asks her*
6 *questions in the direction of the congregation, going partway*
7 *down the aisle, searching.)*
8 **NARRATOR J:** According to the traditional story, Befana never
9 found the infant Jesus and has searched in vain from that day
10 on. Every year on the Eve of Epiphany, the night of the Three
11 Kings, Befana with her broom and her basket of toys, goes
12 from house to house in Italy asking ...
13 **BEFANA:** Is he here? Is the Christ child here? *(Congregation sings*
14 "We Three Kings." *Remain seated. If desired, MAGI can*
15 *pantomime continued journey during song, then return to seats.*
16 *BEFANA returns to seat. NARRATORS I and J return to seats,*
17 *NARRATORS K and L advance to lectern.)*
18 **NARRATOR K:** As we lower the flaps and bring our airship back
19 to the home runway, we hope that this little adventure has
20 been meaningful to you. During this season of traditional
21 goodwill, we wanted to introduce you to your Christian
22 neighbors. For all over the world, in every Christian nation
23 and in every Christian family, the children eagerly await their
24 own special Christmas traditions.
25 **NARRATOR L:** These Christmas traditions occur year after year
26 after year. And in this ever changing, confusing world, these
27 traditions are constant and permit the child to know the never
28 changing eternal love of our heavenly Father and to
29 experience the excitement of the birth of our Savior.
30 **NARRATOR K:** Yes, the traditions are different. The various
31 forms of these celebrations may occur on Saint Nicholas Day,
32 or Boxing Day, or the Feast of Saint Stephen; on Christmas
33 Day, or New Year's Day, or on the Eve of Epiphany. The
34 various treasures of the season may come in Christmas
35 stockings, or wooden shoes, from near a manger, or from

1   under a tree.

2   **NARRATOR L: But, from this world of differences in tradition,**

3   **there exists only one star, and the bright light from that star**

4   **binds all of the Christian children of the world into one. The**

5   **story of that star is found in one book.**

6   **NARRATOR K: In many different nations, the children reach for**

7   **that one book. In different languages the children ask for, and**

8   **listen to, that one story. The story of that bright star is forever**

9   **written on the child's heart and soul; it is the greatest story**

10   **ever told ...** *(Organ provides traveling music to set up live*

11   *Nativity with Mary, Joseph, Angels, Shepherds, and Magi, using*

12   "Silent Night." *The entire cast should surround the Nativity or sit*

13   *on steps in front of it. NARRATORS K and L join cast,*

14   *NARRATOR M advances to the lectern. Do not sing until after*

15   *Scripture.)*

16   **NARRATOR M: And it came to pass in those days, that there went**

17   **out a decree from Caesar Augustus, that all the world should**

18   **be taxed. And this taxing was first made when Cyrenius was**

19   **governor of Syria. And all went to be taxed, every one into his**

20   **own city. And Joseph also went up from Galilee, out of the city**

21   **of Nazareth, into Judea, unto the city of David, which is called**

22   **Bethlehem; because he was of the house and lineage of David;**

23   **to be taxed with Mary, his espoused wife, being great with**

24   **child. And so it was, that, while they were there, the days were**

25   **accomplished that she should be delivered. And she brought**

26   **forth her first-born son, and wrapped him in swaddling**

27   **clothes, and laid him in a manger; because there was no room**

28   **for them in the inn.**

29   **And there were in the same country shepherds abiding in the**

30   **field, keeping watch over their flock by night. And lo, the**

31   **angel of the Lord came upon them, and the glory of the Lord**

32   **shone round about them; and they were sore afraid. And the**

33   **angel said unto them, "Fear not; for, behold, I bring you good**

34   **tidings of great joy, which shall be to all people. For unto you**

35   **is born this day in the city of David a Savior, which is Christ**

1   the Lord. And this shall be a sign unto you; Ye shall find the
2   babe wrapped in swaddling clothes, lying in a manger." And
3   suddenly there was with the angel a multitude of the heavenly
4   host praising God, and saying "Glory to God in the highest,
5   and on earth peace, good will toward men."
6   And it came to pass, as the angels were gone away from them
7   into heaven, the shepherds said to one another, "Let us now go
8   even unto Bethlehem, and see this thing which is come to pass,
9   which the Lord hath made known unto us." And they came
10   with haste, and found Mary, and Joseph, and the babe lying
11   in a manger. And when they had seen it, they made known
12   abroad the saying which was told them concerning this child.
13   And all they that heard it wondered at those things which
14   were told them by the shepherds. But Mary kept all these
15   things and pondered them in her heart. And the shepherds
16   returned, glorifying and praising God for all the things that
17   they had heard and seen, as it was told unto them (Luke 2:1-
18   20 King James Version). *(Cast sings "Silent Night."*
19   *Congregation sings "Go Tell It on the Mountain." Remain seated.*
     Recessional during song)

Note: All of the suggested hymns in this presentation, with the possible exception of "Bring a Torch Jeannette Isabella," and "Go Tell It on the Mountain," should be readily available in hymnals of most denominations. The two exceptions should be known by most choir directors, but if a problem exists in finding the music, any hymn of your choice may be substituted.

Big Times Day
By Valarie L. Short

Cast of Characters

Scene I	Scene II	Scene III	Scene IV
Lil' Brother	Mama	Peter	Grandmama
Sister	Daughter	Ginny	Mama
Mama	Uncle	Vicki	Grandpa
Papa	Papa	Jimmy	Papa
	Child 1	Party Guests	Child 1
	Child 2	(Nonspeaking	Child 2
	Child 3	extras)	Child 3
			Carolers
			Liturgical Dancers
			(Optional)

Production Notes

This Christmas play demonstrates how the African-American family has thrived for generations due to reliance on God, faith, family values, and observance of traditions. All four scenes take place around Christmas time. The Christmas story is personalized from the perspective of the people telling it, based on their own life experiences.

Setting

Scene 1 — Slave cabin the day before Big Times (Christmas) in the Deep South, 1830s.
Scene II — Syracuse, NY, a few months after Jerry's rescue, Christmas time, same family a generation away in 1850.
Scene III — Same family a hundred years later, Christmas up North in Syracuse, pre-civil rights movement, 1949.
Scene IV —Christmas today for the same family, over fifty years later.

To reflect the change in time, the scenery, costumes and props should change in every scene. The basket of pinecones and a quilt remain in every scene in some way or another. The tree outside the cabin in the first scene may be imaginary or an undecorated Christmas tree. You may also paint a fireplace on cardboard. After the first scene, the walls, kitchen table, and chairs can remain the same throughout the rest of the play. Pieces may be added to the room to suggest modern updates to the home. These updates may include different styles of the broom (the stick broom to electric broom), prints on the wall, a change in the lighting of the room (candles to lamps) or the use of popular colors of the period. In the third scene, you may add a radio, curtains, stockings hung from the fireplace mantel, possibly a new icebox in the kitchen, an area rug, a coat tree, and a rocking chair. In the final scene, the room may be expanded to give the kitchen a combined kitchen/family room updated look. It should hold a sofa, TV, and a decorated Christmas tree.

The director has the option of casting the same actresses/actors for different roles in alternate scenes just by changing the costumes and makeup, or the director may use different people for each of the parts, based upon the availability of talent in the church.

Costumes

The costumes for Scene I (slave scene) were old clothing in earth tones with necklines, pant bottoms, and sleeves cut off and smeared with shoe polish to give the costumes a look of poor fit and poverty. Mama can wear a shawl. Costumes for the women in Scene II (the late 1800s scene) consisted of long, dark, solid-colored skirts and nondescript classic-looking blouses, aprons, and head wraps. If your budget allows, period pieces may be rented but are not necessary. For the men, we used dark-colored slacks and old shirts with Nehru collars found at thrift stores, and the children's clothing mimicked the adults. You will also need boots and coats for Papa, Uncle, and the three children. For Scene III (early fifties), we raided the closets of some of the older members of our church to find wide skirts and pointy-toed shoes. You may also rent a few costumes if needed. As for the men, we found fifties-style suits, white dress shirts, and narrow ties in the thrift stores. We did splurge on accessories for the fifties party scene, such as women's gloves, hats, handbags, cat-eye glasses, shoes, and jewelry that we found in a vintage clothing store and costume shop. You'll also need an apron, bathrobe, and slippers. Finally, for the present-day Scene IV, we just used current everyday clothing minus logos.

Props

Basket, pine cones, a quilt folded into a pallet, a rolling pin (dough can be imaginary), a bowl and green beans for snapping, deviled egg fixings, a photo album, a game (board game or electronic), a newspaper, and cookies.

Lighting

Although lighting instructions are included, theatrical lights are not necessary to the success of the play. In the first scene, when it is night and the cabin is lit by a candle, you may simply shut off the house lights and light a real candle.

Music

The choir may supply most of the music. The choir director may include several Christmas carols. At the end of Scene I, the choir should sing a Christmas spiritual, such as "Mary Had a Baby" or "The Virgin Mary Had a Baby Boy." One good source of appropriate music is Christmas Spirituals for Choirs edited by Bob Chilcott, published by Oxford University Press. It is available from Primarily a Cappella, 1-800-sing-181 or www.singers.com/arrangers/christmasarrangements.html. The order number is 9035. There are other places in the script where you may play recorded music, including Christmas music by B.B. King or another similar artist, swing-style Christmas music, and contemporary Christian Christmas music by Kirk Franklin or another current singer.

1   **Scene I**

2 *(MAMA bustles around the simple kitchen of the family's slave*

3 *quarters. SISTER and LIL' BROTHER sit, talking.)*

4 SISTER: Yes, we gon' see Papa soon. He gon' get a pass to come see

5   us from Master Edwards.

6 LIL' BROTHER: We gon' see him all day. Ain't nobody got to work.

7 SISTER: We gon' eat good too! We gon' have some ham. Some turnip

8   greens. Sweet potatoes. Biscuits.

9 LIL' BROTHER: Biscuits with some sweet sugar. I'm gon' eat

10   eleventeen biscuits.

11 SISTER: Ain't no such a thing as eleventeen biscuits. And if it was,

12   Mama wouldn't let you eat them.

13 LIL' BROTHER: I is too. Big Times Day, Mama say I get to eat all I

14   want. Mama, cain't us have eleventeen biscuits, if'n us want?

15 MAMA: Mmm-hmm. You sho' can, child.

16 SISTER: Eleventeen, Mama? Tell him there ain't no such thing like

17   eleventeen, Mama.

18 MAMA: *(Gathering up her shawl)* Aw baby, he can have as many as

19   his belly can hold. It be Big Times tomorrow. It only be once a

20   year.

21 LIL' BROTHER: *(To SISTER)* See, just lak I tol' you. Mama, us'n

22   gon' get a new shirt from Master too. Ain't us'n?

23 MAMA: I sure hope so. *(Sounding slightly distracted now, she is*

24   *looking around the cabin.)* Come on, git yo basket. We gon'

25   gather up some pine cones for the Big Times tomorry. Fo' it git

26   dark. *(ALL exit and re-enter with SISTER carrying basket near a*

27   *big tree some distance from the cabin.)*

28 MAMA: I brought you two out here, 'cause what I gon' tell you, I

29   don't want nobody to hear. Just us, understand? Y'all won't be

30   able to breathe a word of this to nobody, or else Papa may be

31   hurt.

32 SISTER: What is it, Mama? Papa gon' be all right. We won't say

33   nothing. Right, lil' bro?

34 LIL' BROTHER: No, nothing. I wouldn't hurt Papa for nothing in

35   the world.

1　MAMA: Now, y'all gather up pine cones, but listen good. Don't act
2　　　like nothing is different. *(MAMA moves to a point under the tree,*
3　　　*where she can watch for anyone approaching or walking nearby.*
4　　　*SISTER and LIL' BROTHER pick up pine cones, but listen intently.)*
5　MAMA: Come Big Times Day, Papa gon' leave us and go up North to
6　　　be free.
7　SISTER: Free? Free, Mama?
8　MAMA: *(Nods her head and also acknowledges God.)* Then in due
9　　　time, he'll send for us. You can't breathe a word of it. Act like
10　　nothing happened. He gon' come in the middle of the night, and
11　　you two got to act real quiet. Den before morning, he be gone.
12　　Everyone be so busy up at the big house with Christmas and
13　　goings-on, they won't notice he ain't with us this year, lak he
14　　usually is. He'll have a good head start before they notice and
15　　send the dogs after him. When dey ask you if you seen him, you
16　　say, "Naw, he didn't come this year for Big Times." Dat be all.
17　SISTER: Will Papa be all right, Mama?
18　MAMA: We just got to pray. We just got to pray and trust in the
19　　Lord that everything will be all right. Papa be big and strong.
20　　Ain't nothing gon' happen to him. The Lord will see him safely
21　　up North. One day we'll go to be with him.
22　LIL' BROTHER: What if he don't make it, Mama? I scared, Mama.
23　MAMA: Now lil' bro, it be your time to act like a man with Papa
24　　gone. You got to be strong. *(She gives him a hug and looks into his*
25　　*face for agreement.)*
26　LIL' BROTHER: I will. *(Blackout. It's nighttime, with only one candle*
27　　*lit in the cabin. MAMA, SISTER and LIL' BROTHER are seated on*
28　　*a quilt pallet on the floor around PAPA.)*
29　PAPA: I'm gon' be all right, children. Be brave for your mama. Now,
30　　hush. If God can deliver Daniel out of the lion's den, he can
31　　deliver us. You just pray for me, and I'll come back for you.
32　　Y'all just pray. *(PAPA reaches to pull his family closer to him.)*
33　　Now, let me tell you about the very first Big Times Day. A little
34　　bitty baby was born in Bethlehem, a very long time ago. Now,
35　　the prophet Micah told the world, way back before the baby was

1   born, a long time ago, that God would send his Son. This
2   prophet knew that there was going to be a very special night in
3   Bethlehem. The angel came to Mary one day and told her that
4   she was gon' be the one to have God's only Son.
5   SISTER: What did the angel look like, Papa?
6   PAPA: Well, now, let's see. He was wearing the finest pearly white
7   robe. It was laid with diamonds. My, how that robe sparkled. It
8   was one fine garment.
9   LIL' BROTHER: Was she scared, Papa, when she see'd the angel?
10   PAPA: Well, she might have been scared, maybe just a little. But
11   Mary believed that angel. Now the man that was going to marry
12   her, his name was Joseph. Joseph was a good man, a carpenter
13   by trade, just like your papa. But Joseph had a problem with
14   Mary being with baby and all before they was to get married,
15   but then an angel came to him too.
16   SISTER: Another angel, Papa?
17   PAPA: Mmm-hmm. This angel told Joseph that everything was going
18   to be all right, and that he should go ahead with his plans and
19   marry Mary. After all, they was going to be the parents of this
20   very special baby. Now, wouldn't you know, when it came close
21   to the time that this baby was going to be born, Caesar Augustus
22   made everybody report back to their family home to be
23   counted. They called that the census. Now, when they got to
24   Bethlehem, there was no place for them to stay. All the places to
25   spend the night were taken. And, well, Mary was big with the
26   baby, and she was tired from the long trip.
27   LIL' BROTHER: Have mercy!
28   SISTER: What did they do, Papa, what did they do?
29   PAPA: It seems that there was an innkeeper who made a 'lowance for
30   them to stay in the barn out back with the animals. And
31   wouldn't you know, that was the very place she had the baby.
32   That very night. Right there in the stable with the animals. He
33   didn't have no fancy place to be born. No siree, God picked a
34   stable for his very special Son to be born. And do you know
35   what they named that baby?

1   **SISTER and LIL' BROTHER:** *(Together)* **Jesus!**

2   **SISTER:** **I like that story, Papa.**

3   **LIL' BROTHER:** **Me too.** *(PAPA holds all of them close while lights dim*

4   *on cabin scene. Choir sings softly "Mary Had a Baby" or any other*

5   *song in keeping with the time period.)*

6

7   **Scene II**

8   *(LIL' BROTHER and SISTER are now middle-aged. Their mother*

9   *and father have passed on. Scene takes place in the home of SISTER*

10   *[now known as MAMA]. She is preparing for Christmas, rolling*

11   *dough in the kitchen and singing softly to herself. Her DAUGHTER*

12   *is seated at the table, snapping beans. Times have changed. They*

13   *don't have much, but they are free. They are making a living for*

14   *themselves up North. The tattered quilt from the first scene remains*

15   *in this scene. A basket of pine cones is the main Christmas*

16   *decoration.)*

17   **DAUGHTER:** **Mama, can you believe it's almost Christmas time**

18   **once again? I love this time of the year.**

19   **MAMA:** **Yes, daughter, you can feel it in the air up here. Syracuse**

20   **weather gets mighty cold in the winter. Not like where I came**

21   **from. When Big Times came, it was still nice out. Just a little nip**

22   **in the air is all.**

23   **DAUGHTER:** **When Grandmama was still alive, she'd tell us about**

24   **how Big Papa made his escape during Big Times. Every year she**

25   **would tell that story.**

26   **MAMA:** **She just wanted y'all to know just how blessed you were to**

27   **have been born free up here in Syracuse, New York.**

28   **DAUGHTER:** **Yes, I was feeling mighty grateful till they passed that**

29   **fugitive slave law. I can't hardly believe it, can you? The law say**

30   **they can send a slave catcher after you, all the way up here in**

31   **the North. They're allowed to hunt down a runaway slave and**

32   **take that slave back to their old master in the South.**

33   **MAMA:** **Yes, it's not safe in New York these days. Used to be you**

34   **could have your freedom forever, if you made it this far. These**

35   **are troubled times, mighty dangerous for us folks.**

1 DAUGHTER: Do you think they will come for you, Mama? Or
2 Uncle?
3 MAMA: Naw, I don't believe so. Old Master been long gone himself.
4 They wouldn't even know what we'd look like. We was just little
5 children when we left. Besides, we be too old to be any good to
6 them folks now.
7 DAUGHTER: But Mama, aren't these Syracuse white folks
8 something else? Made us proud, just this pass October. Can you
9 believe it, Mama? The whole community rallied around and
10 fought back to free Jerry from the jail.
11 MAMA: Naw, I still can't believe it. But ain't up to me to believe it.
12 It all be in the Lord God's plan.
13 DAUGHTER: *(She is lively and animated, acting out the rescue.)* The
14 search man come to find Jerry and return him back down
15 South to his old master. Jerry was living up here in Syracuse,
16 had his own metal shop, making a living for himself. Well, the
17 whole town got word about his capture. The news spread like
18 wildfire. They say there were thousands gathered right there at
19 Clinton Square, come to free Jerry. Shouting, "Free Jerry. Free
20 Jerry." Some men figured out they shouldn't storm the front of
21 the jail, so they decided to go 'round the back. A man stationed
22 up front sent the signal to the ones around back when they
23 heard the jail guards had fired their last shot. You see, they
24 come on up to rescue Jerry after all the powder had been fired.
25 Some men tore off a big plank of wood and took it and rammed
26 it into the courthouse. Knocked the door clean off!
27 MAMA: Praise the Lord! Poor Jerry, I heard he had most of his
28 clothes snatched off him in the process of them taking him out
29 and guards trying to keep him in jail. Everyone down at the
30 courthouse quickly lifted him over the heads of the crowd and
31 delivered him to a safe house.
32 DAUGHTER: Next thing you knew, Jerry had been taken to Oswego
33 secretly, and from there, he took a ship to Canada. Safe.
34 MAMA: Hallelujah!
35 DAUGHTER: Yes, I guess Syracuse, New York, ain't a bad place to

1   be right now. Them white folks won't allow the slave catchers to
2   take us back down South.
3   MAMA: Lord, have mercy! I just hope they don't get the notion to
4   take Reverend Loguen. They after him and want him bad.
5   DAUGHTER: That's because he talk so strong about freeing the
6   slaves in the South. He say he ain't going nowhere, ain't gon' be
7   taken back as a slave. A man ought to be free, not made a slave
8   just because of the color of his skin. And he's ready to fight to
9   prove it. His wife and children are so scared for him. I hope they
10   talk him into leaving for Canada soon. Even if it's just for a little
11   while, just till things settle down.
12   MAMA: Well now, that is something for him to decide. I know the
13   Lord will help him make the right decision. Now, go on and get
14   the table ready. When your Uncle and Papa get here, they gon'
15   want to eat.
16   DAUGHTER: For sure. I ain't never seen nobody eat as many
17   biscuits as Uncle Bro can eat.
18   MAMA: He always has loved those sweet biscuits, even as a little boy.
19   *(Door opens; PAPA, UNCLE, and CHILD 1, 2, and 3 enter,*
20   *stomping snow off their boots and taking off their coats and hanging*
21   *them up.)*
22   UNCLE: Sho' smells good in here. Sho' is bitter cold and snowy out
23   there. Weather in Syracuse sho' tell you Big Times is near.
24   CHILD 1: You mean Christmas, Uncle?
25   UNCLE: *(Grabbing MAMA and swinging her around)* Naw, Sister, we
26   mean Big Times. Don't us'n.
27   MAMA: Aw, stop it, Bro. The children call it Christmas now.
28   UNCLE: We gon' have plenty of biscuits, Sister?
29   MAMA: We sho' is!
30   UNCLE: Then it's Big Times! *(The CHILDREN begin running around*
31   *On-stage at the excitement.)*
32   MAMA: Y'all children, stop running around in here. Uncle, tell them
33   the Christmas story while we get dinner on.
34   UNCLE: Did I ever tell y'all the story of the very first Big Times? All
35   the fuss is about a little itty-bitty baby born long ago. Come on,

1   y'all. Have a seat. I'm gonna tell you a story. *(CHILD 1, 2 and 3*
2   *seat themselves on the floor close to UNCLE, who is seated in a*
3   *chair.)*
4   CHILD 2: Yes, Uncle, tell us.
5   CHILD 1: Please tell us.
6   CHILD 3: This story is about Jesus! Right, Uncle?
7   UNCLE: Well, let's see now. Mary and Joseph — that's the Mama
8   and Papa of this here baby — were making their way to
9   Bethlehem, because Caesar Augustus had ordered them to
10   return to their home town directly. Mary was big with baby. It
11   was just about time for the baby to be born. That very night, out
12   in the field, shepherds were tending to their sheep. It was a cool
13   night — not as cold as up here in Syracuse — and it was clear
14   out. A few of them was just settling down near the fire they built
15   when all of a sudden, an angel appeared!
16   CHILD 1: A real angel, Uncle?
17   CHILD 2: Ain't no such thing as an angel. I ain't never see'd no
18   angel.
19   CHILD 3: Hush. Let Uncle tell the story. What was this angel
20   wearing, Uncle?
21   UNCLE: This angel, well, you ain't never seen the likes of it before.
22   It wore a long, shiny robe. So shiny, you couldn't look directly
23   at it. It was magnificent. Ooo-wee! You know, when the good
24   Lord does something, he does it right. The Lord wouldn't send
25   no angel just looking any old kind of way. That's how you knew
26   this angel here was real.
27   CHILD 1: What did the Shepherds do?
28   CHILD 2: Was they scared, Uncle?
29   UNCLE: Was they scared? Yes, they was scared! A couple of them
30   saw that angel standing there in that bright, shiny robe and took
31   off running. Just as they was getting away, the angel stopped
32   them. This here angel told them to quit they running and listen.
33   Angel tol' em not to be afraid. He said in a soothing voice, "Fear
34   not: for, behold, I bring you good tidings of great joy, which
35   shall be to all people. For unto you is born this day in the city of

1   David a Savior, which is Christ the Lord. And this shall be a sign
2   unto you: Ye shall find the babe wrapped in swaddling clothes,
3   lying in a manger" (Luke 2:10-12). Then something very special
4   happened. A night like never before! A host of heavenly angels
5   surrounded those shepherds, saying, "Glory to God in the
6   highest, and on earth peace, good will toward men" (Luke 2:14).
7   Well, them shepherds had never seen the whole sky light up with
8   angels before. They just stood there, couldn't move. Till one of
9   them shepherds said, "Hey, what is we waiting for? Let's go see
10   the baby." They gathered up their stuff, and the way I hear tell,
11   they practically ran all the way to Bethlehem. And do you know
12   who they saw when they got to the stable?
13   CHILD 1, 2 and 3: *(Together)* The baby Jesus!
14   UNCLE: That's right, and they was so happy. Imagine that. God
15   picked them, lowly shepherds, to be the first ones to welcome the
16   new baby.
17   CHILD 1: Just lowly shepherds. *(Lights fade to black On-stage. The*
18   *choir may sing an appropriate Christmas carol at this time.)*
19
20   **Scene III**
21   *(This scene takes place approximately one hundred years later. The*
22   *characters are from the same family, several generations later. This*
23   *family appears to be prospering now, as can be seen by the radio,*
24   *curtains at the windows, Christmas stockings on the fireplace and*
25   *new icebox in the kitchen. A battered quilt [the remnants of the same*
26   *one from the Scene I] and a basket of pine cones are displayed.*
27   *PETER and GINNY are preparing for a Christmas Eve party.*
28   *Christmas music from the era, such as that by B.B. King, is playing*
29   *softly in the background.)*
30   GINNY: *(At the kitchen table, making deviled eggs)* I want everything
31   to be just right. Set those chairs out around the wall, Peter. I
32   want everything to be just right for cousin Jimmy's birthday
33   party. Give us all a chance to get together just before the
34   holiday. Jimmy's been so down lately since coming back from
35   the war. He hasn't been able to find any work.

1 PETER: That's because he don't want to work. *(PETER rolls up the*
2 *area rug and puts out extra chairs.)*
3 GINNY: That ain't right, Peter. You know he's been getting up early
4 looking for work every day.
5 PETER: But he too particular. Won't just take any kind of job.
6 Won't sweep floors or be the elevator porter at the hotel. I told
7 him about the porter job just last week. Naw, seems like he too
8 good for that. He want a real job in that new auto factory. He
9 know they only hiring white men over in that factory.
10 GINNY: Now Peter, can't say as I blames him. Said he put his life on
11 the line, fighting for all Americans' freedom in the war. Say he
12 deserve to be treated just like any other man.
13 PETER: Times haven't changed for the colored people. He just
14 better git used to being back over here, all I'm saying, Ginny.
15 GINNY: Maybe times need to change for us. Maybe there is
16 something colored folks can do for themselves to make times
17 better.
18 PETER: Aw Ginny, I wish things was different for us. They still
19 lynching young black men down South for looking at white
20 women. We just needs to be thankful we're up North.
21 GINNY: But are we free if our brothers in the South are not free?
22 Remember the story of Jerry's rescue? I mean, that happened
23 right here in Syracuse. Folks have to work together to change
24 things.
25 PETER: Yes, but we can't be bothered about everything. It's hard
26 enough trying to survive ourselves.
27 GINNY: Yes, I know what you mean, but still. Isn't it a blessing that
28 Vicki is the first one of the family to go to college? Imagine that!
29 Who would've thought that our daughter would be going to
30 college? Our great ancestors would have been so proud. Who
31 knows? Maybe they're bursting with pride up there in heaven.
32 VICKI: *(Entering Stage Right, wearing robe and slippers and carrying*
33 *a photo album)* Somebody call my name?
34 GINNY: Lord, child. I thought you would have been dressed by now.
35 You still lounging around? Folks be coming soon.

1   VICKI: I know, I'll get dressed in a minute. I just love this time of the
2   year, Mama. I was just looking at some of the old photographs.
3   *(Flipping through the pages in the scrapbook)* Seems like
4   Christmas time was always a special time of the year for our
5   family. *(Looking up)* I'm glad I was able to catch a ride home
6   from college with Julie. I would hate to miss this home cooking.
7   What is that I smell?
8   PETER: Aw girl, same as we always eat come Christmas time. We got
9   sweet potatoes, collard greens, ham ... mmm, and sweet biscuits.
10   I just love those sweet biscuits you make, Ginny.
11   GINNY: Years ago, they used to call it Big Times Day. Christmas Day
12   we always ate good. Even if we didn't have much, we sure ate
13   good. And how we couldn't wait to hear Grandpapa tell the
14   Christmas story. He couldn't read or write, but he knew the
15   Christmas story by heart.
16   VICKI: Do you remember how they used to tell the story, Mama?
17   GINNY: Oh, I remember bits and pieces of it. He would start out
18   talking about the very first Big Times Day, when an itty-bitty
19   baby was born. You should have seen his eyes light up when he
20   got to the part about the three wise men. His eyes would sparkle.
21   He would tell us that the mean and wicked King Herod couldn't
22   fool the wise men. Old King Herod heard that there was another
23   King, a King of the Jews that had been born. Now, King Herod
24   became concerned about this new King. He found out that some
25   wise men were going to try and find this new King, so he sent for
26   those wise men. The wise men told the King that they were
27   following a star from the east. They had come from far away.
28   King Herod told them, "When you find that itty-bitty baby, let
29   me know where that baby was, so that I can go and worship
30   him." Well, do you think those wise men fell for that? No siree,
31   they didn't. Why do you think they were called the wise men?
32   God warned those three wise men in a dream. God told them
33   that they should not return back to Herod. No siree. They didn't
34   trust old King Herod, so they went back to their own country,
35   but this time they went a different zigzag way back, to throw the

1   King off their trail.

2   VICKI: Gee, Mama, that's a swell story.

3   GINNY: Now you hurry and get ready for the party. Cousin will be

4   here soon with the rest of the folks. *(GINNY and PETER make*

5   *final preparations for the party and turn the music up. Doorbell*

6   *rings. They go to welcome GUESTS.)*

7   GINNY: Jimmy, how you doing? This your friend? Well, come on in.

8   Welcome, everybody.

9   PETER: Y'all come on in out the cold. *(GINNY and PETER welcome*

10   *the party guests, dressed up in party clothes. GINNY takes off her*

11   *apron. A few GUESTS begin to jitterbug to swing-style Christmas*

12   *music. Or, if preferred, Christmas music is played in the background*

13   *and conversation and laughing are heard as the lights dim.)*

14

15   **Scene IV**

16   *(Present-day Christmas, many generations removed from the first*

17   *Big Times. Family is doing well financially. Now there is a TV,*

18   *beautifully decorated Christmas tree, and a large sofa. The*

19   *CHILDREN are playing a board game or electronic game. PAPA is*

20   *reading the paper. GRANDPA is napping in the rocking chair.*

21   *GRANDMAMA and MAMA are at the kitchen table making cookies.*

22   *Soulful contemporary Christian Christmas music by Kirk Franklin*

23   *or a similar artist is playing in the background. There are still*

24   *remnants of the beat-up quilt and a basket of pine cones as part of*

25   *the Christmas decorations.)*

26   GRANDMAMA: Well, ain't this nice to see. Everybody home for

27   Christmas. What a blessing! You know, years ago they used to

28   call Christmas Big Times Day. Your great-great-great-great-

29   great grandpapa escaped up North to Syracuse from slavery,

30   then sent for his family. That's how come we ended up in

31   Syracuse.

32   CHILDREN: *(Ad lib)* We know, Grandma! Un-huh, right, etc.

33   MAMA: Children, show some respect. Grandmama just going over a

34   little family history.

35   PAPA: *(Putting his newspaper down)* These children need to know

1   their history. Seem like children today don't know how hard it
2   was for us years ago — just what the black people's struggle was
3   about. If they knew, maybe they would show their older
4   relatives some respect. If they knew their history, they would
5   know how important it is to stay in school. They would work
6   hard to get a good education so they could provide for their
7   families.
8   GRANDPA: That's right. You tell 'em, son. They just don't
9   understand today. If they knew the trials and tribulations our
10   people had to go through, just to be able to learn how to read.
11   They don't know how many people risked their lives fighting the
12   battle to end segregated schools — just so we could have the
13   same opportunity as the white children. Dr. Martin Luther King
14   would hang his head to look around and see the lack of progress
15   if he were alive today. How we gonna get ahead today without
16   an education? What's we gonna do? What kind of job will we
17   get? How can we make enough money to support ourselves? If
18   these children today only knew their history, wouldn't be no
19   dropouts. Wouldn't be no such thing as a high school dropout.
20   These young folks need to take advantage of the opportunities
21   they have nowadays.
22   PAPA: That's right, and what about these young men standing
23   around on street corners disrespecting young women? Too
24   many families got absentee fathers. Kids going to visit their dads
25   in jail. What is that all about? If they knew their history, maybe
26   they wouldn't be so quick to join a gang or get strung out on
27   drugs.
28   GRANDPA: Yeah, I've heard that bad mouth dirty talk on some of
29   those rap records. Dirty and disrespectful language. Don't seem
30   like they have any respect for each other. Don't they know the
31   sacrifices strong black women have made so their children could
32   have a better life? Our women have been used and abused by
33   the white man. Don't get me started about what they did to our
34   slave women to satisfy their own selfishness. What a young
35   black man look like today, using such language referring to

1   young black women? Don't make no sense. That's what I mean,
2   if they only knew their history.
3   PAPA: If they knew their history, maybe the young black women
4   today wouldn't be having so many babies while they're in their
5   teens, not to mention the HIV epidemic. Seem like young people
6   today don't know the sacrifices our people made so that they
7   could have the right to vote or to get a good education.
8   GRANDPA: Don't get me started on the right to vote. Don't they
9   know we had to get up early in the morning? We stood in line
10   all day waiting to register. 'Course they would publish the
11   wrong time for the office to open, just so we wouldn't show up.
12   Get up to the front of the line, only for them to ask you a
13   ridiculous question like how many bubbles in a bar of soap. Any
14   answer you gave would be the wrong answer. If they only knew
15   their history, young people today would run downtown to
16   register to vote. Then they need to be the first ones at the polls
17   in the morning, as soon as they open the voting polls. How else
18   you going to able to select people to represent us that are
19   sensitive to our needs? Lord, Lord, Lord! If they only knew
20   their history, they would know the Lord was always there for us.
21   How could we have made it this far? They need to get back into
22   church. Get down on their knees. That's where they need to be.
23   PAPA: That's right. If they knew the stuff we were made of, and how
24   God has seen us through, young people wouldn't give up so
25   easy. They would hold on to hope. They would always believe in
26   God and family. Don't they know the only reason we have
27   survived is because God has brought us this far?
28   GRANDMAMA: Well, we just got to pray on it. And keep praying
29   for the children. It is only the Lord God that has seen us
30   through this far along.
31   MAMA: And we have to work on it. More of us have to go out into
32   the communities and reach out to these young people. It is our
33   responsibility to let them know about their history. We need to
34   remind them. God can see them through. Otherwise, what kind
35   of future are our folks going to have?

1 CHILD 1: *(Cleverly distracts the older members of the FAMILY from*
2 *such a deep conversation.)* **So, what we gon' have for Christmas**
3 **dinner this year, Mama?**
4 MAMA: **Well, let's see. They'll be ham and collard greens, candied**
5 **sweet potatoes, macaroni and cheese, green bean casserole …**
6 **We'll have all the trimmings.**
7 CHILD 1: **Sweet biscuits too, Mama? Right, Mama?**
8 MAMA: **Yeah, we'll have plenty of sweet biscuits. That's our family**
9 **tradition. And black-eyed peas, rice and gravy, sweet potato pie,**
10 **pecan pie, Christmas cookies … All that too.**
11 CHILD 2: **I can't wait! Santa Claus comin', and we gon' get toys. And**
12 **the day after that, we have Kwanzaa. A whole week of**
13 **celebrations, and a big feast day and other presents too.**
14 PAPA: **That reminds me, children, have you learned your parts for**
15 **the Christmas play at church this year?**
16 CHILD 3: **Yes, and I get to be a sheep. Baa, baa, baa.** *(CHILD 3*
17 *gallops across the stage and back, baaing.)*
18 CHILD 2: **I get to be an angel. Mama, is my costume almost ready?**
19 MAMA: **Yes, I'll finish it today.**
20 PAPA: **Did I ever tell you the story of the very first Big Times Day?**
21 **When the itty-bitty baby was born?**
22 CHILD 1: **Yes, Papa. Every year!**
23 PAPA: *(Feigning hurt feelings)* **Well, I don't have to tell you, being**
24 **that you know it already.**
25 CHILD 2: **Please, Papa, I don't remember it.**
26 PAPA: **A long time ago, it all started with Mary and Joseph. That's**
27 **the baby's Mama and Papa. Do you know what swaddling**
28 **clothes are?** *(Doorbell rings.)*
29 MAMA: **Who could that be out on Christmas Eve?** *(Going to the door,*
30 *hearing Christmas carols sung faintly)* **Well, it's Christmas**
31 **carolers.**
32 GRANDPA: **Well, let them in. I didn't know they still did that.**
33 *(CAROLERS come in. They exchange Christmas greetings, then*
34 *raise their voices in a Christmas carol medley. LITURGICAL*
35 *DANCERS may also appear in the aisles and dance to the carols in*
36 *celebration if desired.)*

The Eyes of El Cristo

By George P. McCallum

Adapted for Readers Theatre by Melvin R. White

Cast of Characters

Narrator

Tio Juan — a middle-aged character, congenial and understanding.

Pablocito — a lively seven-year-old boy.

Mama Conchita — Palocito's mother, twenty-five to thirty; pleasant motherly type.

Señora Condora — a sweet old lady; quite frail.

Production Notes

This script's Hispanic flavor will delight your audience with young Pablocito's adventures. No special settings or props are required. This story lends itself to colorful character costuming and will be enhanced by special attire if available — serapes, sombreros, sandals etc.

1   NARRATOR: **Christmas has a rich and varied tradition in many**
2   **cultures and countries. Let's visit Old Mexico in this**
3   **adaptation of George P. McCallum's story entitled "The Eyes**
4   **of El Cristo."** *(If desired, a different NARRATOR "Storyteller"*
5   *may take over at this spot.)*
6   NARRATOR: **Tio Juan, uncle to Pablocito, was lying on the**
7   **ground in Mama Conchita's back yard, leaning against the**
8   **yucca tree. He had been there a long time, his hat down over**
9   **his eyes, dozing and being philosophical in his thoughts.**
10   **Occasionally there would be a puff of smoke from his pipe, but**
11   **he said nothing. Then, finally, he spoke:**
12   TIO JUAN: **It is good to be good.**
13   NARRATOR: **Pablocito, sitting near his uncle, said nothing, but**
14   **waited for Tio Juan to speak again. But to himself he said:**
15   PABLOCITO: **It is nice to be here with Tio Juan, just sitting in the**
16   **sun, doing nothing, nothing at all.**
17   NARRATOR: **Once in a while Pablocito's uncle would puff**
18   **furiously on his pipe and emit huge clouds of smoke. That was**
19   **always a sign that he had reached some important conclusion**
20   **in his thoughts. Then he would reach up, take his pipe from**
21   **his mouth, push his hat back, and speak what was on his**
22   **mind — in as few words as possible, of course. Just now there**
23   **had been the cloud of smoke, and Tio Juan removed his pipe,**
24   **spat on the ground to his left, and said, looking ahead and not**
25   **at Pablocito:**
26   TIO JUAN: **Si, it is good to be good.**
27   NARRATOR: **Then he put his pipe back in his mouth, closed his**
28   **eyes, pulled his hat down, and began dozing again. Pablocito**
29   **wrinkled his small, otherwise unfurrowed brow, as his uncle's**
30   **philosophy gave him much food for thought. He repeated to**
31   **himself:**
32   PABLOCITO: **It is good to be good. I don't quite understand, but**
33   **if Tio Juan says so, it must be so. But when I am good, I don't**
34   **get anything for it. It is much more fun — and much easier —**
35   **to do as I please and just enjoy myself. When I am good, no**

1   beautiful angel comes and says, "Fine work, Pablocito. Here
2   is a bagful of centavos." Nor when I am bad does a devil come
3   and carry me off to punish me. *(Deciding)* No, Tio Juan is not
4   right this time. It is not necessarily good to be good. It is more
5   fun just to take life as it comes. It is not always good to be
6   good.
7   NARRATOR: Pulling his hat down over his eyes, Pablocito
8   assumed his uncle's position. He had hardly closed his eyes
9   when Mama Conchita came to the back door and called:
10   MAMA: Juan! Pablocito! Where are you? *(Looks around, and then*
11   *spots them under the yucca tree.)* Ah, just as I thought, you lazy
12   ones! Come now! Get up!
13   NARRATOR: Slowly the two rose, gradually aware of the din of
14   Mama Conchita's voice. Slowly they started toward the
15   house, Pablocito stumbling along a few feet behind his uncle.
16   MAMA: Fine ones you are! Half an hour it is now since I asked you
17   to go gather wood for me, and here you sit, sleeping in the sun.
18   How can you expect me to make anything for you to eat if you
19   do not bring me wood to cook with? Now get along, both of
20   you, and do not come back until you have your arms full of
21   wood! You hear me?
22   NARRATOR: She turned without another word and went into the
23   house. Tio Juan blinked twice and looked at Pablocito, who
24   also blinked and stared at his uncle.
25   TIO JUAN: Come, Pablocito. I think we'd better do as your
26   mother says and go after the wood.
27   PABLOCITO: Si, Tio Juan.
28   TIO JUAN: She is right, your mother. If she has no wood, she
29   cannot cook anything for us to eat. Tomorrow is the day of the
30   Christmas fiesta, and she is cooking many things for the
31   celebration — the fiesta of La Navidad, si, the birthday of the
32   Christ child. It is a wonderful fiesta.
33   PABLOCITO: Si, si! La Navidad. It's the best of all the fiestas!
34   NARRATOR: The best of all the fiestas. Pablocito always looked
35   forward to it, counting the days and anticipating the good

1   times he would have. Always there were presents from his
2   mother, and even something from Tio Juan.
3   PABLOCITO: The presents! All the good things to eat! Mother is
4   the best cook in the world, and at Christmas she makes better
5   things than you can ever think of! La Navidad is the most
6   wonderful fiesta!
7   TIO JUAN: Let's cut across the village. There's a place on the
8   other side where we can get lots of wood. It isn't very far. And
9   we can look in the shop windows on the way over, si?
10   PABLOCITO: Si!
11   NARRATOR: On their way through the village they stopped at the
12   many shops to gaze through the windows at the good things
13   inside. Some had all sorts of good things to eat. Some had toys
14   such as Pablocito had never seen before. It was the shop
15   window of Miguel Juarento that caught their attention,
16   however. Miguel's shop was usually filled with all kinds of
17   beautiful pictures, but now, for the Christmas season, he had
18   just one picture in his display window, a portrait of Christ. Tio
19   Juan and Pablocito stopped and looked for a long while at the
20   picture. Christ was portrayed with a wreath of thorns on his
21   head, his eyes closed.
22   TIO JUAN: El Cristo. It is a beautiful picture of the Son of the
23   Blessed Virgin, verdad?
24   PABLOCITO: Ah, si. He looks so kind — and good.
25   TIO JUAN: It is one of the most famous portraits of Christ ever
26   painted.
27   PABLOCITO: Tio Juan, he looks sad, too. *(Seeing a card under the*
28   *picture)* What are the words under the picture?
29   TIO JUAN: *(Reading)* For those who are worthy and have the faith,
30   the Christ's eyes will open. *(Read in a halting fashion)*
31   PABLOCITO: Those who are worthy?
32   TIO JUAN: It means those who are good and obey El Cristo's
33   teachings.
34   PABLOCITO: Oh. *(Stares at the picture.)* The eyes remain closed.
35   TIO JUAN: Come, Pablocito, we must hurry and get the wood, or

1   your mother will be very angry.

2   **PABLOCITO:** *(More to himself than to his uncle)* The eyes did not

3   open. I must not be any good at all.

4   **NARRATOR:** All of the rest of the way to the wood, and then all of

5   the way back home, his arms filled with sticks of wood,

6   Pablocito said nothing, thinking only of El Cristo and the eyes

7   which would not open for him. It made him very sad to think

8   they had remained closed. He would give anything to have

9   them open! Open for him! *(Transition)* The day of the fiesta La

10   Navidad came.

11   **MAMA:** Pablocito, eat your breakfast! Then go to the church for

12   Mass. Don't forget to take the candle you saved your pennies

13   to buy just for Mass this morning.

14   **NARRATOR:** Of course he could have purchased a much nicer

15   one, but there had been those tempting candies in Señora de

16   Lara's sweet shop and the cakes in the bakery which had cut

17   down his small pile of pennies, so his candle was not the

18   majestic offering it might have been.

19   **MAMA:** Come right home after Mass. We want to be all ready for

20   the fiesta when it begins.

21   **PABLOCITO:** When does it begin, Mama?

22   **MAMA:** This afternoon, right after we eat a bit. Tio Juan and I

23   went to early Mass this morning so we can get everything

24   ready for fiesta, so remember — come right home after Mass.

25   **PABLOCITO:** Yes, Mama!

26   **NARRATOR:** The good Padre had a beautiful Mass for the

27   birthday of El Cristo. Even to seven-year-old Pablocito, it

28   meant much: the story of the birth of our Savior, the three

29   wise men, and the shepherds on the hill — the Padre told the

30   story simply and beautifully. Pablocito thought it was the

31   most beautiful story he had ever heard. *(Transition)* When

32   Mass was over, Pablocito started for home, trotting along as

33   fast as he could because he lived clear across the village, and

34   it was getting late. As he dashed around the corner by Señora

35   de Lara's sweet shop, he almost ran into an old, old lady

1   loaded down with bundles, trying to make her way along over
2   the rough, cobblestone road. Pablocito watched her. Every few
3   feet she would have to painfully bend down to pick up one of
4   the bundles which had dropped. His first instinct was to help
5   her.
6   PABLOCITO: But if I help her, I'll be late for the fiesta! I don't
7   want to miss the fun!
8   NARRATOR: Just then the old lady tripped on a protruding stone
9   and fell, her bundles flying every which way. There was no
10   alternative; Pablocito could do nothing but hurry to her
11   assistance.
12   OLD LADY: *(Moaning)* Ay! These packages have caused me more
13   trouble than they are worth.
14   PABLOCITO: *(Helping her to her feet)* Did you hurt yourself?
15   OLD LADY: No, no. I'm all right. *(Winces as she bears down on left*
16   *foot.)* Maybe I did hurt my foot a little.
17   PABLOCITO: Let me pick up your bundles for you ... and help
18   you to your home.
19   OLD LADY: Gracias a Dios. It is only a step to my house. See, the
20   little one between those two big ones, just over there.
21   NARRATOR: She pointed down the street to a tiny house squeezed
22   in between two larger ones. In a few minutes they were there
23   and in the house, and the little old lady, they told him her
24   name was Señora Condora, was able to rest her foot which
25   had been turned but not badly sprained.
26   OLD LADY: I'll be all right now.
27   PABLOCITO: *(Getting up to leave)* I hope so. I must go now, as this
28   afternoon —
29   OLD LADY: *(Interrupting)* Oh, please don't go. It's so nice to have
30   someone here to talk to. You see, I live here all by myself, and
31   sometimes I get so very lonely.
32   PABLOCITO: Well, all right — but just for a little while.
33   NARRATOR: He sat down again. Already the fiesta was beginning
34   and he would miss part of it, but that was all right. It was
35   much better for him to be helping Señora Condora, this little

1   old lady who seemed to appreciate it so much. *(Transition)* **By**
2   **the time Pablocito was able to leave, the fiesta was nearly over.**
3   **He had tried to get away several times, but each time she had**
4   **asked him to stay just a little longer.**
5   OLD LADY: Just a little longer. I'll make us some chocolate — and
6   I have some bizcochos we can share. Today is La Navidad, and
7   I am too old and tired to go — and now, with my ankle. Please,
8   stay with me a little longer. It is so good to have someone to
9   talk to.
10   NARRATOR: Finally, Pablocito was able to leave. In a way he was
11   glad he had been able to help her, but the fiesta! He had been
12   looking forward to it for so long, and now he would miss it all.
13   He walked slowly down the street. Now he would have to wait
14   a whole year before the fiesta of La Navidad. A whole year! At
15   the window of Miguel Juarento's shop, he stopped. In the
16   window was the wonderful picture of El Cristo.
17   PABLOCITO: El Cristo who would not open his eyes for me. *(Face*
18   *lights up.)* Si, it's true! The eyes are open. El Cristo is looking
19   at me — at me! Si, it's true, Tio Juan, it is good to be good!
20   NARRATOR: All his troubles were forgotten — the fiesta he had
21   missed, his lost afternoon, everything!
22   PABLOCITO: For those who are worthy and have the faith, the
23   Christ's eyes will open.
24   NARRATOR: So it was true. He had been rewarded. The eyes,
25   which opened only for the worthy, had opened for him! What
26   did he care for fiestas or anything else now? The happiness
27   which filled his very being as he again started down the street
28   toward home could not be equaled. There was nothing like it!
29   PABLOCITO: Si, Tio Juan spoke the truth, just as he always does;
30   it is good to be good!

Children's Pageants

A Pageant of Love
By Arthur L. Zapel

A Christmas/breakfast program with parts for young children.

Cast of Characters

Pastor
Reader 1
Reader 2
Eleven Children: 5 boys and 6 girls (flexible)
   1. Boy 1 with symbol of light
   2. Girl 1 with stump of Jesse
   3. Girl 2 with Holy Spirit symbol
   4. Boy 2 with scroll
   5. Girl 3 with Star of David
   6. Boy 3 with heavenly host symbol
   7. Girl 4 with monogram
   8. Girl 5 with gold
   9. Boy 4 with frankincense
  10. Girl 6 with myrrh
  11. Boy 5 with dove

Production Notes

This program is an informal Christmas presentation for children and their parents for use on any Sunday morning during the Christmas season. It may also be used as part of a worship service, if preferred. The presentation is easily staged indoors in an assembly hall or in the chancel of your church. Only a few brief lines need be memorized by the children. The parent-readers may do their brief narrations from the script. The children carrying the pageant symbols should all enter from the same side, walking briefly to Center Stage on cue with the narrative. After their biblical quotation lines are spoken, they should retire in a line behind the readers.

The readers may be placed on opposite sides of the line of children if two microphones are available. Their speeches alternate from side to side.

Reader One is the narrative storyteller who leads into the lines from Scripture spoken by each of the children carrying a symbol.

Reader Two responds to each of the symbolic moments in the story of Christ's birth by reading the words of a well-known hymn. If a piano or organ is available, you may want to softly play the melody of the hymn under his spoken words. Another option would be to have Reader Two replaced by a singer in all or some of the responses. We did not indicate this as our first recommended choice only because the singing of each of these hymns may slow the flow of the action.

Also, we feel that having the verses of these hymns read aloud may serve to acquaint the listeners with the poetic beauty of the words by themselves.

The symbols may be constructed as indicated in the drawings. Other symbols may be substituted if you prefer. Costumes are optional for the children. This script was written with minimum requirements for easy staging.

Symbol Construction

Most of the symbols carried by the children can be made with corrugated cardboard and dowel rods. Fome-Cor, a lightweight durable material found in art supply stores, may also be used. Cutting should be done with an X-acto knife for best detail. Tempera paints and markers can be used to add colors and details. Other materials needed are: glue, colored construction and tissue paper, silver glitter, tooling foil, metallic gold paint, and masking tape or a hot glue gun to attach the cardboard symbols to the dowels.

The illustrations offer a suggestion for how to construct each symbol. Size is not an important consideration, except for visibility. Colors, shapes, and designs may be changed to suit individual needs and availability of supplies. The colors should be bright rather than realistic. They are symbols, not representative props.

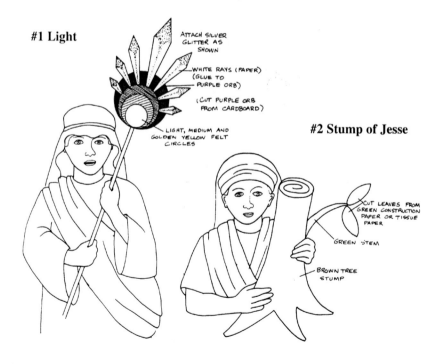

#1 Light

ATTACH SILVER GLITTER AS SHOWN

WHITE RAYS (PAPER) (GLUE TO PURPLE ORB)

(CUT PURPLE ORB FROM CARDBOARD)

LIGHT, MEDIUM AND GOLDEN YELLOW FELT CIRCLES

#2 Stump of Jesse

CUT LEAVES FROM GREEN CONSTRUCTION PAPER OR TISSUE PAPER

GREEN STEM

BROWN TREE STUMP

#3 Holy Spirit

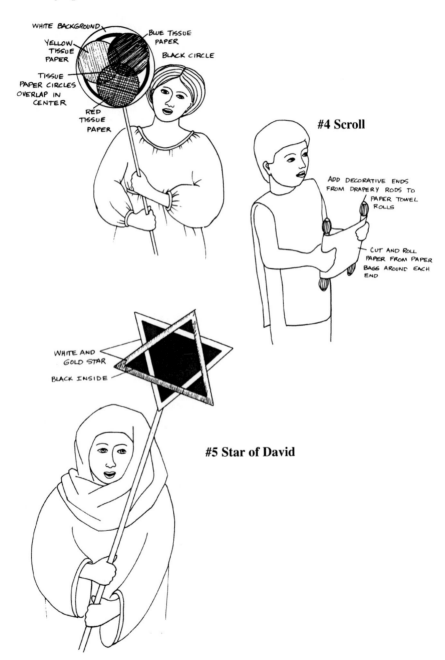

WHITE BACKGROUND

YELLOW TISSUE PAPER

BLUE TISSUE PAPER

BLACK CIRCLE

TISSUE PAPER CIRCLES OVERLAP IN CENTER

RED TISSUE PAPER

#4 Scroll

ADD DECORATIVE ENDS FROM DRAPERY RODS TO PAPER TOWEL ROLLS

CUT AND ROLL PAPER FROM PAPER BAGS AROUND EACH END

WHITE AND GOLD STAR

BLACK INSIDE

#5 Star of David

#6 Heavenly Host

PAINT HALO
YELLOW/GOLD

SILVER
GLITTER OVER
GLUE LINES

CUT STRIPS
OF SILVER
TOOLING FOIL
(HEAVIER THAN
ALUMINUM FOIL)
AND ATTACH TO
BACK OF HALOS

PAINT
WINGS
GREY

ANGELS
WHITE

PENCIL DETAILS
BEFORE PAINTING

CUT BASIC SHAPE
AS SHOWN

PURPLE
MONOGRAM

BLUE
FISH

WHITE
INSIDE

#7 Monogram

#8 Gold

#9 Frankincense

#10 Myrrh

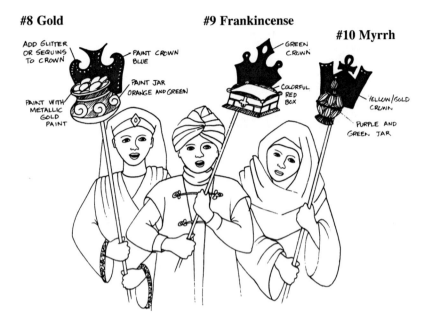

ADD GLITTER
OR SEQUINS
TO CROWN

PAINT CROWN
BLUE

PAINT JAR
ORANGE AND GREEN

PAINT WITH
METALLIC
GOLD
PAINT

GREEN
CROWN

COLORFUL
RED
BOX

YELLOW/GOLD
CROWN

PURPLE AND
GREEN JAR

#11 Dove

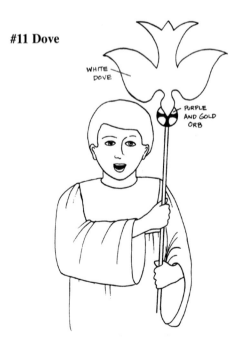

WHITE
DOVE

PURPLE
AND GOLD
ORB

Staging Diagram

The illustration above shows all eleven children in their final positions as they join with the congregation in singing "Joy to the World." This carol is the climax of the pageant staging. If a riser is available, or if there is a stage in your assembly room, this will add the visual drama of the pageant concept.

If neither a riser or a stage is available, an effective alternative can be a single box riser that may be used by each child during his/her key moment. After his/her appearance or speech he/she can step down and back into the line.

Lines to be spoken by the children

You may want to reproduce copies of this page to give to each of the children who carry a symbol and speak a line or more of Scripture. Put a check in front of the lines assigned for memorization and give a copy to each child.

Boy 1: (Page 78) "A child will be born to us! A son will be given to us! And he will be our ruler. He will be called, 'Wonderful Counselor,' 'Mighty God,' 'Eternal Father,' 'Prince of Peace'" (Isaiah 9:6). (This is the longest speech of any assigned to the children. Choose your most advanced and confident boy for this. He will in turn give confidence to each of the other children who follow.)

Girl 1: (Page 79) "Wolves and sheep will live together in peace and leopards will lie down with young goats" (Isaiah 11:6).

Girl 2: (Page 80) "I am the Lord's servant. May it happen to me as you have said" (Luke 1:38).

Boy 2: (Page 81) "Everyone must be registered, each to his own home town" (Luke 2:2-3).

Girl 3: (Page 81) "While they were there ... she gave birth to her firstborn son, wrapped him in cloths, and laid him in a manger" (Luke 2:6-7).

Boy 3: (Page 82) "Glory to God in the highest heaven and peace on earth to those with whom he is pleased" (Luke 2:14).

Girl 4: (Page 82) "Now, Lord, you have kept your promise ... with my own eyes I have seen your salvation" (Luke 2:29-30).

Girl 5: (Page 84) "Gold"

Boy 4: (Page 84) "Frankincense"

Girl 6: (Page 84) "and myrrh."

Boy 5: (Page 85) "This is my own dear Son, with whom I am pleased" (Luke 3:18).

List of Hymns Read

(Page 78) "O God Our Help in Ages Past" — (Verses one and six) Psalm 90. Isaac Watts 1674-1748.

(Page 79) "O Worship the King" — (Verses one and five) Psalm 104. Robert Grant 1779-1838.

(Page 80) "Light of the World, We Hail Thee" — (Verses two and three) John S. B. Monsell 1811-1875.

(Page 81) "Walk in the Light" — (Verse one) 1 John 1:7. Bernard Barton 1784-1849.

(Page 81) "Away in a Manger" — (Verses one and two) Anonymous.

(Page 82) "Angels We Have Heard on High" — (Verses one and three) Traditional French Carol.

(Page 83) "Jesus Shall Reign" — (Verses one and five) Psalm 72. Isaac Watts 1674-1748.

(Page 84) "The First Noel" — (Verse five) Traditional English Carol.

(Page 85) "Now Thank We All Our God" — (Verse one) Ecclesiastes 50:22-24. Martin Rinkart 1586-1649. Translated by Catherine Winkworth 1827-1878.

1   **PASTOR: Joy to the world, Christmas is here! Our savior was born**

2   **this day. Through his life and sacrifice our sins are forgiven.**

3   **"Love came down at Christmas, Love all lovely, Love divine;**

4   **Love was born at Christmas; Star and angels gave the sign."**

5   **It is a day of celebration — a day to remember.**

6   **Using symbols of the Christmas story, many of our church**

7   **children are here this morning to present for you their**

8   ***Pageant of Love* — a visual witness, with passages of Scripture**

9   **that will retell the beautiful story of the birth of Christ.**

10   **READER 1: Over seven hundred years before the day Christ was**

11   **born, an angry prophet named Isaiah reprimanded his people,**

12   **the people of Judah, for their sinful ways and their idol**

13   **worship of false gods. But he also brought good news in**

14   **prophecy, the news of a future king.** *(BOY 1 enters wearing a*

15   *robe and holding high the symbol of light.)* **The lost people of this**

16   **land had been walking in darkness but now the bright light of**

17   **prophecy was shining down on them.**

18   **BOY 1:** *(Holding his symbol of light high above his head he moves to*

19   *a position Center Stage and speaks his lines.)*

20   **"A child will be born to us!**

21   **A son will be given to us!**

22   **And he will be our ruler.**

23   **He will be called 'Wonderful Counselor'**

24   **'Mighty God,' 'Eternal Father,'**

25   **'Prince of Peace' "** (Isaiah 9:6). *(BOY 1 steps back to be the first*

26   *of a line between the READERS.)*

27   **READER 2: "O God, our help in ages past,**

28   **Our hope for years to come,**

29   **Our shelter from the stormy blast,**

30   **And our eternal home!**

31   **O God, our help in ages past,**

32   **Our hope for years to come,**

33   **Be thou our guide while life shall last,**

34   **And our eternal home!"**

35   **READER 1: A child would be born to rule over all, but who would**

1   this child be? What would be his origin? The prophet Isaiah
2   said, "There shall come forth a shoot from the stump of
3   Jesse." By this he meant the royal line of David. From this
4   stump a new branch will grow, fed from the roots of David's
5   descendants. *(GIRL 1 holding the symbol of the stump of the*
6   *Jesse tree steps forward in preparation for her lines.)* The new
7   branch will be the new king to whom the spirit of the Lord
8   will give wisdom and knowledge to rule his people ... He will
9   judge the poor fairly and defend the rights of the helpless.
10 GIRL 1: *(Holding her symbol high, she walks to Center Stage and*
11   *speaks her lines.)* "Wolves and sheep will live together in
12   peace, and leopards will lie down with young goats" (Isaiah
13   11:6). *(GIRL 1 steps back to the second in the line beside BOY 1.)*
14 READER 2: "O worship the King, all glorious above,
15   O gratefully sing his power and his love;
16   Our Shield and Defender, the Ancient of Days,
17   Pavillioned in splendor and girded with praise.
18
19   Frail children of dust, and feeble as frail,
20   In thee do we trust, nor find thee to fail;
21   Thy mercies how tender, how firm to the end,
22   Our Maker, Defender, Redeemer, and Friend."
23 READER 1: The prophecy was told and remembered, but how
24   would it come to be? It happened like this: There was a town
25   in Galilee named Nazareth. Living there was a young woman
26   whose name was Mary. She was promised in marriage to a
27   man named Joseph who was a descendant of the royal line of
28   David. One evening, God sent the angel Gabriel to speak to
29   Mary. "Oh favored one," he said, "the Lord is with you. He
30   has greatly blessed you. God's power will rest upon you, and
31   you will give birth to a son. You shall call him Jesus. He will
32   be great and he will be called the son of the Most High God."
33   Mary was overwhelmed. "How can this be?" she said. "I am
34   a virgin. I do not yet have a husband!" *(GIRL 2 carrying the*
35   *symbol of the Holy Spirit steps forward in preparation for her*

1   *lines.)* Gabriel answered, "The Holy Spirit will come to you. For
2   this reason, your holy child will be called the 'Son of God.' "
3   **GIRL 2:** *(Holding her symbol high, she speaks.)* **"I am the Lord's**
4   **servant. May it happen to me as you have said"** (Luke 1:38).
5   *(GIRL 2 steps back to join the others in a line behind the*
6   *READERS.)*
7   **READER 2:** "Light of the world, thy beauty
8   Steals into every heart
9   And glorifies with duty
10   Life's poorest, humblest part;
11   Thou robest in thy splendor
12   The simple ways of men
13   And helpest them to render
14   Light back to thee again.
15
16   Light of the world illumine
17   This darkened earth of thine
18   Till everything that's human
19   Be filled with the divine;
20   Till every tongue and nation,
21   From sin's dominion free,
22   Rise in the new creation
23   Which springs from love and thee."
24   **READER 1:** Soon after the angel Gabriel appeared to Mary, she
25   left Nazareth to go to a country place where dwelt Zechariah
26   and his wife, Elizabeth, who was Mary's cousin. Elizabeth
27   herself had been visited with a miracle of the Holy Spirit. The
28   angel Gabriel had appeared to Zechariah in the temple and
29   told him that a son would be born to his wife, Elizabeth, and
30   that he would be named John. He would be a great man and
31   would prepare the way for the kingdom of the Lord Jesus who
32   would follow. *(BOY 2 steps forward carrying a scroll in*
33   *preparation for the speaking of his lines.)* It was at that same
34   time that Emperor Caesar Augustus ordered a census to be
35   taken throughout the Roman Empire. The official order from

1   Quirinius who was then governor of Syria read:

2   **BOY 2:** *(Holding up a scroll and reading from it)* **"Everyone must be**

3   **registered, each to his own home town"** (Luke 2:2-3). *(BOY 2*

4   *steps back to join the line of the others behind the READERS.)*

5   **READER 2: "Walk in the light! So shalt thou know**

6   **That fellowship of love**

7   **His spirit only can bestow**

8   **Who reigns in light above."**

9   **READER 1: Because Bethlehem was the birthplace of King David**

10   **and Joseph was from the lineage of David, it was required that**

11   **Joseph and Mary be enrolled in that city. It was a difficult**

12   **journey for Mary, for she was large with child.** *(GIRL 3, with*

13   *the symbol of the Star of David, steps forward in preparation for*

14   *speaking her lines.)* **But Joseph and Mary quietly and patiently**

15   **traveled the one hundred miles from Nazareth to the city of**

16   **David, symbolized by the Star of David, so that the prophecy**

17   **of Isaiah would be fulfilled.**

18   **GIRL 3:** *(Holding her symbol, Star of David, she speaks her lines.)*

19   **"While they were there ... she gave birth to her first-born son,**

20   **wrapped him in cloths, and laid him in a manger"** (Luke 2:6-7).

21   *(GIRL 3 steps back to join the others behind the READERS.)*

22   **READER 1: There was no room for them in the inn and so the**

23   **baby was born in a stable.**

24   **READER 2: "Away in a manger, no crib for a bed,**

25   **The little Lord Jesus laid down his sweet head.**

26   **The stars in the sky looked down where he lay,**

27   **The little Lord Jesus asleep on the hay.**

28

29   **The cattle are lowing, the baby awakes,**

30   **But little Lord Jesus, no crying he makes.**

31   **I love thee, Lord Jesus, look down from the sky**

32   **And stay by my cradle till morning is nigh."**

33   **READER 1: As the baby Jesus slept in his manger bed, there were**

34   **some shepherds nearby watching after their flocks. An angel**

35   **of the Lord appeared to them. They were frightened but the**

1   angel calmed them, saying, "I am here with good news that
2   will bring joy to all people. This day in David's city your
3   Savior was born — Christ the Lord! And this will be a sign to
4   you — the baby is wrapped in cloth and is lying in a manger."
5   *(BOY 3 with the symbol of the Heavenly Host steps forward in*
6   *preparation for speaking his lines.)* **Suddenly a great army of**
7   **heaven's angels appeared, singing praises to God.**
8   **BOY 3:** *(Stepping forward with his Heavenly Host symbol)* **"Glory to**
9   **God in the highest heaven, and peace on earth to those with**
10   **whom he is pleased"** (Luke 2:14). *(BOY 3 retires to a position*
11   *behind the READERS in line with the other children.)*
12   **READER 2:** **"Angels we have heard on high**
13   **Sweetly singing o'er the plains.**
14   **And the mountains in reply**
15   **Echoing their joyous strains.**
16   **Come to Bethlehem and see**
17   **Him whose birth the angels sing.**
18   **Come adore on bended knee**
19   **Christ, the Lord, the newborn King."**
20   **READER 1:** **A week or so after the birth of the Holy Baby, Mary**
21   **and Joseph took their infant son to the temple in Jerusalem**
22   **for the ceremony of purification as commanded by the Law of**
23   **Moses. Every first-born male was to be dedicated to the Lord**
24   **and named.** *(GIRL 4 steps forward holding the symbol of the*
25   *name Jesus.)* **There was at that time, living in Jerusalem, an**
26   **old man named Simeon who had been waiting all of his**
27   **prolonged life for Israel to be saved. He had been assured by**
28   **the Holy Spirit that God was with him, and that he would not**
29   **die until he had seen the promised Messiah. It was this same**
30   **Simeon who was at the temple to greet Joseph and Mary when**
31   **they came to fulfill the requirements of the Law. Taking the**
32   **child in his arms, Simeon knew instantly that this baby was**
33   **the promised one. He looked upward, and with tear-filled**
34   **eyes, he said:**
35   **GIRL 4:** *(Holding symbol high, she speaks his lines.)* **"Now, Lord, you**

1   have kept your promise ... with my own eyes I have seen your
2   salvation" (Luke 2:29-30).
3   READER 2: And then, having said this, he named the baby Jesus,
4   the very name the angels had given him before he was born.
5   It was *Jeshua*, the Hebrew form of the Greek word, Jesus,
6   which means "God is Savior," "God Saves," and "God is With
7   Us." Or, as Isaiah had said, "The Prince of Peace,"
8   "Wonderful Counselor."
9   READER 1: "Jesus shall reign wher-e'er the sun
10   Does his successive journeys run;
11   His kingdom spread from shore to shore,
12   Till moons shall wax and wane no more.
13
14   Let every creature rise and bring
15   His grateful honors to our King;
16   Angels descend with songs again,
17   And earth repeat that loud amen!"
18   READER 2: In a land east of Jerusalem, there lived three men who
19   were called the Magi — this name given to define them as
20   scholarly philosophers, scientists, and astrologers. They had
21   seen a new star. It was different from any they had ever seen
22   before. Or was it a comet, or a planet, or two or more stars in
23   a unique conjunction? Whatever it was, they knew that it
24   signaled an event of world portent. They studied their scrolls
25   until they came upon an old prophecy by Balaam saying that
26   a star shall rise out of Jacob and a scepter shall spring up
27   from Israel. This star must mean that a King was about to be
28   born. Would it be a king for those of Israel only, or a King of
29   Kings for all people? They must find the answer.
30   They followed the path of the star until they came to
31   Jerusalem. There, they asked, "Where is the child born to be
32   king?" King Herod heard of this and commanded that the
33   Magi be brought before him. He was very upset. But he kept
34   his feelings hidden from the wise men of Persia. Instead,
35   wearing a mask of friendship, he told them in secret to go to

1   Bethlehem. It was there that a prophet had said a leader
2   would come to lead the people, Israel.
3   "Go there and find the child, and when you do, come back
4   and tell me so that I, too, may worship him," Herod said.
5   Caspar, Melchior, and Balthazar left the king's palace and
6   followed the star to a place in Bethlehem that gave them great
7   surprise. It was a stable! A king born in a stable! They knew
8   then that this was to be the "King of Kings" — a savior for all
9   people, rich and poor, Jew and Gentile, young and old. *(Two*
10   *GIRLS and one BOY step forward carrying three symbols*
11   *representing the gifts of the wise men.)* The three wise men
12   donned their best robes, entered the stable, and knelt before
13   the manger in worship. Then each of them presented a gift to
14   the Holy Child.
15   **GIRL 5:** *(Holding up a plaque with a symbol of gold, she speaks one*
16   *word.)* **"Gold,"**
17   **BOY 4:** *(Holding up a plaque with a symbol of frankincense, he speaks*
18   *one word.)* **"Frankincense,"**
19   **GIRL 6:** *(Holding up a plaque with a symbol of myrrh, she concludes*
20   *with two words.)* **"and myrrh."** *(All three retire to the line of the*
21   *other children behind the READERS.)*
22   **READER 1:** "Then entered in those wise men three,
23   Fall reverently upon the knee,
24   And offered there, in his presence,
25   Their gold and myrrh and frankincense.
26   Noel, Noel, Noel, Noel,
27   Born is the King of Israel."
28   **READER 2:** After Herod died, an angel of the Lord appeared in a
29   dream to Joseph in Egypt and said, "Get up, take the child
30   and his mother, and go back to the land of Israel." This Joseph
31   did. He returned to Nazareth and resumed his trade as a
32   carpenter, raising Jesus as one of his own sons until he
33   reached manhood. It was then that Jesus left Galilee to go to
34   his cousin, John, asking to be baptized in the Jordon River.
35   John, the Baptizer, protested, "I ought to be baptized by you,

1   and yet you have come to me!" "Let it be so," Jesus replied.

2   So John agreed and it was done. As soon as Jesus came out of

3   the water, heaven was opened to him ... *(BOY 5 steps forward*

4   *carrying a symbol in preparation for his lines)* **and he saw the**

5   Spirit of God coming down like a dove and lighting on his

6   shoulder. Then a voice said from heaven:

7   BOY 5: *(Holding high his symbol of the dove)* "This is my own dear

8   Son, with whom I am pleased" (Luke 3:22).

9   READER 2: "Now thank we all our God

10   With heart and hands and voices,

11   Who wondrous things hath done,

12   In whom his world rejoices;

13   Who, from our mothers' arms,

14   Hath blessed us on our way

15   With countless gifts of love,

16   And still is ours today."

17   READER 1: Let us all celebrate how love was born at Christmas

18   by singing "Joy to the World."

19   EVERYBODY SINGS: "Joy to the World"

Creatures Christmas
By Nancy Amondson-Pitts

Cast of Characters (In order of appearance)

Camel 1
Camel 2
Camel 3
Cow 1 and 2
Donkey
Bull
Lambs 1 and 2
Dog
Goat
Gophers 1 and 2
Mice 1 and 2
Spider

Production Notes

The charm and effectiveness of this playlet will best be served with simple production techniques. Scenery is not necessary, and the costuming need only be suggestive to achieve believability.

We recommend that each of the animals wear only one or two items suggestive of the animal they represent. The camels, for example, can be outfitted with attached "humps" and long ears. The bull can have "horns"; the lambs, some lamb's wool clothing; the gophers, small ears; the mice, a tail; the spider, extra legs; and the dog, a collar. Face makeup will help also in suggesting the character of the animal. Make large eyes for the spider, add whisker marks for the mice and a goatee for the goat. Let your imagination take over. The costuming and makeup will be as much fun as putting on the play itself.

The Christmas carols suggested are all well-known and the music is available from almost all church hymnals or any church music library. It will not be necessary for the children who enact the roles of the animals to overplay the animal's characteristics. The script will keep the identities clear. The charm will be found in the audience's "willing suspension of disbelief" as they watch the children perform.

Music Sources

These songs may be found by using an Internet search engine or in the following printed sources.

The familiar carols "We Three Kings," "Away in a Manger," "While Shepherds Watched Their Flocks by Night," and "What Child Is This?" may be found in any hymnal.

The old Appalachian carol, "I Wonder as I Wander," may be found in *170 Christmas Songs and Carols* (page 22), a Big 3 publication, copyright © 1983, Columbia Pictures Publications. Address: CPP/Belwin Inc., 15800 NW 48th Ave., Hialeah, FL, 33014. Phone: 305-620-1500.

"There's a Song in the Air" may be found in the United Methodist Church's hymnal, *The Book of Hymns* (#380), copyright © 1964, The United Methodist Publishing House.

"The Friendly Beasts" may be found in *170 Christmas Songs and Carols* (page 119), or *Tomie dePaola's Book of Christmas Carols* (page 26), copyright © 1987 by G.P. Putnam's Sons.

"What Can I Give Him?" may be found in *170 Christmas Songs and Carols* (page 188).

1   *(Camels enter through the audience to stage singing "We Three*
2   *Camels" to the tune of "We Three Kings".)*
3   CAMELS: We three camels from Orient are,
4   bearing kings who traveled so far.
5   Field and fountain, moor and mountain,
6   Following yonder star.
7   O, star of wonder, star of night,
8   Star with royal beauty bright.
9   Westward leading, still proceeding,
10   Guide us to thy perfect light.
11 CAMEL 1: Sure was a long, hot ride.
12 CAMEL 2: You better believe it! The sand kept blowing in my eyes,
13   and that smelly stuff I was carrying on my back — phew!
14 CAMEL 3: You mean the frankincense and myrrh?
15 CAMEL 2: No, the rotten bananas.
16 CAMEL 3: You think you had it bad. You should've been carrying
17   that heavy gold I had on my back.
18 CAMEL 2: I still can't figure out why the kings came all this way
19   following that star.
20 CAMEL 3: It has something to do with what they read in an old,
21   old book about a new king being born.
22 CAMEL 1: Then why didn't we stay at the palace in Jerusalem
23   where what's-his-name was?
24 CAMEL 2: You mean King Harold?
25 CAMEL 3: Herod.
26 CAMEL 2: Harold, Herod, same difference. I heard one of the
27   Magi say Harold wanted them to come back and tell them
28   where the baby was so he could worship the new king, too.
29 CAMEL 3: That was nice.
30 CAMEL 2: No. He didn't mean it. An angel told them they
31   shouldn't go back.
32 CAMEL 3: I sure hope we go home soon. I miss our fancy stables
33   back east.
34 CAMEL 1: Me, too! This sure is a mangy old stable. *(CATTLE and*
35   *DONKEY enter in time to hear last comment.)*

1   COW 1: Hey! Wait a minute! This isn't a mangy stable. This is our
2   home.
3   CAMEL 1: *(Rolls eyes and holds nose higher in the air.)* Well, we're
4   awfully sorry you have to live here.
5   COW 2: Don't be. We like it. Besides, it's a special place. There are
6   three kings in there right now.
7   BULL: And there's a lady who just had a brand new baby boy.
8   *(CATTLE sing "We Cattle Were Lowing" to the tune of "Away in*
9   *a Manger.")*
10 CATTLE: We cattle were lowing and donkey sang, too,
11 While Mary and Joseph prayed all the night through.
12 Then Shepherds and wise men who followed a star,
13 Came to our small stable with gifts from afar. *(End song)*
14 COW 1: Are your masters here in town to be counted like everyone
15 else?
16 CAMEL 2: Oh, no. They came to find the new king that's been
17 born. We've traveled for months following that star up there.
18 COW 2: Then why are they here at our stable? There's no king in
19 there — just a tiny baby asleep in our manger.
20 CAMEL 1: Beats me. All I know is that star we've been chasing
21 stopped dead in its tracks right above this place.
22 CAMEL 2: Maybe they're inside asking directions.
23 CAMEL 3: Why are those people with a baby in there anyway?
24 I've never heard of *people* spending the night in a barn, and
25 especially having a baby born in a barn!
26 DONKEY: They didn't have anywhere else to go. Every other
27 place was full. I brought them all the way from Nazareth. And
28 poor Mary — that's the lady's name — she was soooo tired
29 and soooo ready to have her baby, she begged to stay
30 anywhere, as long as it wasn't outside.
31 COW 1: Did this Mary and what's-his-name ... ?
32 DONKEY: Joseph.
33 COW 1: Joseph. Did they say anything about a king?
34 DONKEY: No. They talked about an angel Gabriel who came to
35 Mary and told her she was special — that God had chosen her

1   to give birth to God's very own son — and they were supposed

2   to call him Jesus.

3   **BULL:** A *real* angel? *(LAMBS enter.)*

4   **LAMBS 1 and 2:** Did you say angel?

5   **BULL:** Uhhhh ... yes.

6   *(LAMBS sing "While Shepherds Watched Us Lambs Tonight" to*

7   *the tune of "While Shepherds Watched Their Flocks by Night.")*

8   **LAMBS:** While shepherds watched us lambs tonight,

9   All seated on the ground.

10   The angel of the Lord came down

11   And glory shone around,

12   And glory shone around *(End song)*

13   **BULL:** You actually saw the angels?

14   **LAMB 1:** Right! They sang songs and said "Glory to God in the

15   highest, and on earth, peace to men of goodwill."

16   **LAMB 2:** Our shepherds were afraid, and when they ran away, so

17   did we. We didn't hear the whole story, but there's the dog and

18   goat. *(DOG and GOAT enter.)* They were there. Maybe they

19   know something.

20   *(DOG and GOAT sing "Fear Not, the Angel Said" to the tune of*

21   *"While Shepherds Watched Their Flocks by Night.")*

22   **DOG and GOAT:** "Fear not," the angel said tonight, but we were

23   not afraid.

24   **GOAT:** With my sharp horns,

25   **DOG:** And my loud bark,

26   **DOG and GOAT:** While others ran, we stayed.

27   While others ran, we stayed. *(End song)*

28   **GOAT:** We heard the angels tell the shepherds to go to Bethlehem

29   and find a baby in a manger.

30   **DOG:** They said a savior was born this very day.

31   *(From behind a rock we hear arguing "You go first" "No! You!"*

32   *"I don't want to get stepped on." "Oh, all right!")*

33   **COW 1:** Look, there are the gophers.

34   *(GOPHERS sing "We Wonder as We Burrow" to the tune of "I*

35   *Wonder as I Wander.")*

1   GOPHERS: We wonder as we burrow down under the earth,
2   Why all this commotion for one baby's birth.
3   But high in God's heaven a star's light did shine,
4   So those in the darkness would have a bright sign. *(End song)*
5   GOPHER 1: It's so noisy I can't sleep. All day and all night people
6   and animals are stomping on the roof of our house.
7   GOPHER 2: Yeah, this used to be a nice, quiet town. Now I can't
8   even stick my head out of the hole without someone stepping
9   on me.
10   GOPHER 1: And that new star is so bright it keeps me awake at
11   night.
12   GOPHER 2: I'm used to the dark — that light hurts my eyes.
13   COW 1: Do you gophers know what's happening?
14   GOPHER 1: How can we? All we hear lately is stomp, stomp,
15   stomp. All day, all night.
16   GOPHER 2: And all we see is legs, legs, legs. We barely made it out
17   of our hole this time without being trampled by all those legs,
18   legs, legs.
19   COW 1: How are we ever going to solve this mystery?
20   BULL: Look! Here come the mice and spider.
21   COW 2: What would *they* know?
22   BULL: Let's listen.
23   *(MICE and SPIDER sing "Just a Bug and Some Mice" to the tune*
24   *of "There's a Song in the Air.")*
25   MICE and SPIDER: Just a bug and some mice, "What do they
26   know?" you say.
27   Well, while you talk and talk, we've been listening all day.
28   And inside in the stable this beautiful morn,
29   The King, the Messiah, yes, Jesus was born. *(End song)*
30   MOUSE 1: We were sitting quietly in the corner of the stable and
31   we saw all kinds of things.
32   MOUSE 2: Kings and shepherds.
33   SPIDER: All bowing down and worshiping the baby.
34   MOUSE 1: Some called him Savior.
35   MOUSE 2: Some called him King.

1   SPIDER: The lady called him Jesus.

2   ALL: *(Singing "What Child Is This?" to the tune of "Greensleeves")*

3   What child is this, who, laid to rest, on Mary's lap is sleeping?

4   Whom angels greet with anthems sweet,

5   While shepherds watch are keeping?

6   This, this is Christ the King,

7   Whom shepherds guard and angels sing;

8   Haste, haste to bring him laud,

9   The babe, the son of Mary. *(End song)*

10   CAMEL 1: So the new King is actually inside there?

11   SPIDER: Yes, and everyone is bringing him birthday presents.

12   GOPHER 1: What could all of us give him?

13   CAMEL 1: We already gave him our part.

14   DONKEY: So did I.

15   COW 1: I'm sure we'll think of something.

16   *(Each in turn sings this revised version of "The Friendly Beasts.")*

17   DONKEY: "I," said the donkey, shaggy and brown.

18   "I carried his mother up hill and down.

19   I carried her safely to Bethlehem town."

20   "I," said the donkey, shaggy and brown.

21   CAMELS: "We," said the camels, so proud and bold.

22   "We carried rich treasures of myrrh and gold.

23   We carried three kings through heat and cold."

24   "We," said the camels, so proud and bold.

25   CATTLE: "We," said the cattle, all white and red.

26   "We'll give him our manger for a bed.

27   We'll give him our hay to pillow his head."

28   "We," said the cattle, all white and red.

29   SHEEP: "We," said the sheep, all shaggy and shorn.

30   "We'll give him our wool for a blanket warm.

31   He'll wear our warm coat on a cold, bleak morn."

32   "We," said the sheep, all shaggy and shorn.

33   DOG and GOAT: "We," said the dog and billy goat, too.

34   "We'll then keep a watch the whole night through,

35   So nothing can harm the baby new."

1   "We," said the dog and billy goat, too. *(End song)*

2   MOUSE 1: What could we give him?

3   MOUSE 2: All we have is a tiny, dried-up piece of cheese.

4   SPIDER: I have a couple of juicy flies in my web.

5   GOPHER 1: Flies!

6   GOPHER 2: Dried-up cheese!

7   GOPHER 3: *Yuck!*

8   MOUSE 1: Well! What do *you* two have to give?

9   GOPHERS: ... Nnnnothing.

10   MOUSE 1: Come here, gophers. *(SPIDER, MICE, and GOPHERS*

11   *get in a huddle and whisper about what they'll give. Then they*

12   *come out and sing this version of "What Can I Give Him?")*

13   SPIDER, MICE and GOPHERS: What can we give him, poor as

14   we are?

15   We cannot bring rich gifts from a land afar.

16   We can only give him such a little part.

17   Oh, what can we give him? *(Pause)*

18   We'll give him our heart.

Little Fir's Vision

By Myrtle L. Forsten

A Christmas folktale for children

Cast of Characters

Reader 1
Reader 2
Reader 3
Reader 4
Narrator
Little Fir
Oak
Sycamore
First Woodsman
Second Woodsman
Christmas Star
Young Boy
Joseph
Mary
Choir of Trees

The first eight characters may be played by either boys or girls.

Production Notes

This one-act musical drama is based on the traditional folktale of three trees in a forest near Bethlehem. The presentation emphasizes the spiritual meaning of the birth and death of Jesus through the conversation of the trees. Also, what Little Fir becomes serves to enhance the spiritual meaning of the Christmas tree. The drama uses a minimum of eight characters (not including the four short presentations in the prologue) and an unlimited number in the Choir of Trees. The playing time is about 20 minutes.

The prologue is a nice touch, and the four small banners are easily made from green felt (see illustration). The basic tree design is the same for each banner, with the only difference being the words: peace, life, joy, and love, which tell what the fir tree symbolizes. However, you may eliminate the banners and readers if you wish and simply have the narrator read their parts.

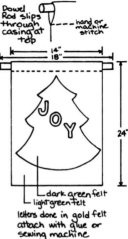

Staging

A bare stage is adequate, but if you wish you may have a sky with a backdrop of clouds (painted on a bed sheet).

The Sycamore, Oak, and Little Fir should be at Center Stage, with the Narrator at a lighted lectern at Stage Left. The Sycamore is planted "on a craggy hill," so have the Sycamore stand on a low stool and in front of it put a pile of crumpled newspapers with a brown blanket draped over it for an impromptu "hill." The Oak can be on a similar "hill" as well, so Little Fir really does appear little. The Choir of Trees stands in a row or semi-circle behind the three main tree characters. Place a microphone on a stand at Stage Right for the four prologue readers and a stool or small platform for the Christmas Star to stand on.

Lighting

Normal lighting is adequate — simply turn off and on the lights as indicated. If you have access to a spotlight, use it to highlight the Christmas star.

Costumes

The Choir of Trees may wear green poster board cutouts of fir trees. These trees hang down in front from cords around their necks. Leave the tips of the trees off below the children's faces as shown in the costume illustration. (Optional: Each child may wear a green cone-shaped hat on his or her head as the top of the tree.)

95

The Sycamore, Oak, and Little Fir are costumed as illustrated. In the original presentation, these three characters' trees were painted on the front of large refrigerator boxes. The backs of the boxes were removed and shrubs were painted on the sides to provide a screen for the reader inside. He/she sat on a stool and read the script into the microphone, eliminating the need for memorization. You may choose this option if you wish, remembering to select your best readers for vocal inflection and emphasis.

The Christmas Star should wear a yellow poster board cutout of a star (worn hanging in front like the trees). The star may be decorated with gold glitter.

The First Woodsman, and the Second Woodsman, the Young Boy, and Joseph should wear biblical costumes, i.e., simple robes in earth tones made of a rough weave of cloth. They should wear a simple belt of cord or made from a strip of the same fabric as their robes. Their matching headpieces should be tied to their heads with cord.

Mary also wears a biblical costume, but her robe and headpiece should be made of blue or white to set her apart from the others. Her matching headpiece should be loosely draped over her head.

Props

A hatchet for one of the woodsmen. Use a plastic toy one if available. If not, improvise with gray construction paper cut into a hatchet shape and taped to a stick.

Cardboard stump for when Little Fir is chopped down. This should be hidden On-Stage prior to the performance. Prop it up against a rock or make a stand for it.

Flashlight for the Christmas Star to shine on Little Fir.

Manger with doll wrapped in white cloths.

Suggested Music Source

1. "The Trees of the Field," based on Isaiah 55:12, by Stuart Dauermann, performed by Steffi Geiser Rubin. May be found in a number of collections of Scripture songs, such as *Contemporary Classics* (arrangement by Ken Thomas), copyright © 1983 by Lillenas Publishing Company, Kansas City, MO.
2. "Be Planted," by Myrtle L. Forsten. Music and motions included in script.
3. "O Come Let Us Adore Him" is the chorus from the well-known Christmas carol, "O Come, All Ye Faithful," by Frederick Oakeley. It may be found in any hymnal or in many collections of Christmas songs.
4. "O Little Town of Bethlehem," by Phillips Brooks is another well-known Christmas carol which may be found in any hymnal.
5. "One Day," by Dr. J. Wilbur Chapman may be found in the songbook *To Know Your Heart* compiled by Bruce Greer, copyright © 1989 by Word Inc., Dallas, TX. (Toll-free order number: 1-800-933-9673.)

Songs

(In order of appearance)
1. The Trees of the Field
2. Be Planted
3. O Come Let Us Adore Him
4. O Little Town of Bethlehem
5. One Day

Be Planted

Music by Myrtle L. Forsten
arr. by Mary Cupecy

Be Planted
2

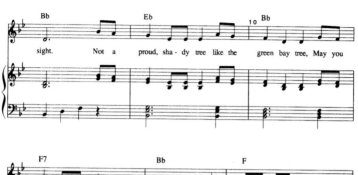

Be Planted
3

praise like a crown of glo - ry and spread forth His joy to the

world. You will fear not the heat of the sum - mer, nor

faint in the win - ter of pain, For the Lord of the har - vest is

Be Planted
4

with you, and the sun-shine a way to the rain, In His

wis-dom be bold, Be a win-ner of souls, And you'll see what the Lord had in

mind. For the rest of your days, To be filled with praise, that His

name may be glo-ri-fied.

1   **Prologue**

2   *(Four READERS enter with banners, each with green trees*

3   *lettered to match the meaning of the fir tree: peace, life, joy, love.*

4   *They line up at Stage Right and hold up their banners, stepping*

5   *forward and speaking into the microphone at the appropriate*

6   *time.)*

7   **READER 1: The fir tree is the sign of peace. The angels said,**

8   **"Glory to God in the highest, and on earth peace to men on**

9   **whom his favor rests" (Luke 2:14).**

10   **READER 2: It is the sign of eternal life, for its leaves are always**

11   **green. " ... the gift of God is eternal life in Christ Jesus our**

12   **Lord" (Romans 6:23).**

13   **READER 3: It is a sign of rejoicing. The angel said, "I bring you**

14   **good news of great joy..." (Luke 2:10).**

15   **READER 4: It is a sign of love. "For God so loved the world that**

16   **he gave his one and only Son" (John 3:16).** *(READERS exit. The*

17   *OAK, SYCAMORE, LITTLE FIR, and CHOIR OF TREES enter*

18   *and take their places.)*

19

20   **Song: The Trees of the Field**

21   *(CHOIR OF TREES claps with song.)*

22

23   **NARRATOR: It was cool and windy on that day when the trees got**

24   **together in the forest of that far-off land. But the sun spread**

25   **its cheer to the creatures of the woodland while the trees**

26   **chatted freely with one another.**

27   **OAK:** *(To little fir)* **What a beautiful little fir tree you are. I hope**

28   **you can grow up to be a strong, tall tree like I am.** *(Flexes*

29   *muscles, arms out.)*

30   **FIR: Me, too! I take my vitamins from the soil every day and drink**

31   **lots of water through my roots. And every morning I stretch**

32   **my branches** *(Raises arms up)* **and say, "Yoo-hoo, Mr. Sun!**

33   **Remember me — the shortest tree in the forest? How about**

34   **sending some rays down here? I want to grow up to be what**

35   **the Lord of the Trees wants me to be."**

1   **Song:** *Be Planted* **(see pages 98-101.)**
2   *(TREES sway back and forth. As the music begins, the CHOIR OF*
3   *TREES performs the motions to the song.)*
4   **May the *Lord* of the trees**
5   *(Right hand pointing up.)*
6   **Give you days of *peace*;**
7   *(Left hand comes up to right, then both hands sweep down and out*
8   *at sides.)*
9   **May you grow tall and *strong* in His sight.**
10   *(Hands up in front of shoulders, fists inward.)*
11   ***Not* a proud, shady tree, like the green bay tree,**
12   *(Hands with palms outward cross over each other, while shaking*
13   *heads at same time.)*
14   **May you bear forth your *fruit* with delight.**
15   *(Hands with fingers hanging out and down.)*
16   **Be planted by the *streams* of His Spirit,**
17   *(Fingers waving up and down; hand sweeping left to right.)*
18   **Be *rooted* in the law of the Lord.**
19   *(Hands side by side in front, pointing down.)*
20   **Wear His praise like a *crown* of glory.**
21   *(Hands encircle head.)*
22   **And spread forth His joy to the *world*.**
23   **You will fear not the heat of the summer,**
24   **Nor faint in the winter of pain,**
25   **For the Lord of the harvest is with you,**
26   *(Hands and arms form big circle in front, then CHOIR OF TREES*
27   *sways back and forth.)*
28   **And the *sunshine* give way to the rain.**
29   *(Make circle in air for sun with right hand, then fingers of both*
30   *hands move up and down for rain.)*
31   **In His wisdom be *bold*, Be a winner of souls,**
32   *(Index finger of right hand goes up firmly.)*
33   **And you'll see what the Lord had in *mind*.**
34   *(Bring index finger to forehead.)*
35   **For the rest of your days, to be filled with *praise*,**

1   *(Clapping hands)*
2   That His name might be *glorified.*
3   *(Right hand, palm out, thrusts up to sky.)*
4
5   OAK: Little Fir, you have lofty ambitions. But you must remember
6   that the finest ambition for the trees of the forest is to die, so
7   we may be useful to others. I feel certain that my time here in
8   the forest is drawing to a close.
9   FIR: Oh? Why is that?
10 OAK: Well, I heard the woodsmen talking as they came by to
11   inspect the trees. *(WOODSMEN enter and pantomime talking as*
12   *they point at the OAK.)* They said that my straight, sturdy
13   trunk would make a fine mast for the ship that is being built.
14   *(WOODSMEN exit.)*
15 FIR: A ship — wow! That's great! *(Sadly)* But I don't want you to
16   leave. You're like a big brother to me.
17 OAK: Don't cry for me, little one. Death is not the end. I have
18   heard a word from heaven that I may be chosen to become a
19   very famous ship. The Son of God is coming into the world —
20   and I will become the stage that he stands on to teach
21   thousands of people about the kingdom of God. I am willing
22   to give my life for this purpose.
23 FIR: Oh, how majestic you are! How magnificent you shall
24   become. But what about little ol' me? I'm hardly more than a
25   sapling! I'll never get to have a purpose!
26 OAK: You will grow, little sister *(or brother)*. You must be patient
27   and do all the things God has commanded you to do. I'm sure
28   he has a great plan for you.
29 CHOIR OF TREES: *(Chants and shakes fingers at FIR.)*
30   Little Fir, you must be patient!
31   You must learn to grow and wait.
32   The Lord of the Trees will answer
33   And he will not be late!
34 FIR: *(Sighs and waves arms sadly.)* Be patient — be patient — that's
35   all I ever hear. But it's lonely down here! Just me and the

1   earthworms. *(To OAK)* **How's the weather up there, anyway?**
2   **Must be nice to feel the breeze.**
3   **OAK: Sometimes the wind is very rough up here, Little Fir. When**
4   **the wind blows gently,** *(CHOIR OF TREES rocks arms, sighing*
5   *in unison, "Ahhhh!")* **I cradle the birds in their nests, rocking**
6   **them to and fro. But when the storms come,** *(CHOIR OF*
7   *TREES shakes arms and says "Woooo!")* **I envy you, for you are**
8   **well protected by all of us older trees in the forest. See? It's**
9   **not so bad.**
10   **SYCAMORE: I must be patient, too, Little Fir. But I'm glad to**
11   **wait. I don't** *want* **to hasten the day when I see for myself what**
12   **the Lord of the Trees has planned for me.**
13   **FIR: How come, old friend? Your trunk is twisted and your**
14   **branches are broken. And what about the cold winds that**
15   **make your limbs ache?**
16   **SYCAMORE:** *(Sighs.)* **Oh, to be young and beautiful again! I know**
17   **I'm, uh, weathered, shall we say? I can't get by with saying I**
18   **have twenty-nine rings on my trunk anymore. Perhaps the**
19   **trees of the forest would be glad to see me go. The forest would**
20   **be more beautiful without me.**
21   **FIR: Oh, no, great Sycamore! I don't mean that I want you to**
22   **leave. I just feel bad that you must suffer each day.**
23   **SYCAMORE: Ah, little friend, don't feel sorry for me. I didn't**
24   **mean to complain when I told you of my suffering. I only**
25   **wanted you to see how lucky you are. God has allowed me to**
26   **live on this craggy hill for a reason. He wanted me to learn to**
27   **suffer and to feel pain so that I would be ready for the job he**
28   **has called me to do.**
29   **FIR: You mean you know what your purpose is, too?**
30   **SYCAMORE: Yes, little one. That's why I'm not anxious to die,**
31   **although it** *is* **the highest calling that any tree could know. I**
32   **am most honored that the Lord of the Trees has chosen me.**
33   *(Bows branches in reverence.)*
34   **FIR: Then why are you afraid to die, mighty Sycamore?**
35   **SYCAMORE: I'm not afraid for** *myself*, **little one. I'm afraid for**

1   those who will see me. *(Trembles, shakes arms.)* **You see, I have**

2   **been chosen — me, the ugliest of all the trees — to be the cross**

3   **upon which the Lord of all the earth will be crucified. Oh-h-**

4   **h-h! Oh-h-h-h!** *(TREES in CHOIR moan, in echo: "Oh-h-h-h!*

5   *Oh-h-h-h!," with heads down and limbs folded in front of them.)*

6   **FIR: Oh, I see. When you moan and suffer in the wind, you are**

7   **thinking of the day when you must suffer with him.**

8   **SYCAMORE: That's right. But I am not ashamed to be made into**

9   **this cross. For I know that many people will start to believe**

10   **when they see it. They'll see that God loves them so much that**

11   **he gave his son to die for them.**

12   **FIR: You're brave, Sycamore. God's given you an important job to**

13   **do.** *(Turns to OAK, waves arm.)* **Don't you agree, big brother?**

14   **OAK: Yes, I do.** *(To Sycamore)* **Your death — and his death —**

15   **means new life for many. I'm sure this wooden cross will be**

16   **remembered far longer than my ship.**

17

18   **Song:** *O Come Let Us Adore Him*

19   *(The second time through, sing "For He Alone Is Worthy" to the*

20   *same tune. TREES sing choruses softly.)*

21

22   **FIR: I see now that God hasn't forgotten about me. He's just**

23   **waiting for the right time to reveal his plan for me. But now**

24   **the sun is sinking below the hill.** *(Lights dim.)* **It's getting dark.**

25   *(FIR yawns and stretches.)* **I'm tired and need to get my rest.**

26   **NARRATOR: All the trees in the forest were silent as the night**

27   **owls came out and little creatures began to roam through the**

28   **woods. A blanket of darkness settled over them all, and the**

29   **stars began to twinkle in the sky. The little fir had been**

30   **sleeping soundly through the night when suddenly**

31   *(CHRISTMAS STAR enters Stage Right, stands on stool or*

32   *platform and shines flashlight on FIR)* **she was awakened by a**

33   **bright light. The light seemed to be shining directly upon her.**

34   **FIR: Wh-what is it?** *(With arm towards light)* **Is it time to wake up**

35   **already?**

1   STAR: I am the Christmas Star, Little Fir. You must wake up early,
2   while it is still dark. You must be ready when the woodsmen
3   come to the forest. They are looking for a tree to make a
4   manger. The baby King will soon be born and you have been
5   chosen to hold this Savior.
6   FIR: You — you — you mean me?! *(Stammers.)* But I'm not even
7   full grown. Surely it's not time for me to die!
8   STAR: Little Fir, I have searched this whole forest and have found
9   no finer tree for this service to the King. You have a very
10   loving heart and you have obeyed the Lord of the Trees. Since
11   you are a young tree, you will understand the needs of this
12   baby King. Be ready, for I must go now — to guide the visitors
13   to the newborn King.
14 FIR: The baby King! Oh, yes! I would gladly give my life to help
15   this baby King, for he is Lord of all the trees. He is Lord of
16   everything and everyone! *(CHRISTMAS STAR exits.)*
17 NARRATOR: Little Fir could hardly believe what was happening.
18   *(WOODSMEN enter, one with hatchet. FIR voice character moves*
19   *behind shrubbery of OAK and remains there.)* It still seemed like a
20   dream, for as suddenly as the Christmas Star had appeared, its
21   light was swept away. Then the beautiful vision became a reality.
22 FIRST WOODSMAN: *(To SECOND WOODSMAN)* It's getting cold
23   out here. Let's just cut down this small fir tree to make the
24   manger. It'll be less work than cutting down a big tree.
25 SECOND WOODSMAN: Suits me! *(Character playing LITTLE FIR*
26   *slips Off-stage as unobtrusively as possible, leaving the*
27   *WOODSMEN to hold up her cardboard tree. Optional: Sound effect,*
28   *such as a hammer on board from Off-stage, to suggest the chopping*
29   *down of the tree, as FIRST WOODSMAN pantomimes the act.*
30   *FIRST WOODSMAN picks up the tree while SECOND*
31   *WOODSMAN leaves the stump, which has been hidden On-stage, in*
32   *its place.)*
33 NARRATOR: *(As lights come up)* And just as the last stars faded from
34   the sky, the woodsmen began to leave with their small fir tree.
35 BOY: *(Running On-Stage)* Sirs — have you heard the news? A baby

1   is going to be born here very soon. He'll need a bed to sleep in.
2   Can you spare any wood?
3   FIRST WOODSMAN: A bed for a baby? What nonsense! We just
4   cut down this small fir tree, but we're using it to make a
5   manger for our master's barn.
6   BOY: But where will the baby sleep?
7   SECOND WOODSMAN: That's no concern of ours. Like he
8   said — we only came out to get wood for a manger.
9   BOY: *(Disappointed)* Oh! But I only wanted to help ...
10 FIRST WOODMAN: Sorry, lad. *(He drags the fir tree Off-stage.*
11 *SECOND WOODSMAN and BOY follow.)*
12 CHOIR OF TREES: *(Lifting hands up and down slowly and ad-*
13 *libbing)* Oh, no! Little Fir is gone! *(WOODSMEN enter with*
14 *manger and place it at Stage Right.)*
15 FIRST WOODSMAN: This is one sturdy manger.
16 SECOND WOODSMAN: Gotta keep those donkeys fed.
17 *(WOODSMEN exit.)*
18
19 SONG: *O Little Town of Bethlehem*
20 *(During the song, JOSEPH and MARY enter and seat themselves*
21 *on the floor on either side of the manger. MARY places the doll in*
22 *the manger. They remain in position for the entire song. After the*
23 *song, the lights dim. MARY and JOSEPH exit, taking the manger*
24 *with them.)*
25
26 NARRATOR: In the morning, the sun came up over the hill. *(Lights*
27 *come up.)* The Sycamore tree looked down where the young fir
28 had been. All he could see was a short stump where the little
29 fir had been and the footprints of the woodsmen who had
30 felled her. He shook his branches sadly for the loss of his
31 friend. *(SYCAMORE shakes arms.)*
32 OAK: *(To SYCAMORE)* Oh mighty Sycamore, we shouldn't be sad
33 for our little friend. It may seem that her life was cut short too
34 soon. But remember that she desired, most of all, to be what
35 the Lord of the Trees wanted her to be.

1   **SYCAMORE: That's right, my friend!** *(Lifts arms and waves them*
2   *back and forth.)* **Little Fir lives on — to serve the baby King. It**
3   **can only mean that God's great plan for us is soon to be**
4   **fulfilled. I'm ready to offer myself to him.**
5   **CHOIR OF TREES:** *(Lifting and waving arms with joy and ad-*
6   *libbing)* **Yes! Yes! Little Fir lives on!**
7
8   **SONG:** *One Day*
9   *(Verses 1, 2, 4, and 5. Whole cast sings.)*

The Nutcracker Story
By Pat Hall

A play version of the famous Christmas ballet

Cast of Characters

Clara — a girl about ten.
Fritz — Clara's brother, about twelve.
Uncle Drosselmayer — an old toymaker, absent-minded.
Nutcracker Prince — a handsome prince.
Furch — a mouse.
Fuzz — a mouse.
Gumdrops — or other assorted candy people.

Production notes and suggestions

Costumes

Clara and Fritz wear contemporary clothing suitable for a family Christmas dinner. Fritz wears pajamas in the last scene.

Uncle Drosselmayer also wears contemporary workman-type clothes — jeans, flannel shirt, a bibbed work apron, winter coat. As the Golden Knight, he could wear brown or yellow pants, yellow or gold shirt and a gold cape. His helmet could be made of a round cardboard ice-cream carton fitted over the head. Cut away enough to show the face. Paint gold. Attach strings to tie under the chin and any padding needed inside to make it comfortable. Plumes can be glued to the top. Or, check a costume rental store for a knight or Roman helmet.

The Nutcracker Prince should match wooden nutcracker as close as possible — same color pants, boots, coat, belt. Make a helmet/mask out of a box, gluing on fabrics, fake fur, felt, etc., to also resemble the head of your wooden nutcracker.

The mice could wear gray hooded sweatsuits. Attach ears to hoods and tails to backsides. Chief Mouse could also have military stripes on sleeves, ribbons and medals on chest, an eye patch, and a silver helmet with a spike. Make the helmet with an ice-cream carton or rent a Prussian-style helmet.

The Gumdrops can wear colored, long-sleeved leotards and tights. Make two "sandwich-board" candy shapes of cardboard and tie them on at the shoulders and sides.

Props

Wooden nutcracker for Clara.

Workbench with paints and brushes.

Nuts.

Alarm clock.

Wooden horse marionette for Fritz — make one out of cardboard tubes if you can't find a toy one.

Wooden blocks for Clara.

Coat tree.

Glue bottle and magic bottle — decorate empty plastic detergent bottles.

Large cartons decorated to look like Clara's wooden blocks grown large.

Swords for Nutcracker, Chief, and Uncle.

Crown for Clara — paper or cardboard.

Swan boat to hold two people — cut a large swan shape out of a sheet of cardboard or 4'x8'x1' building insulation Styrofoam. On the back attach a box toward the front and one toward the rear so the swan will stand up, but two people can stand between the boxes and appear to be in the boat. The swan is pulled across the stage by a tow line attached near the bottom. Uncle and Clara can rock the boat back and forth while they are "riding."

Bandages for Chief — white cloth for head bandage and arm sling.

Dragon costume — The dragon is made in three segments. Each segment is a cardboard box that fits over a mouse, leaving the legs showing. The segments are connected by about three feet of rope or fringe. The head segment fits over the Chief Mouse and has smaller boxes or Styrofoam pieces glued on to shape a dragon head. The middle and tail segments fit Furch and Fuzz. The last segment should have a long, dragging fabric tail attached. The whole dragon should be brightly colored and menacing. Check pictures of Chinese parade-style dragons for ideas.

Bed for Fritz — use a cot.

Sets

Uncle Drosselmayer's toyshop can be a cluttered workbench in front of the curtain.

Room of Fritz and Clara's house needs a Christmas tree backdrop that can grow larger. This can be painted on fabric and pulled upward to make it "grow." Or, real or artificial branches can be attached to fabric, decorated (non-breakable ornaments!) and pulled upward. Put coat tree at Stage Right near "door."

Sugar Plum Land needs a castle backdrop. Paint a gingerbread and candy castle on a curtain or on large cardboard screens. One-inch-thick building insulation Styrofoam could also be used — it is lightweight, rigid, easily cut, and comes in 4'x8' sheets. Remember the castle needs to appear smoothly and quietly in the last scene. Use other "candy" walls and arches as desired. They also can be made out of decorated cardboard boxes or building Styrofoam.

Fritz's bedroom has a bed near Stage Right. Toys and clothing are scattered around, including wooden blocks and the marionette.

Sound Effects

Excerpts recorded from Tchaikovsky's *Nutcracker Ballet* may be used throughout the play.

Ringing of alarm clock.

Dinner bell.

Tick-tock sounds — use a tick-tock block found in preschool rhythm sets or knock on two different-sized pieces of wood.

Clock striking midnight — strike on a cymbal or metal bowl.

Hissing and squeaking.

Roaring wind sounds — blow gently across a microphone.

Clash of cymbals for fights with dragon — time carefully with sword strikes.

1	**Scene 1**
2	*(Music from Tchaikovsky's "Nutcracker Overture" plays before,*
3	*and as curtain rises. UNCLE DROSSELMAYER is in his toy*
4	*workshop painting the Nutcracker.)*
5	UNCLE: **Just a little touch of paint here ... and there ... perfect! A**
6	**Nutcracker Prince all ready for adventures and excitement!**
7	**And this is no ordinary nutcracker either. Most nutcrackers**
8	**open their mouth,** *(Does so)* **you pop in a nut, close the mouth,**
9	*(Does so)* **and the nutshell is cracked. But this is a special**
10	**nutcracker ... there's something secret about him ...** *(Alarm*
11	*clock goes off.)* **Oh drat! Where is that alarm clock? Quiet!**
12	**Quiet! I'm coming ... as soon as I find you.** *(Finds ringing*
13	*clock and turns it off.)* **There! Now why did I set the alarm? I**
14	**was supposed to remember something ... Good heavens! Yes!**
15	**I'm supposed to go to Clara and Fritz's house for a Christmas**
16	**supper.** *(Takes off apron and puts on coat.)* **That's why I made**
17	**the nutcracker. It's a present for my little niece Clara, and this**
18	*(Shows horse marionette)* **is for her brother Fritz. This could be**
19	**a noble horse, if Fritz will take the time to play with it. But**
20	**you, Prince Nutcracker, I have no doubt that Clara will find**
21	**out your little secret. Oops! Come along! I'm late, I'm late,**
22	**I'm late!** *(Exits with toys.)*
23	
24	**Scene 2**
25	*(Room of Fritz and Clara's house. Christmas tree in background.*
26	*CLARA is building with blocks.)*
27	CLARA: **... And this room of the castle will be where the princess**
28	**keeps all her jewels ... and there'll be a rose garden over**
29	**here ...**
30	FRITZ: *(Enters Stage Left.)* **Gosh, Clara, I'm hungry! When are we**
31	**going to eat supper? I'm starving to death!**
32	CLARA: **Mother said we'll eat as soon as Uncle Drosselmayer gets**
33	**here.**
34	FRITZ: **Oh no! Uncle Drosselmayer is coming here for supper? I**
35	**just lost my appetite!**

1   CLARA: Fritz! That was a nasty thing to say!
2   FRITZ: So what? I wish he wasn't coming. He's so old and creaky
3   and forgetful.
4   CLARA: So what yourself! I don't think he's so awful.
5   FRITZ: And he always brings dumb presents too. Wooden toys! I
6   don't think he's realized that there are such things as
7   batteries! What good is a toy unless you can turn it on and
8   have it do something?
9   CLARA: You have to learn to use your imagination.
10   FRITZ: I can imagine how great it would be if Uncle Drosselmayer
11   weren't coming here.
12   CLARA: I know it'd be great if you weren't going to be here! *(A*
13   *knock at door)* I'll get it! I'll get it! *(Answers door Off-Stage,*
14   *Stage Right.)* Merry Christmas, Uncle Drosselmayer! Mom!
15   Uncle Drosselmayer's here!
16   UNCLE: Merry Christmas, Clara! *(Enters with Clara.)* Merry
17   Christmas, Fritz! *(Hangs up coat.)*
18   FRITZ: *(Unenthusiastically)* Merry Christmas.
19   UNCLE: I have a little something for each of you. I didn't get time
20   to wrap them, but here you go, Fritz — your own horse! Just
21   move this bar back and forth like this, and he's a real, live
22   horse. *(Demonstrates.)*
23   FRITZ: *(Sarcastically)* Oh wow.
24   UNCLE: And for you, Clara, a handsome Nutcracker Prince!
25   CLARA: Oh, thank you, Uncle Drosselmayer! He'll fit right into
26   my story about a princess and a castle. See, here's the jewel
27   room, and the gardens ...
28   FRITZ: *(Grabs nutcracker.)* Princes! Castles! *(Knocks down blocks*
29   *with nutcracker.)* Baby stuff!
30   CLARA: My castle! My nutcracker! Fritz, you broke my
31   nutcracker! *(FRITZ runs out Stage Left.)* My brand new
32   nutcracker and he broke it! *(Cries.)*
33   UNCLE: Don't cry, Clara, let's see what can be done here.
34   CLARA: Can you fix it, Uncle? Can you?
35   UNCLE: Ah yes! The Golden Knight comes to rescue the Prince

1   **again!**

2   **CLARA:** *(Puzzled)* **What? What did you say, Uncle?**

3   **UNCLE: Oh, nothing, nothing, just daydreaming for a minute. I**

4   **like to think about castles and knights and adventures.**

5   **CLARA: I do too!**

6   **UNCLE: Let's see now, yes, I can just glue this back on, and he'll**

7   **be good as new ... I always carry a glue bottle with me.**

8   *(Glues.)* **There we go.** *(Dinner bell Off-stage)*

9   **CLARA: That's mother's little bell to tell us supper is ready!**

10   **UNCLE: We'll let the glue dry now and after supper he'll be ready**

11   **to play with again. Mmmmm! Supper does smell good!**

12   *(Exeunt Stage Left. Lights dim. The "Arabian Dance" from the*

13   *ballet plays during the interlude and during the first part of the*

14   *next scene until the mice appear.)*

15

16   **Scene 3**

17   *(Dim lighting on stage. CLARA enters Stage Left, yawning and*

18   *stretching.)*

19   **CLARA: That was such a long supper! I'm so tired I could just fall**

20   **over!** *(Yawns some more.)* **But I have to check my nutcracker**

21   **and see if he's all right.** *(Yawns, finds nutcracker, yawns again.)*

22   **Golly, I'm tired!** *(She lies down on stage with nutcracker beside*

23   *her.)* **I'm glad you're fixed, Nutcracker.** *(Pause. Tick-tock*

24   *sounds. The clock strikes midnight. The tree in the backdrop*

25   *grows. Push cartons decorated like blocks On-stage. A hissing*

26   *and squeaking noise starts. CLARA wakes with a start.)* **What**

27   **was that? Where am I?** *(Hisses, squeaks and scratches from Off-*

28   *stage)* **What's that? Let's hide!** *(Takes nutcracker and hides Off-*

29   *stage Stage Right. CHIEF MOUSE peeks around corner at Stage*

30   *Left.)*

31   **FURCH:** *(Off-stage)* **How's it look, Chief?**

32   **CHIEF:** *(Enters.)* **All clear! Come on out, you guys.**

33   **FURCH:** *(Enters.)* **Right, Chief!**

34   **FUZZ:** *(Enters.)* **Right on!**

35   **CHIEF: Furch and Fuzz, the most glorious time of the Christmas**

1   season is now here!

2   FURCH: Here! Here!

3   FUZZ: Lay it on, Chief!

4   CHIEF: The big Christmas supper is over, the presents have been

5   opened, the people have gone to bed ...

6   FURCH: Here! Here!

7   FUZZ: Nobody can say it as well as the Chief can!

8   FURCH: Say on! Say on!

9   FUZZ: Yay, Chief!

10 CHIEF: The people have gone to bed, and loads of new Christmas

11   · toys are right here in this room, defenseless and waiting ...

12   Waiting for what, guys?

13 FURCH: Say it, Chief!

14 FUZZ: Nobody can say it like you, Chief!

15 CHIEF: Those brand new Christmas toys are waiting to be *broken!*

16   And who's gonna do it?

17 FURCH: Here! Here!

18 FUZZ: Say it, Chief!

19 CHIEF: *We* are gonna break 'em!

20 FURCH: Hooray for the Chief!

21 FUZZ: Nobody can break toys like you, Chief! *(MICE sing and*

22   *dance to tune of "Three Blind Mice.")*

23   Three tough mice! Three tough mice!

24   Here we come! Here we come!

25   We all came here to break your toys!

26   We don't care much for Christmas toys!

27   We only want to smash up toys!

28   We're three tough mice!

29   *(While they sing, CLARA peeks out at them and hides again.)*

30 CHIEF: Hold it! Hold it! What did I see? *(Grabs CLARA and drags*

31   *her On-Stage.)*

32 CLARA: Let me go! Let me go!

33 FURCH: Wow! What is it?

34 FUZZ: These dolls get more realistic all the time!

35 FURCH: A walking, talking Barbie doll!

1   **CHIEF: There's work to be done, guys! Should we pull out her**
2   **eyelashes, or should we bite off her toes?** *(MICE shove CLARA*
3   *around and sing.)*
4   **We don't care much for Christmas joys!**
5   **We only want to smash up toys!**
6   **We're three tough mice!**
7   *(Play the first two measures of the "March," like a trumpet, and*
8   *the NUTCRACKER PRINCE leaps On-Stage from Stage Right*
9   *with drawn sword. He wears his mask. FURCH and FUZZ hide*
10   *behind CHIEF. CLARA runs behind PRINCE.)*
11   **FURCH: Who's he? Barbie's friend, Ken?**
12   **FUZZ: Naw! It's a transformer!**
13   **CHIEF: Whatever he is, he wants to fight. Furch? Fuzz? Who's**
14   **gonna fight with him?** *(FURCH and FUZZ look at each other a*
15   *minute, then push the CHIEF toward the PRINCE.)*
16   **FURCH: Nobody can do it like you can, Chief!**
17   **CHIEF: Wait a minute ...**
18   **FUZZ: Go get him, Chief!**
19   **CHIEF: Wait ...**
20   **FURCH: Yay for the Chief!**
21   **CHIEF:** *(Draws a sword.)* **This is stupid!** *(CHIEF fights with*
22   *PRINCE. FURCH and FUZZ cheer "Go Chief!" "Keep it up,*
23   *Chief!" CHIEF gets wounded.)*
24   **CHIEF: Aaaauugh! He got me! I'm bleeding!**
25   **FURCH: Keep it up, Chief!**
26   **FUZZ: Nobody can bleed better than you, Chief!**
27   **CHIEF: You idiots! Help me out of here!** *(MICE retreat Off-stage*
28   *Stage Left.)*
29   **CLARA:** *(To PRINCE)* **Why, you're my nutcracker!**
30   **PRINCE: Actually, your nutcracker is just one of my disguises.**
31   **CLARA: My nutcracker a disguise? I don't understand. Who are**
32   **you really?**
33   **PRINCE: Just let me get this mask off ...** *(Removes nutcracker*
34   *mask.)*
35   **CLARA: Why, you're a handsome prince!**

1   **PRINCE: And you're a beautiful princess! Turn around three**
2   **times ...**
3   **CLARA:** *(Turns.)* **... One ... two ... three ...** *(Lights flash, CLARA*
4   *puts on a crown previously hidden On-stage.)* **Oh my gosh!**
5   **PRINCE: And here comes a boat just right for a beautiful princess.**
6   *(Swan boat enters Stage Left to the "Waltz of the Flowers." They*
7   *board.)* **Come with me and I'll show you my kingdom. It's**
8   **called Sugar Plum Land.** *(Exit in boat Stage Right. MICE push*
9   *on bandaged CHIEF from Stage Left.)*
10   **FURCH: Go get him again, Chief!**
11   **CHIEF: No! No! I'm not going to fight him again! I'm wounded!**
12   **He'll make mincemeat out of me!**
13   **FUZZ: Nobody can be better mincemeat than you, Chief!**
14   **FURCH: Get him, Chief!**
15   **CHIEF: Wait a minute, he's not here!**
16   **FURCH: Where'd he go?**
17   **FUZZ: And where's the Barbie doll?** *(FURCH and FUZZ look*
18   *around.)*
19   **CHIEF: I bet I know where they went! They snuck off to Sugar**
20   **Plum Land! We'll get 'em! I know how to get to Sugar Plum**
21   **Land too! Line up, you guys!** *(FUZZ and FURCH line up behind*
22   *the CHIEF.)* **Now count to three.**
23   **ALL: One ... two ... three** *(Pause)*
24   **CHIEF: What? What's the matter here? Do it again!**
25   **ALL: One ... two ... three ...** *(Pause)*
26   **CHIEF: Can't you guys do anything right? How come it's not**
27   **working?** *(Looks carefully at FURCH and FUZZ.)* **You**
28   **dummies!** *(Bonks their heads.)* **You're in the wrong places!**
29   *(Shoves them.)* **Furch, you go here, and Fuzz, you go here! Now**
30   **do it again!**
31   **ALL: One ... two ... three ...** *(Lights flash, a roaring sound, MICE*
32   *quickly put on dragon costume hidden On-Stage. Head position*
33   *for CHIEF, first hump for FURCH and second hump for FUZZ.)*
34   **CHIEF: There we go! Everybody here? Furch?**
35   **FURCH: Right here, Chief!**

1   **CHIEF: Fuzz?**

2   **FUZZ: Right here, Chief!**

3   **CHIEF: OK, let's go to Sugar Plum Land too.** *(Exit Stage Right with*

4   *a roar and discordant music. Curtain. "Waltz of the Flowers"*

5   *plays during scene change.)*

6

7   **Scene 4**

8   *(Sugar Plum Land background. PRINCE and CLARA enter Stage*

9   *Right in the swan boat.)*

10   **CLARA: Sugar Plum Land is so *beautiful!* *(They get out of boat. It*

11   *drifts Off-stage Stage Left.)*

12   **PRINCE: Now let's go see my castle.**

13   **CLARA:** *(Points to backdrop castle.)* **That's where you live? It's**

14   **more fabulous than anything I ever imagined!**

15   **PRINCE: It's really a very comfortable and jolly place, and we get**

16   **a lot of interesting visitors, sometimes even the Golden**

17   **Knight.**

18   **CLARA: The Golden Knight? Who is he?**

19   **PRINCE: The Golden Knight is one of the great heroes of Sugar**

20   **Plum Land. He always seems to know when there's a disaster**

21   **and he comes to rescue us from the edge of doom.**

22   **CLARA: I didn't think you'd have disasters in Sugar Plum Land.**

23   **PRINCE: Here comes some of the people of Sugar Plum Land!**

24   **GUMDROPS:** *(Enter from both sides and dance around to the*

25   *"Dance of the Sugar Plum Fairy.")* **The Prince is home!**

26   **Welcome back, Prince! He brought Clara!** *(All bow.)*

27   **Welcome, Princess Clara! Welcome to Sugar Plum Land!**

28   **PRINCE: Go and prepare a feast in honor of Princess Clara.**

29   **GUMDROPS: Whoopee! A party! Let's go!** *(Dance off Stage Right.*

30   *They scream Off-stage and come running back.)* **A dragon! Help!**

31   **Help! A dragon in Sugar Plum Land! Save us, Prince**

32   **Nutcracker! Help! Help!** *(Run off screaming Stage Left.*

33   *DRAGON enters Stage Right with a roar and discordant music.)*

34   **PRINCE:** *(Draws sword.)* **Stand back, Clara. This is a disaster!**

35   *(DRAGON and PRINCE fight. DRAGON wounds PRINCE and*

1	*PRINCE falls down Stage Left.)*
2	**CLARA: Prince Nutcracker!**
3	**PRINCE: He got me!** *(DRAGON roars and gets ready to finish off the*
4	*PRINCE.)* **We're doomed! The only thing that can save us now**
5	**is the Golden Knight.** *(Play first two measures of the "March."*
6	*Uncle Drosselmayer as the GOLDEN KNIGHT enters Stage*
7	*Right. DRAGON turns and fights with the KNIGHT. DRAGON*
8	*backs KNIGHT into a corner Stage Right, and it appears the*
9	*DRAGON is going to win.)*
10	**CLARA: This can't happen! The dragon can't win!** *(She grabs*
11	*PRINCE's sword and fiercely hacks at DRAGON and gives him a*
12	*death blow. DRAGON dies. To KNIGHT)* **Are you all right,**
13	**Golden Knight?**
14	**UNCLE: I'm fine ... just got knocked down. How's the Prince?**
15	**CLARA: He's terribly wounded! Can you help him? Can you?**
16	**UNCLE: Ah yes. The Golden Knight comes to rescue the Prince**
17	**again.**
18	**CLARA: Huh? My uncle said that once ...**
19	**UNCLE: Let's see now, yes. I can just put a little magic healing**
20	**potion here and he'll be good as new. I always carry a bottle**
21	**of magic healing potion with me.** *(Pours potion.)* **There we go.**
22	**PRINCE: A thousand thank-yous, Sir Knight. You have saved us**
23	**all once again.**
24	**UNCLE: Oh no, it was really Clara who did it.**
25	**GUMDROPS:** *(Enter from both sides.)* **The Golden Knight! Three**
26	**cheers for the Golden Knight! Three cheers for Clara!**
27	**Whoopee for the heroes!**
28	**CLARA:** *(To KNIGHT)* **Have we met before? You seem awfully**
29	**familiar.**
30	**UNCLE:** *(Laughs.)* **Let me get my helmet off ...** *(Takes it off.)*
31	**CLARA: Uncle Drosselmayer?! You're the Golden Knight? The**
32	**great hero of Sugar Plum Land?**
33	**UNCLE: Well, yes. I do seem to be the Golden Knight. I come here**
34	**quite often. When other people think I'm daydreaming, I'm**
35	**actually here in Sugar Plum Land having adventures.**

1   **GUMDROPS: Yay for Uncle Drosselmayer, the Golden Knight!**

2   **UNCLE: I think it's time for this adventure to go back home now.**

3   *(Swan boat floats Up Stage Left to the sound of the "Waltz of the*

4   *Flowers.")*

5   **PRINCE: I'd better get into my disguise.** *(PRINCE and a*

6   *GUMDROP go Off-stage Stage Right and GUMDROP then*

7   *carries on the wooden nutcracker.)*

8   **GUMDROP: Here's the Prince, ready to go.** *(UNCLE and CLARA*

9   *enter boat with wooden nutcracker.)*

10   **GUMDROPS: Come back for more adventures!**

11   **UNCLE: We will!**

12   **CLARA: Good-bye! Good-bye!** *("Waltz of the Flowers" plays. Swan*

13   *boat goes to front of stage and curtain closes on Sugar Plum*

14   *Land. Dim light.)* **Do you really go to Sugar Plum Land for**

15   **adventures all the time?**

16   **UNCLE: Oh yes. I've been going there for years and years.** *(Pats*

17   *wooden nutcracker.)* **The Prince and I have had many**

18   **adventures.**

19   **CLARA: And this is really truly the Prince in disguise?**

20   **UNCLE: Yes indeed! We planned this carefully. The Prince wanted**

21   **to meet you so I made him a disguise.**

22   **CLARA: Why did he want to meet me?**

23   **UNCLE: Because you like to imagine things about castles and**

24   **adventures.** *(Swan boat starts tilting and rocking.)* **Oooops!**

25   **What's happening? We're sinking! We're going to have to**

26   **make a bigger boat if all of us are going adventuring again.**

27   **Hang on! Steady! Steady!** *(Curtains open to show FRITZ'S*

28   *bedroom. Boat bumps into FRITZ'S bed near Stage Right.)*

29   **FRITZ:** *(Wakes up with a yell of panic.)* **What are you doing? Don't**

30   **smash me!** *(Stands on bed.)* **Clara! I'm sorry I broke your**

31   **nutcracker! I'm sorry I broke the castle! Thanks for the**

32   **horse, Uncle! Don't run over me! Help! Aaaauugh!** *(FRITZ*

33   *hides under bed. UNCLE and CLARA climb out of boat. CLARA*

34   *takes out the wooden nutcracker.)*

35   **UNCLE: Calm down, Fritz. We're not going to hurt you.**

1   **CLARA: We just got back from an adventure!**

2   **FRITZ:** *(Crawls out. Accusingly)* **Where did you go? How come you**

3   **didn't invite me?**

4   **UNCLE: I don't think we need this right now.** *(Gives swan boat a*

5   *push and it drifts Off-stage Stage Right.)*

6   **FRITZ: Holy cow! It went right through the wall! How did you do**

7   **that?**

8   **UNCLE: It's kind of a transformer, Fritz. When you learn how to**

9   **use it you can come on adventures too.**

10   **FRITZ: Learn what? How?**

11   **UNCLE: Learn to use your imagination.**

12   **CLARA:** *(Hands him the marionette horse.)* **You can start with this.**

13   **FRITZ:** *(Tries toy.)* **Like this? Then I think of things to happen?**

14   **CLARA:** *(Piles up some blocks.)* **That's right. Here's the castle**

15   **where the Nutcracker lives.**

16   **FRITZ: And the horse comes galloping up with a message.**

17   **Somebody's in trouble. They need help.** *(Sugar Plum Land*

18   *appears in the background and the "Waltz of the Flowers" plays*

19   *softly.)*

20   **UNCLE: We'll all go on adventures together, won't we?**

21   **FRITZ:** *(Looking up from playing)* **Merry Christmas, Uncle and**

22   **Clara!**

23   *(Curtain)*

Monologues

My Son, the Messiah

By Lia Goens

Advent reflections from Joseph, plus a Christmas Eve service.

Cast of Characters

Joseph
Aaron
Mary

Production Notes

Props

Optional props that add to the authenticity but are not absolutely necessary are tools that would be found in a biblical carpentry work area. One of our carpenters made a crude, unpainted bench, a mallet, and added a handmade handle to a rusted saw. These items were placed on or beside the bench. On the first three Advent Sundays, Joseph can carry one of the tools with him as he enters. Sheets of parchment rolled up into scrolls serve as the letters that Joseph reads. (The script may be hidden in or taped to the parchment.) The edges may be burned to give the pages an older appearance. Non-fusible interfacing (available at fabric stores) or any heavy paper may be stained with tea and used in place of parchment. Also needed is a thick writing utensil resembling a stylus or reed pen and a clay-like "ink well." A straw basket may be used to carry these items in with him on Advent Four and Christmas Eve. For Christmas Eve, the props needed are a manger, straw, and a baby Jesus.

Costumes

Simple biblical-style, long-sleeved robes with sandals for all the characters. All three should have headpieces made from rectangular pieces of cloth. Joseph and Aaron wear theirs tied with cord around the circumference of their heads, *kaffiyeh*-style, while Mary's should drape loosely around her head and shoulders.

Description

This program is designed so that each Advent letter can be read, with occasional memorized commentary to the congregation, as if it were a distant cousin just arrived in Nazareth. This is how we performed it at Church of the Savior, and the congregation enjoyed a kind of intimacy with the drama.

Joseph gives a brief recap of his previous monologue each week. You may wish to supplement this with a small review in your bulletin for those who were not in attendance the previous week.

Aaron can remain an unseen correspondent by simply deleting the Christmas Eve script that involves him, or he may be included in the Christmas Eve service, which is what we did in the original production. Mary has a small speaking role in this script also. If desired, you may add (nonspeaking) shepherds to round out the live Nativity on Christmas Eve. You may also wish to create a stable-like setting for this service, with straw strewn about a platform, a couple of bales intact for Mary and Joseph to sit on, old blankets, and some clay pottery.

Each Sunday of Advent carries a theme, which is indicated. Suggested Scripture readings and hymns have been included but obviously are not required.

Advent One —
Secure in God's Will

Theme
Contentment.
Scripture Reading
Psalm 130.
Setting
Joseph's carpentry workshop. It is Friday evening at sundown — the beginning of the Sabbath.

1   *(There is a blast of a ram's horn, after which JOSEPH enters and*
2   *approaches his tools and bench. He is carrying a scroll and a tool,*
3   *as if he's been working.)*
4   **JOSEPH: It is time for the Sabbath to begin and the work to cease.**
5   *(Places his tool on the bench.)* **As always, the ram's horn calls us**
6   **to prayer at the synagogue. Tonight I will concentrate prayers on**
7   **my good friend, Aaron. Let me read to you a letter I received**
8   **from him this morning.**
9   *(Unrolls scroll and reads.)* **Dear Joseph, I am sorry to tell you**
10   **that Ezra and I have been imprisoned at Caesarea and now**
11   **await a ship which will carry us to Rome for trial. We were**
12   **arrested protesting the census.** *(Looks up.)* **I warned him. I**
13   **warned him not to do it.** *(Reads.)* **I didn't tell Herod that Jews**
14   **resent paying taxes to Rome. I didn't complain or threaten. So**
15   **there wouldn't be so much as a hint of violence, we carried no**
16   **weapons.**
17   *(Looks up.)* **That's because they don't own any weapons. Ezra**
18   **is a scribe, Aaron a potter — or would be, if he'd quit protesting**
19   **everything under the sun.** *(Reads.)* **All I did was explain that**
20   **forcing us to travel long, hazardous journeys to our birthplaces**
21   **for the census was inhumane and could be more easily**
22   **accomplished by sending Roman representatives to each village.**

1   A simple, reasonable request. *(Looks up.)* As if a crazy man like
2   Herod would listen to a simple, reasonable request. And even if
3   he wasn't crazy, Herod would never risk the disfavor of Rome.
4   I told Aaron this, but he didn't hear me. And now this letter.
5   *(Reads.)* Herod called it treason. *(Looks up.)* Of course he
6   called it treason. *(Reads.)* And so we go to Rome. I am not sorry
7   about the petition, Joseph. I feel what I did was right. You want
8   me to be like you: a student of the Torah, an obedient citizen of
9   Nazareth, an unquestioning follower of God's law. I know you
10   want me to avoid risk and patiently and quietly await the
11   Messiah to rescue us. I can't, Joseph. It is not my way; it is
12   yours. I believe God has chosen me to fight and go to prison —
13   maybe even to die. He wants you to live a quiet life, working
14   your trade and rearing your children to be righteous and wise
15   in the Torah. If we are each doing what is right for us, then we
16   are doing what is right for God.
17   My only regret is that I will miss the joyous day of your
18   wedding. How lucky you are to be getting such a beautiful,
19   loving girl and even luckier that your father and Mary's agreed
20   to the betrothal when you two were already in love. Think of me
21   on that great day and know that I rejoice in the union. May God
22   bless each of you and your many sons and daughters. Faithfully
23   yours, Aaron. *(JOSEPH rolls up scroll.)*
24   He will never see my sons and daughters. I know this. It
25   hurts and it makes me angry, but he is right. We all must do
26   what God has called us to do, even if others do not understand.
27   I shall wed Mary, and we shall raise a family in our quiet
28   corner of the world. We shall worship God and wait for the
29   Messiah to free us from tyrants — the tyrants who have taken
30   Aaron from us. But I will miss him. *(Exits.)*
31   Suggested Hymn: "O Come, O Come, Emmanuel"

Advent Two —
A World Turned Upside-Down

Theme
Distress/change of direction in life.

Scripture Reading
Luke 1:26-38. (This Scripture may be read as a dialogue with a female voice for Mary and a male voice for the angel delivering the message.)

Setting
Joseph's carpentry workshop.

1   *(JOSEPH enters and sits on his bench, finishing up a letter to his*
2   *friend Aaron.)*
3   **JOSEPH: I'm glad you have come today. Things have changed**
4   **drastically since we last met. You remember the letter from my**
5   **friend Aaron that I read to you at our last visit. Do you recall**
6   **how he expressed his sorrow at missing my marriage to Mary,**
7   **even though he could not be sorry for his criticism of Rome**
8   **that landed him in prison? He said we were both doing what**
9   **was right for us: He would wait for the Messiah as he battled**
10   **Rome while Mary and I would wait for him here in Nazareth.**
11   **Well, it isn't to be. Everything has changed. Everything. Let**
12   **me read my letter to Aaron. Perhaps then you will understand**
13   **my misery and confusion.** *(Reads letter.)* **Dear Aaron, I warn**
14   **you: This letter imposes on our friendship, for here you are**
15   **imprisoned, awaiting an uncertain future, and I am about to**
16   **use you as a sounding board. It's so hard to come right out and**
17   **say this, but there's no other way. Mary — my beloved,**
18   **beautiful Mary — is pregnant.** *(Pause)* **And I am not the father**
19   **of this child.**
20   **There is so much about this that makes no sense. First of all,**
21   **I know Mary loves me. She loved me long before we were**
22   **officially betrothed. Second, in this small village, I would have**
23   **known if another man had come into her life. Third and most**

1   important, Mary is known for a purity almost divine in
2   nature. It simply isn't possible she could do anything that
3   violates God's laws. The strange fact is, when she told me
4   about the pregnancy, she didn't even act guilty.
5   Actually, between you and me, Aaron, my sweet, gentle
6   Mary acted a little crazy. She seemed to be in a state of shock
7   as well as confusion and couldn't answer my questions
8   rationally. She kept saying, "How can I make you understand
9   when I don't?" Twice she pleaded, "Be patient, Joseph. Surely
10   God will explain."
11   The second time my self-control vanished, and I said,
12   "Maybe while we wait for God's explanation, you might tell
13   me what happened. You might also tell me when you stopped
14   loving me."
15   She burst into tears then and for a long time couldn't say
16   anything at all. Finally she said, "I never stopped loving you,
17   Joseph. I will always love you. But I love God, too." And then
18   as if I wasn't confused enough, she said, "If my parents will
19   send me, I want to visit my cousin Elizabeth." In a kind of
20   daze, she turned away from me, mumbling almost to herself,
21   "When I've seen Elizabeth, I'll know more." And then she was
22   gone.
23   At first I thought she wanted to go to Elizabeth in order to
24   be somewhere besides Nazareth for her confinement, but what
25   could she mean by, "When I've seen Elizabeth, I'll know
26   more"? Know more what? Can you make sense of this? Am I
27   so hurt and angry that I'm missing some obvious truth? Help
28   me, my good friend. You know Mary and me better than
29   anyone. I wish you were here, but since you are not, you must
30   write. And pray. Mary and I both need God's help.
31   Of course I cannot bring her before a jury to be tried.
32   Though she is the cause of my intense suffering, I love her too
33   much to be the cause of hers. I will quietly distance myself
34   from her, hide my grief from everyone but you, and try to lose
35   myself in my work. Such a short time ago, my plans for life

1 were so clear. I knew who I was and where I was headed. I
2 loved God and Mary, and I knew they loved me. Now God has
3 turned his face away, and I no longer know what he wants
4 from me. And Mary? Unbelievably, she has betrayed me.
5 Nothing makes sense anymore.
6   I guess we were wrong about God's will for my life. Let's
7 hope we were equally wrong about his will for yours, and that
8 you will be released to come home rather than sent to Rome
9 for trial. I will pray for you. May God be with us all. Your
10 troubled friend, Joseph. *(JOSEPH rolls up his scroll and exits.)*
11 Suggested Hymn: "Come, Thou Long-Expected Jesus"
12
13   *Advent Three —*
14   *A Change of Heart*
15
16 *Theme*
17   Joy and anticipation.
18 *Scripture Reading*
19   Matthew 1:18-25.
20 *Setting*
21   Joseph's carpentry workshop.
22
23   *(JOSEPH enters and sits on his bench, finishing up a letter to*
24   *Aaron.)*
25 JOSEPH: I look different today, don't I? Not so sad. Not so
26   worried. Not so confused. Well, I'm still confused — just
27   happy and confused instead of sad and confused. I've poured
28   out my feelings to my friend Aaron in another letter. Do you
29   mind if I read it to you? Good.
30   *(JOSEPH unrolls scroll and reads.)* **Dear Friend Aaron, I**
31   **hope my letters bring you some diversion from the dreadful**
32   **conditions of prison life. Though I wish you were**
33   **corresponding from a scribe's shop and not a dark, damp cell,**
34   **I am grateful to be able to talk to someone in these most**
35   **confusing times. In my last letter, I related the shocking**

1   circumstance of Mary being with child and my sorrow at
2   having to leave her. Now the situation has changed entirely.
3   I'm about to tell you an amazing story — one that would be
4   impossible to believe if you didn't know me as well as you do.
5   Several nights ago, an angel came to me. Yes, a real angel. I lay
6   in bed trying to sleep, feeling sad and worrying about Mary. I
7   kept thinking, *How can I turn her away? How can I live without*
8   *her?* Suddenly, a figure stood beside my bed. It was an angel
9   who said, "Don't hesitate to take Mary as your wife, for the
10   child she carries has been conceived by the Holy Spirit." The
11   angel said she will have a son, and that I should call the boy
12   "Jesus" because he is destined to save people from their sins.
13   If this child is to save people from their sins, if an angel is
14   telling me his name is ordained by the Holy Spirit to be Jesus,
15   which means Savior, then Mary is carrying the Messiah. The
16   prophets said, "The virgin shall conceive a child. She shall
17   give birth to a son, and he shall be called Immanuel." Can this
18   mean God is with us in Mary's baby? It must. No wonder she
19   looked stunned. No wonder she couldn't explain what
20   happened.
21   At first I asked myself why God chose Mary for this
22   assignment, thinking I certainly had nothing to do with it; but
23   now I'm not so sure. Maybe I have been chosen, too. I am a
24   descendant of King David. Didn't the prophets say the
25   Messiah would come from the lineage of David? And surely
26   the angel would not have told me to go ahead with my plans if
27   God did not see me as a worthy man and capable father. And
28   so, my dear friend, it appears God's will is for me to wed Mary
29   after all. Later I will consider what all this really means, but
30   for now, I am filled with gratitude. I have earned God's favor,
31   and I will be spending the rest of my life with the woman I
32   love.
33   Your prison sentence works nearly as much hardship on
34   me as on you, my good friend. I wish you were here to share
35   in this incredible experience. Write to me soon and let me

1 know what you think. As for me — I am overcome with joy!
2 Shalom, Joseph.
3 *(The following can be read or memorized and recited either at the*
4 *end of the letter or later in the service in conjunction with*
5 *Scripture reading of the Magnificat, Luke 1:46-55.)*
6 **Joseph's Magnificat**
7 O Lord, I thank you. My mouth shouts forth your praise, my
8 heart is filled with love. I will speak of your glories and grace
9 forever. I will declare your kindness and tell all the
10 discouraged to take heart. You are merciful to the suffering
11 and faithful to the reverent. O God, there is none like you.
12 *(JOSEPH exits.)*
13 Suggested Hymn: "Joy to the World"
14
15 *Advent Four —*
16 *Relying on Jehovah*
17
18 *Theme* ·
19 Dependence on God in the midst of uncertainty.
20 *Scripture Reading*
21 Luke 2:1-5.
22 *Setting*
23 Joseph is waiting outside a home in Bethlehem for a midwife
24 who is busy with another patient. (A bare stage is fine.)
25
26 *(JOSEPH enters with his scroll, inkwell, and pen in a basket and*
27 *sits on the floor to write a letter. He gets up, looks about anxiously*
28 *for the midwife, and sighs. The midwife has run into*
29 *complications, and JOSEPH is beginning to realize that he must*
30 *return to the stable soon or MARY may give birth entirely alone.*
31 *He is hoping against hope that he will not be the only person in*
32 *attendance. He writes a few more lines, then reads.)*
33 JOSEPH: *(Reading)* Dear Aaron, since I haven't heard from you in
34 so long, I write this letter without even knowing if you're still
35 in prison in Caesarea or if you've been moved to Rome for

1   **trial. Maybe God has answered our prayers and you've been**
2   **released. Whether you still languish there in prison or not, I**
3   **have to write. As usual, this is not a calm, newsy letter to quiet**
4   **your soul, but rather an attempt by me to avoid panic. I'm**
5   **hoping that if I concentrate on writing this letter, I'll regain**
6   **some of my composure.**
7   **My emotions have seen such highs and lows lately. When**
8   **we first started corresponding, I was content with my lot in**
9   **life and was eager to wed Mary. Then I sank into despair when**
10   **she told me she was with child. But when the angel visited me**
11   **and I saw clearly that the child she was carrying was the**
12   **Messiah, my disappointment turned to joy! And now — well,**
13   **I still feel the joy, but it is tempered with nervousness and**
14   **concern for Mary and the baby.**
15   **Mary and I arrived in Bethlehem late this afternoon and,**
16   **not surprisingly, the long, rugged trip started her labor. I have**
17   **finally found a midwife, but — if you can believe it — she is**
18   **delivering another baby and can't come right now. I've been**
19   **sitting outside this home for a long time. The midwife tells me**
20   **her patient is suffering complications. Complications! Talk**
21   **about complications. Mary and I are overwhelmed with**
22   **complications. I don't know what else could possibly go wrong.**
23   **Where is God? Isn't this his child we're worried about? He**
24   **chose Mary to bear his son. Why would he leave her alone in**
25   **a stable to do it? She needs a midwife! And she needs me. I'm**
26   **supposed to provide for her and protect her, but I don't know**
27   **what to do. Am I too young for this responsibility? Have I**
28   **failed the woman I love? Have I failed God?** *(Pause)* **No, he**
29   **has failed me.**
30   *(Looks up.)* **What am I saying? Forgive me, oh Lord. I am**
31   **afraid.** *(Looks again for midwife.)* **I don't know what to do, but**
32   **I cannot leave my wife alone any longer. I must go. Oh God,**
33   **my rock, my salvation. Why have you forsaken me?** *(Pause)*
34   **Take courage, my soul.** *(Drops to knees to pray.)* **Oh Lord, hear**
35   **my cry. You, who has done many great miracles, who has**

1 created the earth and the stars, the rushing waters and
2 awesome mountains, you alone can save us. I long for you, oh
3 God. Do not forsake me now. *(He rises.)* I dare not wait any
4 longer. I must go. *(He exits hurriedly.)*
5 **Suggested Hymn: "Let All Together Praise Our God"**
6
7
8 *Christmas Eve Service —*
9 *Father to a Newborn King*
10
11 *Theme*
12 The Messiah completes the picture
13 *Scripture Reading*
14 Luke 2:6-14.
15 *Setting*
16 A stable.
17
18 *(In the original production, JOSEPH and MARY entered the*
19 *sanctuary and took their places around the manger before the*
20 *first worshipers arrived. Some shepherds joined the live Nativity*
21 *scene and remained throughout the service. As the congregation*
22 *entered, MARY alternated between holding the baby and laying*
23 *him in the manger. Likewise, JOSEPH took part in caring for the*
24 *child. Prearranged visitors came up to look at the child*
25 *occasionally.*
26   *At any point after the service begins, JOSEPH moves slightly*
27 *apart from MARY and the baby to his straw basket and removes*
28 *parchment, pen, and ink. He writes a letter during chimes, a*
29 *hymn, etc., while MARY rests and tends to the baby. Following the*
30 *hymn, JOSEPH reads his letter.)*
31
32   **Part I**
33
34 JOSEPH: I am so happy to have you here to share in this
35   marvelous event. Is there anything so joyful, so miraculous, as

1   the birth of a baby? Mother and son are doing well. You and I

2   are together to celebrate. Now, if only Aaron were here also.

3   I'm hoping this letter will make him feel as if he is.

4   *(Unrolls scroll and reads.)* My Dear Friend Aaron, I write to

5   share the good news with you — the child has been born. We

6   have a son. Things were precarious for a while, but mother

7   and child came through perfectly — a miracle in itself. We are

8   situated in a stable some distance from an inn just outside

9   Bethlehem. It doesn't sound like much, but has proved to be

10   warm, comfortable, and much more peaceful than the inn

11   would have been. Bethlehem establishments have grown

12   rather noisy and boisterous because so many visitors are

13   present for the taxation.

14   I look at Mary, so obviously enthralled with this beautiful

15   infant. Only our God and I know how much she has endured

16   these last weeks. So gentle and sweet and small she seems, yet

17   she is strong and sure and confident. Perhaps it was for these

18   qualities she was chosen to be the mother of Jesus. I remain

19   overwhelmed that God has seen me worthy of Mary and

20   capable of raising this special child.

21   I do not pretend to understand even yet why things have

22   happened the way they have, nor do I completely understand

23   who this child is. Jesus, my son, yet not my son, but God's.

24   Mary, my wife, yet not my wife, but God's chosen one. Jesus,

25   a king, yet not a king, but a simple, ordinary baby wrapped in

26   swaddling cloths, not royal robes.

27   I see Mary, cradling her baby in a cave meant for cattle. I

28   see shepherds from nearby fields peering in at Mary and

29   Jesus, their eyes full of wonder. They tell me stories of angels

30   appearing on high and a star guiding their way to this manger.

31   I am deeply moved by all this, yet as perplexed by God's

32   method as before. One can only wonder what is in store for

33   tomorrow.

34   And what is my part in all this? As God has chosen Mary

35   to be Jesus' mother on earth, he has assigned me to be his

1   father. It is my job to see that he is fed and sheltered and
2   protected from all harm. I will see that he is educated. And I
3   will love him. Until our God makes known his plan for the
4   future, I will lead and guide this child as he grows. I pledge
5   myself to this task.
6   But for tonight, I rejoice, wishing only that you were here
7   to celebrate with me. *(JOSEPH kneels beside MARY.)*
8 Suggested Hymn: "What Child Is This?"
9
10   **Part II**
11   **Aaron Arrives in Bethlehem**
12
13   *(Enter AARON from opposite entry to stable. He hesitates just*
14   *inside and proceeds slowly down the aisle, coming around the left*
15   *side of the altar. JOSEPH spots him about halfway around and*
16   *goes to greet him. The two make their way to MARY as they talk.)*
17 JOSEPH: Aaron! I can't believe it.
18 AARON: My friend.
19 JOSEPH: You're here. You're really here.
20 AARON: I thought I would never see you again. *(They hug.)*
21 JOSEPH: I was just writing you a letter, telling you ... but never
22   mind, you're here. Come. You must see Mary. The baby has
23   been born.
24 AARON: I know. I heard.
25 JOSEPH: You heard?
26 AARON: Some shepherds told me on the road to Bethlehem.
27   *(Kneels next to MARY.)* Mary.
28 MARY: Aaron! I'm happy to see you. We've been so worried. Are
29   you all right? *(JOSEPH picks up the baby.)*
30 AARON: I'm tired from the long journey, but I rejoice that I'm out
31   of prison and here with you. Ironic, isn't it? The Romans who
32   arrested me for protesting the census released me to register
33   for that census. But what about you? How are you feeling
34   after this difficult night?
35 MARY: I'm fine, but I'm not the important one. Look. *(JOSEPH*

1   *shows him the baby. AARON looks him over carefully, saying*

2   *nothing.)*

3   JOSEPH: Well, what do you think?

4   AARON: He's ... he's a baby.

5   JOSEPH: Of course he's a baby. What did you expect?

6   AARON: I didn't expect to find him here in a stable!

7   JOSEPH: Neither did I.

8   AARON: In your letters, you said this baby was to be a

9   king — the Messiah, even.

10   JOSEPH: Mary and I were told this, yes.

11   AARON: *(Looks around.)* I mean no disrespect, brother, but this

12   doesn't seem a likely place for the birth of a king. Are you sure

13   you got the message right?

14   MARY: The message was clear, Aaron. You've been looking for the

15   Messiah a long, long time. You needn't look any longer. This is

16   the Savior the prophets promised.

17   JOSEPH: *(Handing AARON the baby)* Immanuel.

18   AARON: In this baby, God is with us. Joseph, do you realize what

19   this means? We are free. Not just from a Roman prison, but

20   all of us from all our prisons. We are free. Praise God!

21   JOSEPH and MARY: *(Together)* Hallelujah!

22   Suggested Hymn: "Silent Night" *(Optional: The congregation,*

23   *carrying candles, may file past the live Nativity scene during the*

24   *hymn.)*

Merry Christmas Plus Peace on Earth

By Art Buchwald

Adapted for Readers Theatre by Melvin R. White

Cast of Characters

Narrator

Mrs. Carstairs — a mature housewife, perhaps gossipy type.

Mr. Carstairs — her husband, a "typical" businessman.

Production Notes

Who hasn't felt some pressure to send Christmas cards? What can be a wonderful tradition to connect with old friends can turn into a source of stress. This sketch takes things to the extreme and skewers the way we view sending — and receiving — Christmas greetings.

The only props you'll need are four pieces of mail. The first is a photo greeting card. The second and fourth are letters in an ordinary white envelope. The third is a letter in a yellow envelope. You may wish to have the actual words on the letters — they need not be memorized.

1   *(NARRATOR is in place behind lectern which is positioned at the*
2   *side of the stage.)*
3   NARRATOR: **Some two-thousand-odd years have passed since that**
4   **night in Bethlehem. The story has been told, retold, written and**
5   **rewritten. But many think that today the celebration of Christ's**
6   **mass has been cheapened. Radio and television blasts**
7   **commercials, advertising gifts to give at Christmas. Millions**
8   **and millions of Christmas greeting cards clog the mail each**
9   **December. Let's listen in on Mr. and Mrs. Carstairs from the**
10   **humorous writings of Art Buchwald. This sketch is used with**
11   **his permission.** *(MR. and MRS. CARSTAIRS move their stools*
12   *Down Center and sit — or sit on a bench Down Center.)*
13   MRS. CARSTAIRS: **Honey, I wonder why the Carbunkles take**
14   **their Christmas cards so seriously.**
15   MR. CARSTAIRS: **I dunno. Maybe it's because he works in the**
16   **credit office of a store.**
17   MRS. CARSTAIRS: **Well, anyway, last Wednesday, December**
18   **first, we got a card from them — our first card this Christmas.**
19   **Can you imagine, this early? Really!**
20   MR. CARSTAIRS: **Expensive?**
21   MRS. CARSTAIRS: **Another photograph of the family — you**
22   **know, like they had last year, only this one was in Mexico.**
23   MR. CARSTAIRS: **Mexico?**
24   MRS. CARSTAIRS: **You remember, they took a trip down there**
25   **one weekend last summer, one of those bargain quickie trips.**
26   *(Pulls out card.)* **Here it is: "Warmest wishes from all the**
27   **Carbunkles for a merry Christmas and a happy New Year."**
28   MR. CARSTAIRS: *(Peering over at it)* **Hmmmh. Say, Carbunkle's**
29   **putting on a little weight, isn't he?**
30   MRS. CARSTAIRS: **Yeah. And will you look at that chintzy dress**
31   **she has on?**
32   NARRATOR 2: **The card was tossed aside,** *(MRS. CARSTAIRS sets*
33   *it down or even throws it)* **and no one thought about it again**
34   **until two weeks later a second item arrived from the**
35   **Carbunkles.** *(MR. CARSTAIRS picks up envelope.)*

1   MR. CARSTAIRS: What's this letter? Marked "Second Notice"?
2   MRS. CARSTAIRS: Open it, honey. I've been too busy getting
3   cards addressed — I couldn't find our Christmas card list —
4   haven't even looked at the mail. "Second Notice!" Are there
5   any bills we forgot to pay?
6   MR. CARSTAIRS: *(Reading)* "Two weeks ago you were sent a
7   Christmas card from the Carbunkles wishing you a merry
8   Christmas and a happy New Year. Probably due to the rush of
9   the holiday season, you were unable to acknowledge it. Now
10   we are very understanding of this, but we would like to
11   remind you that your Christmas card is one week past due,
12   and we are hoping you'll attend to this matter at your earliest
13   convenience. Sincerely, The Carbunkles." *(Sets letter down.)*
14   MRS. CARSTAIRS: Oh dear, I meant to do it! It just slipped my
15   mind. Well, I'll try to get it done tomorrow. Uh — I don't
16   suppose you have time to ...
17   MR. CARSTAIRS: Me? No — not me.
18   NARRATOR 2: Three days later in a yellow envelope arrived a
19   third item. This time all of the holly and mistletoe decorations
20   were missing, and in red letters stamped on the front was:
21   MRS. CARSTAIRS: *(Picks up yellow envelope.)* Third notice!
22   *(Opening letter)* "It has been called to our attention that you
23   are now two weeks in arrears on sending our family a return
24   Christmas card. When we sent you our lovely Mexican photo
25   Christmas card, we assumed you would send us one back by
26   return mail. To put it bluntly, you owe us one. We are
27   enclosing a self-addressed envelope for your convenience, and
28   would appreciate your remittance immediately." *(Sets letter*
29   *down.)*
30   MR. CARSTAIRS: *(Exploding in anger)* You said you'd take care of
31   it! Now look what's happened. I can't check on everything
32   and everybody around here — after all, I have to go to the
33   office every day. Why can't you stay home from that silly
34   bridge club of yours just once and get things done that need
35   doing!

1 MRS. CARSTAIRS: *(Upset; crying a little)* That's right, blame me.
2   After all, the Carbunkles are your friends, not mine. So why
3   don't you get that secretary of yours to take care of their
4   greeting? She does everything else for you. Besides, we don't
5   have any more cards left. I tried to call you at the office to tell
6   you — but they said you had taken your secretary out to
7   lunch.
8 MR. CARSTAIRS: *(Defensively)* It was a business luncheon — we
9   were deciding what I had to give the staff this Christmas.
10   *(Changing subject)* Tell you what. They've waited this long, they
11   can wait until New Year's — we'll send 'em a New Year's card!
12 MRS. CARSTAIRS: Good idea. When I go to Mabel's tomorrow,
13   I'll see if I can find some of those "Thank You for the
14   Christmas Greeting and Have a Happy New Year" cards.
15   Besides, we owe the Huses and the Fenners before we return
16   greetings to the Carbunkles.
17 NARRATOR 2: Two days later came a registered, special delivery
18   letter from the Miseracordia Collection Agency.
19 MRS. CARSTAIRS: *(Picks up envelope)* Honey, this came this
20   morning. I'm afraid to open it. What does it say?
21 MR. CARSTAIRS: *(Opening letter)* "Dear Sir and Madam: The
22   Carbunkles have turned over your bad debt Christmas
23   greeting to this office and have asked us to collect it for them
24   immediately. We are hoping you give us no difficulty in this
25   regard, as we have methods of collecting holiday wishes that
26   are not pleasant. Unless we hear from you by return special
27   delivery mail, we will see to it that you are listed as a bad
28   Christmas card risk, and will never receive another greeting.
29   This is your last warning. Signed, Miseracordia Collection
30   Agency."
31 NARRATOR: Well, I must admit that things have gotten out of
32   hand, what with cards and trees and office parties and all.
33   Sometimes we make all the celebrating much harder than it's
34   supposed to be. At the heart of Christmas is a very simple
35   notion: "Joy to the world! The Lord is come."

Christmas by Injunction

By O. Henry

Adapted for Readers Theatre by Melvin R. White

Cast of Characters

Narrator — An effective storyteller, man or woman.

Cherokee — A middle-aged prospector who strikes it rich.

Baldy — Possibly a bantam-type man, quick of speech, excitable; could be bald.

California Ed — Prospector, contrasting type man.

Man — Prospector, contrasting type man.

Texas — Prospector, Texas drawl.

Shorty — A singing prospector, not tall.

Thirsty Rogers — Perhaps a bit tipsy.

Trinidad — A strong-minded prospector, a leader.

Judge — An older man, pompous, stuffy, perhaps a hard drinker, even a W.C. Fields type.

Parent — Contrasting character, old enough to have seven children.

Section Boss' Wife — Perhaps twenty-five or thereabouts.

Woman — Thirty-five-ish, tired, worried but attractive.

Bobby — Ten, impish, thin, not a very nice kid.

Assayer's Wife — Society type, a bit snooty.

Miss Erma — Aging actress, but trying not to show it.

Production Notes

This humorous O. Henry short story has the typical surprise ending. It calls for a cast of sixteen readers, mostly men, but can be done by six or eight by double-casting. The easiest way to produce it is to provide boxes, chairs, benches, or stools in the playing area for the cast, bring them on and seat them, moving them Downstage, away from their seats, as they are needed, and return them to those seats when they are not required in a scene, or simply have them turn their backs to the audience. The narrator and the storyteller move in and out as needed. This keeps the story moving without interruption.

The main scene takes place in a bar; this will be Down Front Center over much of the playing area. Smaller scenes may be placed Down Front Right, Down Front Center, and Down Front Left, or portions thereof, changing locations to change locales. A few suggestions have been included in the script, but not many, leaving such up to the ingenuity of the director and cast.

One character in this story needs to be costumed, and that is Cherokee when he is playing Santa Claus. It would be fun to have everyone in period attire — but it is not necessary. Props may be real or pantomimed (mainly Bobby's gift).

1   NARRATOR: *(To audience)* Cherokee was the civic father of
2   Yellowhammer. Yellowhammer was a new mining town
3   constructed mainly of canvas and undressed pine. Cherokee
4   was a prospector. One day Cherokee turned up with his pick
5   and a nugget weighing thirty ounces. He staked his claim, and
6   then, being a man of breadth and hospitality, sent out
7   invitations to his friends in three states to drop in and share
8   his luck.
9   When a thousand citizens had arrived and taken up claims,
10   they named the town Yellowhammer, appointed a vigilance
11   committee, and presented Cherokee with a watch chain made
12   of nuggets. Three hours after the presentation ceremonies,
13   Cherokee's claim played out. Yellowhammer was made up of
14   men who took off their hats to a smiling loser, so they invited
15   Cherokee to say what he wanted.
16   CHEROKEE: Me? Oh, grubstakes will be about the only thing. I
17   reckon I'll prospect along up in the Mariposas. If I strike it up
18   there, I'll most certainly let you all know about the facts. I
19   never was any hand to hold out cards on my friends.
20   NARRATOR: In May, Cherokee packed his burro and headed to
21   the north. On the twentieth of December, Baldy, the mail
22   rider, brought Yellowhammer a piece of news.
23   BALDY: *(Coming Down Center to join CALIFORNIA ED, TEXAS,*
24   *SHORTY, and others at the bar.)* What do I see in Albuquerque
25   but Cherokee, all embellished and festooned up like the Czar
26   of Turkey, and lavishin' money in bulk. Him and me seen the
27   elephant and the owl, and we had specimens of this Seidlitz
28   powder wine; and Cherokee, he audits all the bills, C.O.D. His
29   pockets looked like a pool table's after a fifteen-ball run.
30   CALIFORNIA ED: Cherokee must have struck pay ore. Well, I'm
31   much obliged to him for his success.
32   MAN: Seems like Cherokee would ramble down to Yellowhammer
33   and see his friends. But that's the way. Prosperity is the finest
34   cure there is for lost forgetfulness.
35   BALDY: You wait. I'm comin' to that. Cherokee strikes a three-

1   foot vein up in the Mariposas that assays a trip to Europe to
2   the ton, and he closes it out to a syndicate outfit for a hundred
3   thousand hasty dollars in cash. Then he buys himself a baby
4   sealskin overcoat and a red sleigh, and what do you think he
5   takes it in his head to do next?
6   TEXAS: Chuck-a-luck.
7   SHORTY: *(Singing)* "Come and Kiss Me, Ma Honey."
8   THIRSTY ROGERS: Bought a saloon?
9   BALDY: *(Perhaps a bit impatient with these interruptions to his news.)*
10   Cherokee took me to a room an' showed me. He's got that
11   room full of drums an' dolls an' skates an' bags of candy an'
12   jumping-jacks an' toy lambs an' whistles an' such truck. And
13   what do you think he's going to do with such inefficacious
14   knick-knacks? Don't surmise none — Cherokee told me. He's
15   goin' to load 'em up in his red sleigh an' — wait a minute,
16   don't order no drinks yet — he's goin' to drive down here to
17   Yellowhammer an' give the kids, the kids of this here town —
18   the biggest Christmas tree an' the biggest cryin' doll an' Little
19   Giant Boys' Tool Chest blowout that was ever seen west of
20   Cape Hatteras.
21   TRINIDAD: *(Speaks, but after a long silence as they all stare at each*
22   *other in astonishment.)* Didn't you tell him?
23   BALDY: Well, no. I never exactly seen my way to. Ah — you see,
24   Cherokee had this Christmas mess already bought an' paid
25   for; an' he was all flattered up with self-esteem over his idea;
26   an' we had in a way flew the flume with that fizzy wine I speak
27   of; so I never let on.
28   JUDGE: *(Impressively pompous)* I cannot refrain from a certain
29   amount of surprise that our friend Cherokee should possess
30   such an erroneous conception of — ah — his, as it were, our
31   town.
32   BALDY: Oh, it ain't the eighth wonder of the terrestrial world.
33   Cherokee's been gone from Yellowhammer over seven
34   months. Lots of things could happen in that time. How's he to
35   know that there ain't a single kid in this town, an' so far as

1   emigration is concerned, none expected?
2   CALIFORNIA ED: Come to think of it, it's funny some ain't
3   drifted in. Town ain't settled enough yet for to bring in the
4   rubber-ring brigade, I reckon.
5   BALDY: To top off this Christmas-tree splurge of Cherokee's, he's
6   goin' to give an imitation of Santa Claus. He's got a white wig
7   and whiskers that disfigure him up exactly like the pictures of
8   this William Cullen Longfellow in the books, an' a red suit of
9   fur-trimmed underwear, an' eight-ounce gloves, an' a stand-
10   up, lay-down crocheted red cap. Ain't it a shame that an outfit
11   like that can't get a chance to connect with to Annie an'
12   Willie's prayer layout?
13   TRINIDAD: When does Cherokee allow to come over with his
14   truck?
15   BALDY: Mornin' before Christmas. An' he wants you folks to have
16   a room fixed up an' a tree hauled and ready. An' such ladies
17   to assist as can stop breathin' long enough to let it be a
18   surprise for the kids.
19   SHORTY: We ain't got but five women in Yellowhammer.
20   TEXAS: And children, none!
21   BALDY: Christmas comes on Thursday.
22   TRINIDAD: It'll be a disgrace to Yellowhammer if it throws
23   Cherokee down on his Christmas tree blowout. You might say
24   that man made this town. For me, I'm goin' to see what can be
25   done to give Santa Claus a square deal.
26   JUDGE: My cooperation would be gladly forthcoming, for I am
27   indebted to Cherokee for past favors. But, I do not see — I
28   have heretofore regarded the absence of children rather as a
29   luxury — but in this instance — still, I do not see —
30   TRINIDAD: Look at me, and you'll see old Ways and Means with
31   the fur on. I'm goin' to hitch up a team an' rustle a load of
32   kids for Cherokee's Santa Claus act, if I have to rob an
33   orphan asylum.
34   JUDGE: *(Enthusiastically)* Eureka!
35   TRINIDAD: No, you didn't. I found it myself. I learned about that

1   Latin word in school.
2   JUDGE: I will accompany you. Perhaps such eloquence and gift of
3   language as I possess will be of benefit in persuading our
4   young friends to lend themselves to our project. *(Readers*
5   *either move Upstage, turning backs to audience, or sit frozen on*
6   *stools and chairs as provided until needed. The short scenes with*
7   *TRINIDAD and the JUDGE and PARENT that follow are to be*
8   *played at various areas of the stage, Down right, Down Left,*
9   *Down Center, varying the area as the two men move from spot to*
10   *spot.)*
11   NARRATOR: Within an hour, Yellowhammer was acquainted with
12   the scheme of Trinidad and the Judge, and approved it.
13   Anyone who knew of families within forty miles of
14   Yellowhammer came forward and contributed their
15   information. Trinidad made careful notes of all words, and
16   then hastened to secure a vehicle and team. *(PARENT, JUDGE,*
17   *and TRINIDAD move Down Center to meet.)* The first stop was
18   at a log house fifteen miles out of Yellowhammer. The doorway
19   was filled with a mass of youngsters, some ragged, all full of
20   curiosity and health.
21   TRINIDAD: *(Explaining)* You see, it's this way. We're from
22   Yellowhammer, an' we come kidnappin' in a gentle kind of
23   way. One of our leading citizens is stung with the Santa Claus
24   affliction, an' he's due in town with half the knick-knacks
25   that's painted red and made in Germany. The youngest kid we
26   got in Yellowhammer packs a forty-five an' a safety razor. So
27   we're mighty shy on anybody to say "Oh" an' "Ah" when we
28   light the candles on the Christmas tree. Now, partner, if you'll
29   loan us a few kids, we guarantee to return 'em safe and sound
30   on Christmas Day. And they'll come back loaded down with a
31   good time and cornucopias and red drums and such. What do
32   you say?
33   JUDGE: In other words, we have discovered for the first time in
34   our embryonic but progressive little city, the inconvenience of
35   the absence of adolescence. The season of the year having

1   arrived during which it is the custom to bestow frivolous but
2   often appreciated gifts upon the young and tender ...
3 PARENT: *(Interrupting)* I understand. I guess I needn't detain you
4   gentlemen. Me an' the old woman have got seven kids, so to
5   speak; an', runnin' my mind over the bunch, I don't appear
6   to hit upon none that we could spare for you to take over to
7   your doin's. The old woman has got some popcorn candy an'
8   rag dolls hid in the clothes closet, an' we allow to give
9   Christmas a little whirl of our own in an insignificant sort of
10   style. No, I couldn't, with any degree of avidity, seem to fall in
11   with the idea of lettin' none of 'em go. Thank you kindly,
12   gentlemen. *(Turn backs to audience.)*
13 NARRATOR: The two men drove thirty miles, making four
14   fruitless halts and appeals. Everywhere, they found "kids" at
15   a premium. The sun was low when the wife of a section boss
16   on a lonely railroad huddled her available progeny behind her
17   and said: *(Play this short scene Down Left.)*
18 SECTION BOSS' WIFE: There's a woman that's just took charge
19   of the railroad eatin' house down at Granite Junction. I hear
20   she's got a little boy. Maybe she might let him go.
21 NARRATOR: Trinidad pulled up at Granite Junction at five
22   o'clock in the afternoon. On the steps of the eating house, they
23   found a thin and glowering boy of ten smoking a cigarette. A
24   youngish woman reclined, exhausted, in a chair. Trinidad and
25   the Judge set forth their mission. *(Play this scene Down Right.)*
26 YOUNG WOMAN: I'd count it a mercy if you'd take Bobby for a
27   while. I'm on the go from morning till night, and I don't have
28   time to tend to him. He's learning bad habits from the men.
29   It'll be the only chance he'll have to get any Christmas.
30 JUDGE: My young friend, Santa Claus himself will personally
31   distribute the offerings that will typify the gifts conveyed by
32   the shepherds of Bethlehem to —
33 BOBBY: *(Interrupting)* Aw, come off it. I ain't no kid. There ain't
34   no Santa Claus. It's your folks that buys toys and sneaks 'em
35   in when you're asleep. An' they make marks in the soot in the

1   chimney with the tongs to look like Santa's sleigh tracks.

2   TRINIDAD: That might be so, but Christmas trees ain't no fairy

3   tale. This one's goin' to look like the ten-cent store in

4   Albuquerque, all strung up in a redwood. There's tops an'

5   drums an' Noah's arks an' ...

6   BOBBY: Oh, rats! I cut them out long ago. I'd like to have a

7   rifle — not a target one, a real one — to shoot wildcats with;

8   but I guess you won't have any of them on your old tree.

9   TRINIDAD: Well, I can't say for sure; it might be. You go along

10   with us and see.

11   BOBBY: All right, I'll go — but there ain't no Santa Claus. *(They*

12   *turn backs to audience.)*

13   NARRATOR: With this solitary beneficiary for Cherokee's holiday

14   bounty, the canvassers spun along the homeward road. In

15   Yellowhammer, the empty storeroom had been transformed

16   into what might have passed as the home of an Arizona fairy.

17   The ladies had done their work well. A tall Christmas tree,

18   covered to its topmost branch with candles, spangles, and toys

19   sufficient for more than a score of children, stood in the center

20   of the floor. *(CITIZENS OF YELLOWHAMMER come On-stage*

21   *to admire the tree and await the JUDGE and TRINIDAD.)*

22   Trinidad and the Judge, bearing the marks of protracted

23   travel entered, conducting between them a single impish boy,

24   who stared with sullen, pessimistic eyes at the gaudy tree.

25   ASSAYER'S WIFE: Where are the other children?

26   TRINIDAD: Ma'am, prospectin' for kids at Christmas time is like

27   huntin' in limestone for silver. This parental business is one

28   that I haven't no chance to comprehend. It seems that fathers

29   and mothers are willin' for their offsprings to be drownded,

30   stole, fed on poison oak, and ate by catamounts 364 days in the

31   year; but on Christmas Day they insist on enjoyin' the

32   exclusive mortification of their company. This here young

33   biped, ma'am, is all that washes out of our two days'

34   maneuvers.

35   MISS ERMA: Oh, the sweet little boy.

1   BOBBY: *(Scowling)* **Aw, shut up. Who's a kid? You ain't, you bet.**

2   MISS ERMA: **Fresh brat!**

3   TRINIDAD: **We done the best we could. It's tough on Cherokee,**

4   **but it can't be helped.** *(CHEROKEE enters, dressed as St. Nick.)*

5   CHEROKEE: *(After seeing there is only one boy present.)* **Merry**

6   **Christmas, little boy. Anything on the tree you want, they'll**

7   **get it down for you. Won't you shake hands with Santa Claus?**

8   BOBBY: *(Whining)* **There ain't no Santa Claus. You've got old false**

9   **goat's whiskers on your face. I ain't no kid. What do I want**

10   **with dolls an' tin horses? The driver said you'd have a rifle,**

11   **and you haven't. I wanna go home.**

12 TRINIDAD: *(Perhaps shaking CHEROKEE'S hand)* **I'm sorry,**

13   **Cherokee. There never was a kid in Yellowhammer. We tried**

14   **to rustle a bunch of 'em for your party, but this sardine was**

15   **all we could catch. He's an atheist, and he don't believe in**

16   **Santa Claus. It's a shame for you to be out all this truck. But**

17   **me an' the Judge was sure we could round up a wagonful of**

18   **candidates for your knick-knacks.**

19 CHEROKEE: *(Gravely)* **That's all right. The expense don't**

20   **amount to nothin' worth mentionin'. We can dump the stuff**

21   **down a shaft or throw it away. I don't know what I was**

22   **thinkin' about; but it never occurred to my cogitations that**

23   **there wasn't any kids in Yellowhammer.** *(Goes to BOBBY.)*

24   **Where do you live, little boy?**

25 BOBBY: **Granite Junction.** *(CHEROKEE takes off his beard and*

26   *wig.)* **Hey, I know your mug, all right.**

27 CHEROKEE: **Did you ever see me before?**

28 BOBBY: **I don't know — but I've seen your picture lots of times.**

29 CHEROKEE: **Where?**

30 BOBBY: *(Hesitating)* **On the bureau at home.**

31 CHEROKEE: **Let's have your name, if you please, buddy.**

32 BOBBY: **Robert Lumsden. The picture belongs to my mother. She**

33   **puts it under her pillow at night. And once I saw her kiss it. I**

34   **wouldn't. But women are that way.** *(CHEROKEE goes to*

35   *TRINIDAD.)*

1　　CHEROKEE: Trinidad, keep this boy by you till I come back. I'm
2　　　　　　goin' to shed these Christmas duds an' hitch up my sleigh. I'm
3　　　　　　goin' to take this kid home. *(Turn back to audience, or may leave*
4　　　　　　*the stage.)*
5　　TRINIDAD: *(Going to BOBBY)* Well, infidel, and so you are too old
6　　　　　　an' growed up to yearn for such mockeries as candy and toys,
7　　　　　　it seems.
8　　BOBBY: *(With bitterness)* I don't like you. You said there'd be a
9　　　　　　rifle. A fellow can't even smoke. I wish I was at home.
10　 NARRATOR: *(During the narration, CHEROKEE and BOBBY sit*
11　　　　　　*side by side Downstage Center. If selective lights are available*
12　　　　　　*and have been used, blackout all but the two readers as the*
13　　　　　　*narration ends.)* Cherokee drove his sleigh to the door, and
14　　　　　　they lifted Bobby in beside him. The team of fine horses
15　　　　　　sprang away prancingly over the hard snow. Cherokee had on
16　　　　　　his five-hundred-dollar overcoat of baby sealskin. The laprobe
17　　　　　　that he drew about them was warm as velvet. Bobby slipped a
18　　　　　　cigarette from his pocket and was trying to snap a match.
19　　CHEROKEE: *(Quietly)* Throw that cigarette away. *(BOBBY*
20　　　　　　*hesitates, then does so.)* Throw the box, too. *(More reluctantly,*
21　　　　　　*the boy does.)*
22　　BOBBY: Say, I like you. I don't know why. Nobody ever made me
23　　　　　　do anything I didn't want to do before.
24　　CHEROKEE: Tell me, kid, are you sure your mother kissed that
25　　　　　　picture that looks like me?
26　　BOBBY: Dead sure. I seen her do it.
27　　CHEROKEE: Uh — didn't you remark something a while ago
28　　　　　　about wanting a rifle?
29　　BOBBY: You bet I did. Will you get me one?
30　　CHEROKEE: Tomorrow — silver-mounted. *(CHEROKEE takes*
31　　　　　　*out his watch.)* Half-past nine. We'll hit the Junction plumb on
32　　　　　　time for Christmas Day. Are you cold? Sit closer. *(BOBBY*
33　　　　　　*moves over as CHEROKEE puts his arm around the boy's*
34　　　　　　*shoulders.)*

A Brief History of Christmas Customs
By Melvin R. White

Cast of Characters
VOICE 1
VOICE 2
VOICE 3

Production Notes

This overview of Christmas customs is a wonderful addition to Christmas programs. Its short length makes it easy to incorporate without taking up too much time. If desired, PowerPoint projected images of a gift, Santa Claus, a Christmas tree, and the other items may be shown as they are discussed in the script.

1   VOICE 1: Many of our time-honored Christmas traditions are so
2   familiar that we may not take the time to reflect on where they
3   came from ...
4   VOICE 2: Or what they mean.
5   VOICE 3: Let's look at the real meaning behind several of our
6   favorite Christmas customs.
7   VOICE 2: The custom of "giving" is definitely a major part of our
8   Christmas holiday! This hearkens back to the wise men and
9   their gifts of gold, frankincense, and myrrh for the baby Jesus.
10   This spirit of giving is still with us at Christmas today.
11   VOICE 3: But many other traditions have been adopted, too. A bit
12   of history:
13   VOICE 1: All those Christmas gifts are typically placed under a
14   Christmas tree. Saint Boniface, who was an eighth century
15   missionary to Germany, used the three points, or triangle, of
16   the Christmas tree as a symbol for the Trinity.
17   VOICE 2: Evergreens are the tree species of choice, because they
18   symbolize everlasting life.
19   VOICE 1: December twenty-fifth is the holiday started when Pope
20   Julius I established that date as Christ's birthday in 350 A.D.
21   VOICE 2: Christmas was first observed as an English holiday in
22   521 A.D. when King Arthur retook the city of York on
23   December twenty-fifth. To celebrate his victory, he proclaimed
24   the holiday — and a feast at the Round Table.
25   VOICE 3: *(Or alternate between VOICE 1 and 2.)* Pre-Christian
26   Scandinavians celebrated with a holiday whose name is still
27   with us — Yule.
28   VOICE 1: That's the ancient Norse word for feasting.
29   VOICE 3: Yes. They burned a huge log in honor of the god Thor.
30   Later, Christians in Europe adopted the yule log custom —
31   but without its pagan purpose.
32   VOICE 2: What about Santa Claus?
33   VOICE 1: This "gift-bringer" originated in fourth century Asia
34   Minor with Saint Nicholas, a kindly bishop who took presents
35   to the needy. He came to be known as the patron saint of

1   sailors, travelers, bakers, and merchants — but especially
2   children.
3   VOICE 3: Saint Nicholas?
4   VOICE 2: Yes, Dutch settlers brought this Christmas gift-giving
5   custom to New York in the early seventeenth century. But the
6   Dutch name, Sinterklaas, was hard to pronounce, so New
7   Yorkers soon called him simply Santa Claus.
8   VOICE 3: All over the colonies?
9   VOICE 2: No. The fact is that a few hundred miles north of
10   Sinterklaas-cheering New Amsterdam, the seventeenth
11   century colony of Massachusetts took a different view. They
12   attacked the — as they called it — "heathen celebration of
13   Christmas," and passed a law forbidding any festive
14   observance of the Nativity in 1659 — and this remained the
15   law until 1681. In fact, Christmas was not made a legal
16   holiday in Massachusetts until 1859, almost two hundred
17   years later.
18   VOICE 1: *(Laughing a bit)* And now we have Santa Claus, St. Nick,
19   and even Rudolph the Red-Nosed Reindeer. *(VOICES 1, 2, 3*
20   *may break into song here if a longer performance is desired.)*
21   VOICE 3: Even that sweet treat we enjoy at Christmas time, the
22   candy cane, leads us back to the real meaning of Christmas.
23   VOICE 2: Its shape resembles a shepherd's crook to remind us of
24   those who first heard the news of the birth of Jesus. Turn it
25   upside down, and it becomes a "J" as in the first letter of
26   Jesus' name.
27   VOICE 1: The red stripes symbolize the blood he shed for all of
28   humankind.
29   VOICE 3: The white stands for his purity.
30   VOICE 2: Candy canes are hard, because Jesus is our rock.
31   VOICE 1: The candy cane's sweet taste reminds us that God's gift
32   of Jesus is the sweetest gift of all.
33   VOICE 3: The candy cane's peppermint flavor has a taste similar
34   to hyssop, which was used for cleansing and purifying in Old
35   Testament times. This reminds us that Jesus cleanses us from
36   our sins.

1 **VOICE 2: So many customs!**

2 **VOICE 1: They remind us of the reason why we celebrate.**

3 **VOICE 3: They remind us of the Christ child, born in Bethlehem.**

Christmas Kingdom

By Brian Bopp

A Christmas dinner theatre for the whole family.

Schedule of Events

Christmas Kingdom is a dinner theatre featuring a three-course meal. The dramatic action is interspersed with the dining. Although times for the various courses and scenes are suggested, they are merely a guideline to assist in your planning. Actual times may vary.

6:45 p.m. — Guests arrive and are introduced. Hot chocolate and punch.
7:05 p.m. — Scene 1 ("The Shepherdsons at Home.")
7:15 p.m. — Latecomers seated.
7:18 p.m. — Scene 2 ("The Shepherdsons Arrive at Christmas Kingdom.")
7:30 p.m. — Soup/salad. Scene 3 ("Eunice and Dorothea Reminisce.")
7:45 p.m. — Entrée. Scene 4 ("Encounter With Mr. Fleckman.")
8:00 p.m. — Scene 5 ("Special Guests Visit Christmas Kingdom.")
8:15 p.m. — Dessert and coffee. Scene 5 ("Stan Sees the Light.")
8:23 p.m. — Dismissal

Optional activities after dismissal: caroling, tree decorating, sledding, kitchen clean up (OK, the last one isn't optional!)

Cast of Characters (With costume suggestions)

Frosty the Maître d'/Emcee

Male/female in a snowman suit with a big black hat. Laughs a lot and *shshshivers* when *spppeaking*.

Elves

May wear green tunics, green tights or leggings, pointy green hats, and green cloth shoes with pointy toes.
Greeter Elves (2 or more) — Male/female. They meet people at the door. Some may be stationed in the parking lot to direct cars.
Seater Elves (3-4) — Male/female. They escort guests to their tables in banquet hall.
Wait Elves (1 per table) — This is what the greeter/seater elves do when everyone is in place.

Barb Shepherdson

Late thirties. Wears a dress. She is a woman who is heavily involved with being a mom, a church volunteer, and other duties.

Stan Shepherdson

Early forties. Wears a shirt and tie or sweater. He is a mid-management guy in a local industry.

Emily Shepherdson

Sixteen-years-old or so. She is dressed in the latest fashion. She just got her driver's license, and her major difficulty in life is Garth, her younger brother.

Garth Shepherdson

Eleven. He is just old enough to bug his sister to death and enjoy it. He is dressed casually.

Eunice

Wrote, directed, and did all the costumes for every Christmas pageant since 1903. Old, but not senile. She wears an "old lady" dress and perhaps even a hat.

Dorothea

Eunice's right-hand woman. At sixty-eight, she is spunky, light-hearted, and still able to keep the kids in line. She is dressed similarly to Eunice.

Mr. Fleckman

The town's undisputed champion of gaudy outdoor "Yuletide" display. Nobody knows his first name. He is kind of a mysterious character. He should wear a shirt and a loud tie — a Christmas one, if available.

St. Nicholas

He wears a red suit and white beard. He holds a bag with goodies inside and is always ready with a hearty "Ho! Ho! Ho!"

Joseph of Nazareth

He wears biblical attire. He is a bearded man with the hands of a craftsman. (Nonspeaking role)

Mary, Mother of Jesus

She also wears a biblical robe. She is a first-time mother who shows special anointing from God, plus the real-world strain of coping with a newborn. (Nonspeaking role)

Baby Jesus

Real baby if you can, or a lifelike doll if necessary.

You will also need kitchen helpers to plan the menu and prepare the meal, and your pastor to pray before the meal and conclude the evening.

Production Notes

Setting: The banquet hall is decorated to look like a "winter wonderland" complete with fake snowmen, lots of fake snow, tinsel, hanging icicles, gaily wrapped empty boxes scattered about, etc. The main entrance should be through some sort of archway, where the guests will be introduced and then escorted to their tables. See Stage Diagrams on pages 166 and 167. Christmas carols should be playing in the background, of course. "Away in a Manger" and "O Come, All Ye Faithful" should be on this tape, as they are needed to set the mood for Scene 5.

Microphones

In a smallish banquet (fifty to seventy-five guests), microphones may not be necessary. With seventy-five or more guests, the ideal would be for each main character to wear a wireless lapel microphone which may be rented from an audio supply house if necessary.

Lighting

If you have access to theatrical lighting in your playing area, there are lighting instructions included throughout the script. If a lighting system is not available, simply disregard the lighting instructions. While lights *can* enhance the drama, they are not vital to the production. The dialogue will set the mood and carry the action.

Sound Effects

TV noise (may be taped).

Stage Diagrams

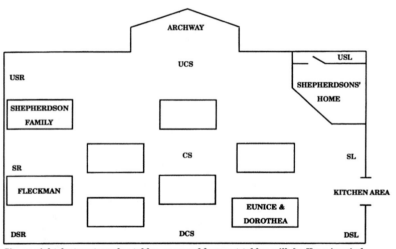

Six- or eight-foot rectangular tables, or round banquet tables will do. Keep in mind that people must be able to easily see both the archway and the Shepherdson home, as well as the tables for the Shepherdsons, Fleckman and Eunice and Dorothea.

SHEPHERDSON HOME

Ideally this set should be raised from the level of the banquet hall.

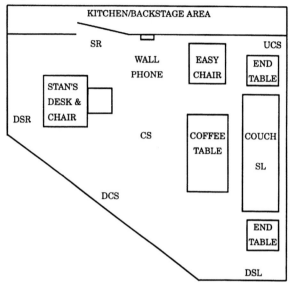

Props (By scenes)

Introductions:
Sleigh bells — Frosty
Snowflakes (may use fake snow available in craft stores or instant mashed potato flakes) — Elves
Snowflake stickers — Elves
"Honorary Elf" badges — Elves

Scene 1:
Telephone — Barb
Bills, checkbook, calculator, credit card, etc. — Stan
Christmas catalog — Emily (This prop should be pre-cut to rip at the proper time.)
Pan of cookie bars and kitchen knife — Stan
Pen and long Christmas list — Garth
Bundle of packages wrapped for mailing — Barb
Coat — Barb
Car keys — Emily

Scene 2:
Sleigh bells — Frosty
Plan B envelope — Messenger Elf
Coat — Garth
Coat — Barb
Pan of cookie bars — Barb
Coat — Emily
Coat — Stan
Snowflakes — Elf

Scene 3:
None

Scene 4:
Floodlight bulb — Mr. Fleckman

Scene 5:
Sleigh bells — Frosty
Bag with candy canes and other goodies — St. Nicholas
Baby Jesus — Mary
Salvation Army bell — St. Nicholas

Scene 6:
Coat — Barb
Coat — Stan
Coat — Emily
Coat — Garth
Bible — Stan
Floodlight bulb — Stan

Dismissal:
Sleigh bells — Pastor

1	**Introduction**
2	*(6:45 p.m. — As guests enter the hall, GREETER ELVES will take*
3	*their coats to the cloakroom or hang them up on the rack. Hot*
4	*chocolate or punch may be served in the lobby/foyer/fellowship*
5	*hall while the guests wait to be seated. A "Please Wait to be*
6	*Seated" sign should help to keep the guests from going in on their*
7	*own. FROSTY welcomes guests at the archway, gets their names,*
8	*then shakes sleigh bells loudly. He then announces: "MMMr. and*
9	*Mrs. John Johnson [inserting their real names of course],*
10	*wwwelcome to CCChristmas KKKingdom!" this includes the*
11	*players, who will enter in character and remain in character all*
12	*evening. [Note: The SHEPHERDSON FAMILY is not seated until*
13	*Scene 2.] SEATER ELVES then throw snowflakes into the air, cry*
14	*"Welcome!" or "So glad you're here!" and then escort the*
15	*couple/family to their seats. Elf voices should be somewhat*
16	*"chipmunk-like" and fun. Elves also put stick-on snowflakes upon*
17	*the cheeks of all and give special "Honorary Elf" badges to the*
18	*kids. All actors enter as if they were regular dinner guests and are*
19	*introduced in the same way.)*
20	
21	**Scene 1**
22	**The Shepherdsons At Home**
23	*(7:05 p.m. — done as a "prelude" on stage platform after dinner*
24	*guests have been seated. House lights dim and stage lights come*
25	*up on platform area. Latecomers must stay at the archway until*
26	*this scene is complete.)*
27	**Setting:** The family room of a typical middle-class American home on
28	an evening just a few weeks before Christmas.
29	**At Rise:** (BARB is on the phone Up Center, impatiently pacing,
30	waiting for an operator to take her call. She keeps looking
31	anxiously Off-stage and looking at her watch. STAN is seated at
32	his desk Down Right, examining a stack of bills and the
33	checkbook, with a calculator close by. EMILY is on the sofa Stage
34	Left looking through the clothes section of a Christmas catalog.
35	GARTH is on the floor in front of the TV Down Center, sitting too

1   close as usual. It is after dinner. The TV is on with some sort of
2   Christmas special.)
3   **STAN:** *(To GARTH)* **Garth, would you please turn that TV down?**
4   **We've been hearing those same carols since before**
5   **Thanksgiving.**
6   **GARTH: OK, Dad.** *(He turns down the TV, then joins his sister on the*
7   *sofa Stage Left.)*
8   **BARB:** *(To STAN)* **Honey, would you go peek at the bars in the**
9   **oven? I'm afraid they'll burn.**
10   **STAN:** *(Frustrated)* **I'm trying to do the bills, Barb. Can't you do**
11   **it?**
12   **BARB: If I hang up now, I'll lose my place, and I'll have to wait**
13   **another ten minutes to place my order ... for ... something.**
14   *(Points at GARTH as if to indicate she's ordering his present on*
15   *the sly.)*
16   **STAN:** *(Getting up)* **Oh, all right. These bills can wait awhile. They**
17   **may have to wait a long while with the way our bank account**
18   **looks.** *(He exits to kitchen Up Right shaking his head.)*
19   **GARTH: C'mon, Emily, turn the page ...** *(He tries to flip to the toy*
20   *section of the catalog.)*
21   **EMILY:** *(Holding the pages down with her hands)* **No way, Garth!**
22   **You had the catalog all afternoon. Now I get to look at it for**
23   **awhile.**
24   **BARB:** *(To KIDS)* **Kids ...** *(They ignore her.)*
25   **GARTH: Yeah, but clothes? Who'd want clothes for Christmas?**
26   **You are way weird, sister!**
27   **EMILY:** *(Indignant)* **You should talk!** *(Teasing)* **You wear Power**
28   **Rangers underwear!**
29   **BARB:** *(Somewhat louder)* **Emily! Garth!** *(They still don't hear.*
30   *GARTH and EMILY are now fighting over the catalog. They ad lib*
31   *arguing loudly. BARB yells, with the phone still to her ear.)* ***You***
32   ***kids stop it! You are driving me crazy!*** *(Finally the operator picks*
33   *up her call.)* **Oh no, not** *you,* **Operator! I'm terribly sorry! You**
34   **see, my kids were fighting over ... What? That's right, the**
35   **Christmas catalog. Your kids do that too? Oh, I'm so glad**

1   **mine aren't the only ones** … *(She continues to talk with the*

2   *operator. During preceding conversation, the catalog rips in two.*

3   *The KIDS stop fighting and begin to page through their half. After*

4   *a few moments they realize they have the wrong half and*

5   *sheepishly exchange with each other.)*

6   STAN: *(Comes in from the kitchen carrying a pan of bars.)* **Honey!**

7   **Honey, I think they're done** … *(Crosses to Stage Left in front of*

8   *the coffee table.)*

9   GARTH: *(Smells the pan)* **Ewwww! What's that?**

10   STAN: **Just some bars Mom made** …

11   GARTH: **They look gross!** *(He returns to catalog.)*

12   BARB: *(Holding her hand over the phone mouthpiece)* **Give me our**

13   **Visa number, quick!**

14   STAN: *(Line said with reluctance)* **Yes, dear** … *(He goes to desk, picks*

15   *up card and hands it to her. She recites numbers quietly to*

16   *operator.)*

17   EMILY: *(Gets up from sofa and crosses to desk Stage Right with*

18   *STAN. Both are looking at the bars.)* **Do they have nuts?**

19   STAN: **Don't know** … **Guess there's one way to find out.** *(He pulls*

20   *out a kitchen knife and begins to cut the bars.)*

21   EMILY: **They smell kinda good. You try them.**

22   STAN: **I consider it a duty and a privilege.** *(He takes out a bar and*

23   *is just about to bite, when …)*

24   BARB: *(Slamming down the phone just in time, she declares with*

25   *ultimate authority …)* **Those are *not* for you!**

26   STAN: **I should have known** … *(He puts the bar back.)*

27   BARB: *(Snatching the pan away from STAN)* **Yes, you *should* have**

28   **known. When I make something good for you, I'll *tell* you.**

29   EMILY: *(Shrugs.)* **They've probably got too many fat grams**

30   **anyway** … *(She returns to the sofa and the catalog.)*

31   STAN: *(To BARB)* **May I ask who they *are* for?**

32   BARB: *(Trying to remember)* **Well, it's either the Women's**

33   **Fellowship Pre-Christmas Craft Bazaar or the WWCCD**

34   **December Clean-Up.**

35   EMILY: **WWCCD? What's that?!**

1   BARB: Women With a Compulsive Cleaning Disorder.
2   STAN: Barb, I thought you didn't like that group. *(He returns to his*
3   *desk and bills.)*
4   BARB: I don't. But if I quit the group, they'll think my house is
5   messy. *(To EMILY)* Did you make your bed today?
6   EMILY: *(Exasperated)* Yes, Mom ...
7   BARB: *(Trying to remember)* Hmmmm, there was something else
8   these bars were for ... *(Still wondering, she exits into the kitchen*
9   *Up Right.)*
10 GARTH: *(Holding the catalog, he runs to STAN at desk and says*
11   *excitedly.)* Dad, look! Can we get this?
12 STAN: *(Suspiciously)* What now?
13 GARTH: This cool neon manger scene! *(Points to picture in the*
14   *catalog.)* See how the shepherds and animals all bow down to
15   Jesus in the manger? *(He imitates jerky motion of bowing.)*
16 STAN: *(Responding with fake amazement)* What will they think of
17   next?
18 GARTH: And look at this awesome blinking star! Dad, we could be
19   the first ones on the block with that baby. We could even outdo
20   Mr. Fleckman across the street!
21 STAN: *(Mildly interested, he takes the catalog.)* Hmmmm, that
22   would show old Fleckman a thing or two. I've been getting
23   pretty tired of those sad-looking reindeer on his roof.
24 GARTH: Yeah, Dad. We gotta show him what Christmas is really
25   about!
26 STAN: *(Standing up)* Yeah!
27 GARTH: "Neon Christmas," here we come!
28 STAN: Wait a second. Let's look at the price here. *(Consults*
29   *catalog, then slumps back down on chair in shock.)* O holy night!
30 GARTH: *(Looks at the price too.)* What's the matter, Dad? Is that
31   too much? *(STAN is still in shock.)* Dad? *(GARTH shrugs it off,*
32   *goes to sofa and consults long Christmas list, adding things.)*
33 BARB: *(Rushes in from Up Right with her coat on. She is carrying a*
34   *large bundle of packages wrapped for mailing and can hardly see*
35   *where she's going.)* Emily, do you have the car keys? I've got to

1   get to the post office today, or these things will never make it
2   on time.
3   **EMILY:** *(Still absorbed in the catalog, she pulls the keys from her*
4   *pocket and holds them out to BARB.)* **OK, Mom, but don't**
5   **forget to be back in time for the banquet.**
6   **BARB:** *(Reaching for the keys)* **Banquet! What ...** *(A look of sudden*
7   *realization. BARB gathers her breath, screams and throws the*
8   *packages up into the air.)* **Ahhh!** *(Her scream shakes STAN out of*
9   *his daze.)* **The Christmas Banquet!** *(Instant drill sergeant)*
10   **Emily, do your hair! Stan, warm up the car! Garth, get our**
11   **coats! We've got five minutes to get to the** *Christmas*
12   *Kingdom!* *(They all stare at her in a daze.)* **Move it, people! Go!**
13   **Go! Go!** *(They scramble.)* **Now, where did I put those bars?**
14   *(Lights blackout on platform. House lights up.)*
15
16   *(Allow a few moments here for the latecomers to be seated at their*
17   *tables.)*
18
19   **Scene 2**
20   **The Shepherdsons Arrive at Christmas Kingdom**
21   *(7:18 p.m. – Begins immediately after Scene 1, lights up on*
22   *FROSTY at the archway.)*
23   **FROSTY:** *(Shakes sleigh bells to get everyone's attention.)* **It is my**
24   **ppprivilege and ppppleasure to welcome one and all to our**
25   **Christmas KKKKingdom. It is the royal wish that you all**
26   **enjoy the feast and fellowship to the utmost. If there is**
27   **anything you need, please ask your Wait Elf. This evening it is**
28   **our ddddistinct pleasure to introduce a very sssspecial guest,**
29   **the King of Christmas Kingdom, who ...** *(FROSTY looks Off*
30   *stage to locate KING, but doesn't see him)* **... has not yet**
31   **arrived.** *(MESSENGER ELF runs in to present FROSTY with*
32   *large envelope obviously labeled "Plan B." ELF exits. FROSTY*
33   *opens envelope, scans message.)* **I would like to invite our**
34   **ppppastor forward at this time for a blessing.**
35   **PASTOR:** *(PASTOR sincerely welcomes the guests on behalf of the*

1   *church, then prays a brief prayer something like this:)* **Heavenly**
2   **Father, we give thanks for this day, and these people, and this**
3   **food. We pray that it will nourish our bodies so that we will be**
4   **able to serve you. Amen.** *(He/she returns to his/her seat.)*
5   **FROSTY: Thank you, PPPPastor. I have been informed that the**
6   **King of Christmas Kingdom has been delayed by *heavy**
7   **traffic, but will arrive shortly.** *(*If play is presented in a small*
8   *town, use "heavy traffic." If play is presented in a large city, use*
9   *"heavy fog" or some other unlikely occurrence.)*
10   **GARTH:** *(Enters through the outer doors by FROSTY at archway.*
11   *Calls back to family.)* **Mom! Dad! We made it! They don't even**
12   **have their** *(Notices everyone staring at him)* **... food ... yet.**
13   *(Swallows hard.)*
14   **BARB:** *(Coming up behind GARTH and FROSTY, she is carrying the*
15   *pan of bars.)* **Oh, good. I'd hate for people to think that**
16   **we ... forgot.** *(To FROSTY)* **Was I supposed to bring bars?**
17   *(STAN and EMILY have arrived at archway now, too.)*
18   **FROSTY:** *(Shakes sleighbells.)* **Shepherdson family, wwwwelcome**
19   **to CCCCChristmas KKKKingdom!** *(SEATER ELF is fed up.*
20   *He/she rolls eyes, throws snowflakes, motions for family to follow*
21   *him/her. The SHEPHERDSONS all sheepishly follow SEATER*
22   *ELF to their table Up Right. BARB and STAN ad-lib greeting*
23   *people at the table as they move. When they reach their table,*
24   *BARB gives bars to ELF, who takes them back to the kitchen*
25   *intending to eat them him/herself.)* **As I wwwwas saying, the**
26   **KKKKing will appear shortly. Until then, I invite you to relax**
27   **and enjoy the first course of our meal.** *(Lights down on*
28   *archway. WAIT ELVES enter with soup/salad course.)*
29
30   **Scene 3**
31   **Eunice and Dorothea Reminisce**
32   *(About 7:30 p.m. — This scene takes place during the soup/salad*
33   *course. House lights dim for a moment and come back up.*
34   *Spotlight hits EUNICE and DOROTHEA throughout their scene*
35   *Down Left.)*

1   EUNICE: *(Getting up from her chair)* **Excuse me, Dorothea, dear.**

2   DOROTHEA: **Where are you going, Eunice?**

3   EUNICE: **Oh, I thought they might need a little help in the kitchen.**

4   *(Heads toward kitchen door.)*

5   DOROTHEA: *(Chastising, she gets up to stand near her.)* **Oh,**

6   **Eunice, that's just like you. Can't keep your fingers out of**

7   **anything, can you?**

8   EUNICE: *(She looks over the crowd to DOROTHEA.)* **Dorothea, isn't**

9   **this special?**

10 DOROTHEA: **Yes, Eunice, it really is. And you know the best thing**

11 **about it?**

12 EUNICE: **What's that, dear?**

13 DOROTHEA: **We didn't have a thing to do with it!**

14 EUNICE: **You got that right, honey. If we had a nickel for every**

15 **banquet or pageant or program we put together we'd —**

16 DOROTHEA: *(Finishing her sentence)* **Be rich!** *(They both chuckle.)*

17 EUNICE: *(Looking around)* **You know, Dorothea, as I look around,**

18 **I think we've coached every adult in this room through one**

19 **show or another ...**

20 DOROTHEA: **I believe you're right! Look, there's little**

21 **_____.** *(Insert name of prominent church board member*

22 *here.)* **Wasn't he the kid who thought angels' wings really**

23 **worked?**

24 EUNICE: **Yes, he was. He fluttered off the top row of the risers ...**

25 DOROTHEA: **... and wiped out three hosts of angels in front of**

26 **him. Lucky thing there were no broken bones.**

27 EUNICE: **Not that year.** *(She spots someone else.)* **Oh, Dorothea,**

28 **there's _____.** *(Insert name of prominent soprano or alto,*

29 *or the choir director, if possible.)* **Wasn't she the captain of the**

30 **angelic host or something?**

31 DOROTHEA: *(Thinking)* **Yes ... yes. But she refused to rejoice!**

32 EUNICE: **Of course. When I took her aside and asked why she**

33 **couldn't smile, she said, "My haw-wo is bwoken."**

34 DOROTHEA: **Do you remember Pastor _____** *(Insert head*

35 *pastor's first name here.)* **when he was in the first grade?**

1	EUNICE: **Who could forget? He kept poking the girls with his**
2	**shepherd's staff.**
3	DOROTHEA: **We finally got him to stop by threatening to re-cast**
4	**him as the donkey.**
5	EUNICE: *(Laughing)* **Nobody wanted that job ... Oh, my dear,**
6	**we've had some good times, haven't we, Dorothea?**
7	DOROTHEA: **You bet we have, Eunice. Every year we'd collapse**
8	**after it was over, throw our feet up and ask, "Was it all worth**
9	**it?"**
10	EUNICE and DOROTHEA: *(Together, doing a high-five)* ***Yessss!***
11	DOROTHEA: *(Misty-eyed)* **Looking at all these grown-up kids**
12	**here, I'd say we really are rich.**
13	EUNICE: *(Patting DOROTHEA's hand)* **Come on, honey. Let's see if**
14	**we can keep those elves on their pointy little toes.** *(EUNICE*
15	*and DOROTHEA exit into kitchen for a short time and are*
16	*ushered out again by a gang of KITCHEN ELVES.)*
17	
18	*(Spotlights out. WAIT ELVES serve main course.)*
19	
20	**Scene 4**
21	**Encounter With Mr. Fleckman**
22	*(About 7:45 p.m. — This scene takes place during the main*
23	*course, after everyone has been served. House lights dim and*
24	*come up again. Spotlights come up on the Shepherdsons' table.*
25	*STAN and BARB are seated with their backs to MR. FLECKMAN.*
26	*They should all be eating their meal throughout this scene.*
27	*GARTH stands up, obviously straining to see someone across the*
28	*room.)*
29	BARB: *(Trying to maintain decorum)* **Garth, please sit down. People**
30	**are staring.**
31	EMILY: *(Sarcastically)* **So what else is new?**
32	STAN: **Son, what** *are* **you looking at?**
33	GARTH: *(Finally spots MR. FLECKMAN.)* **Aha! I knew I saw him.**
34	*(Sits back down.)*
35	BARB: **Saw who, dear?**

1   GARTH: Mr. Fleckman, that's who.

2   BARB: Fleckman. Fleckman? *(To STAN)* Do we know a Mr.

3   Fleckman?

4   STAN: Sure we do. He's that obviously frustrated man who lives

5   across the street from us.

6   EMILY: Isn't that the guy with all the gaudy Christmas lights and

7   junk on his house?

8   STAN: The very same ...

9   BARB: *(Lightly)* Oh. I didn't know he was a member here.

10   GARTH: Sure, Mom. He's the guy who put the fluorescent bulbs

11   behind the cross so it kind of "glows," you know?

12   STAN: Not to mention those flashing dollar-sign lapel pins he made

13   for the ushers.

14   BARB: *(Now she remembers him.)* Oh, that Mr. Fleckman.

15   STAN: That man has the biggest outdoor lighting display in the

16   whole county!

17   BARB: Well, I like it.

18   EMILY: *(Incredulous)* Mom, how can you even say that? Twinkling

19   lights make me wanna barf.

20   BARB: *(Warning)* Emily ...

21   GARTH: *(Excitedly)* Dad and me are really gonna show him this

22   year ...

23   BARB: *(Correcting)* Dad and I, dear ...

24   GARTH: You too, Mom? Cool. Our neon manger scene will make

25   old Fleckman want to pull the plug on his whole yard.

26   STAN: Now, son, I didn't say ...

27   BARB: *(Wary)* Garth, did you say "neon"?

28   GARTH: *(Ignoring her)* C'mon, Dad. Say what you really think. Go

29   ahead.

30   STAN: Well, it's no secret in this town that Fleckman has a screw

31   loose. Think of it. Every November twenty-six the man climbs

32   up on his roof, anchors eight "not-so-tiny reindeer" up there

33   complete with sled. Then he strings thousands of lights

34   through his trees, lights up seventy-five little plastic snowmen,

35   and places them all along his driveway. I mean, really, the

1   **man is obsessive.** *(GARTH looks up to see MR. FLECKMAN*
2   *walking toward their table. His eyes pop open. STAN is oblivious*
3   *and continues his tirade.)* **As if that's not enough, he fills his**
4   **yard with a life-sized manger scene complete with the**
5   **mechanized baby in the manger. Now I could live with all that**
6   **if it weren't for the way he pipes "angelic" choruses out of that**
7   **loudspeaker on his garage.** *(EMILY notices MR. FLECKMAN*
8   *approaching and tries to warn STAN, but he doesn't notice — he*
9   *just gets more worked up.)* **I swear, if I hear one more verse of**
10   **"Angels from the Realms of Glory," I will run over his camels.**
11   **That's how fed up I am ...**
12   **BARB: Now calm down, Stan. It's Christmas.** *(MR. FLECKMAN is*
13   *now standing right behind them.)*
14   **STAN: He has gone too far! That laser-image star of Bethlehem is**
15   **just too much! I'll bet the electric company awarded him their**
16   **"Consumer of the Year" trophy. He's using so much juice that**
17   **every time he turns his stuff on, the lights dim in the whole**
18   **neighbor —** *(Notices MR. FLECKMAN and stops abruptly. This*
19   *line said with false sincerity.)* **Hi, neighbor! Merry Christmas!**
20   **MR. FLECKMAN:** *(It is obvious he has heard STAN's tirade. He*
21   *swallows hard, then offers his hand to STAN. They shake hands.)*
22   **Merry Christmas to you, Stan. I just thought I'd mention**
23   **something to you. It's about your manger scene. I couldn't**
24   **help but notice that one of your spotlights burnt out, so I**
25   **thought that you might need one, and ...** *(Pulls a floodlight*
26   *bulb out of his coat pocket)* **well, here. Take one of mine.**
27   **STAN:** *(Embarrassed)* **Oh no, I couldn't**
28   **MR. FLECKMAN: No, really, I want you to. I get them cheap from**
29   **the electric company.**
30   **STAN:** *(Accepting the bulb)* **Thanks, Fleckman. That's real decent**
31   **of you.**
32   **MR. FLECKMAN: After all, we don't want the Light of the World**
33   **to suffer for want of a little old light bulb, now do we?**
34   **STAN:** *(Realizing what FLECKMAN has said)* **No indeed.** *(Sincerely)*
35   **Thanks again, neighbor.**

1   **MR. FLECKMAN: Don't mention it, Stan. See ya.** *(He turns to go*
2   *back to his table.)*
3   **STAN:** *(Catching him as he goes)* **Hey, Fleckman, Merry Christmas.**
4   *(Lights go down on scene.)*
5
6   **Scene 5**
7   **Special Guests Visit Christmas Kingdom**
8   *(About 8:00 p.m. — This scene takes place toward the end of the*
9   *main course.)*
10   **FROSTY:** *(Shakes sleigh bells to get everyone's attention.)*
11   **LLLLadies and ggggentlemen, I have just been informed that**
12   **our esteemed guest has nnnnow arrived. I would ask that all**
13   **cccconversations now cease, and I call our Wait Elves to**
14   **attention. It is with ggggreat ppppleasure I now present ...**
15   **ST. NICHOLAS:** *(Enters from the kitchen with a bag of goodies over*
16   *his shoulder.)* **Ho! Ho! Ho!** *Meeeerrrry* **Christmas!** *(To someone*
17   *seated nearby)* **Am I in time? Hope I didn't miss anything**
18   **good ...** *(He moves through the tables in the direction of the*
19   *archway, handing out candy canes to the kids as he goes.)* **You**
20   **wouldn't believe the traffic!** *(Various ad-libs. WAIT ELVES may*
21   *be needed to make sure every kid gets a candy cane without mass*
22   *pandemonium.)*
23   **FROSTY:** *(Said as ST. NICHOLAS nears the archway.)* **St.**
24   **NNNNicholas, you're just in ttttime. WWWWelcome to**
25   **Christmas Kingdom.**
26   **ST. NICHOLAS:** *(At archway with FROSTY)* **Thank you, Frosty.**
27   **You certainly have done a marvelous job with the place. Did I**
28   **miss anything?**
29   **FROSTY: JJJJust the meal, but then I guess you won't go hungry.**
30   *(Pokes him in the tummy.)*
31   **ST. NICHOLAS:** *(Returns the poke, laughing.)* **Nor you, my chilly**
32   **friend.**
33   **FROSTY: YYYYou made it just ttttime.** *(He rings the sleigh bells*
34   *one more time.)* **Ladies and ggggentlemen, boys and girls,**
35   **elves, elfettes, and whomever else, I nnnnow present to you his**

1   **Majesty, the KKKKing of Christmas KKKKingdom!** *(Taped*
2   *background music of "Away in a Manger" begins softly. There*
3   *should be sort of a "sacred hush." FROSTY looks Off-stage Right*
4   *and kneels. At the same time, all ELVES go down on one knee*
5   *wherever they are in the room. ST. NICHOLAS kneels also, so that*
6   *he and FROSTY are on either side of the archway. Spotlight shines*
7   *Up right, following the baby KING. MARY, JOSEPH, and BABY*
8   *JESUS enter Up Right, go to the archway, and stop for a moment.*
9   *Then they walk slowly through the hall, winding between tables,*
10   *giving folks a peek at His Majesty. After "Away in a Manger," "O*
11   *Come All Ye Faithful" begins. ELVES, ST. NICHOLAS, and*
12   *FROSTY join in singing as many verses as it takes for the*
13   *procession to pass each table. Everyone should be encouraged to*
14   *sing along on this song. MARY, JOSEPH, and JESUS exit through*
15   *the archway. As they do, ST. NICHOLAS rises and presents MARY*
16   *with a candy cane for JESUS. She takes it, and they exit Up Left in*
17   *the same quiet way they entered.)*
18 **FROSTY:** *(After motioning that all may rise and/or take their seats.)*
19   **Thank you, friends. Somehow, I don't feel like shivering**
20   **anymore.** *(From this point on, FROSTY speaks normally.)*
21 **ST. NICHOLAS:** *(Wipes a tear from his eye.)* **Yes, Frosty. It fills a**
22   **heart with warmth to remember that first and most precious**
23   **gift of all.**
24 **FROSTY:** **"Yet to all who received him, to those who believed in his**
25   **name, he gave the right to become children of God"** (John 1:12).
26 **ST. NICHOLAS:** *(Shaking FROSTY's hand)* **Until next year, my**
27   **friend. I have to leave for my next appointment.** *(He takes small*
28   *Salvation Army bell out of his pocket and begins to ring it as he*
29   *leaves Up Left.)*
30 **FROSTY:** *(Waving ST. NICHOLAS out)* **Good-bye!** *(To audience)*
31   **Speaking of fat grams** *(Pats his tummy)***, our Wait Elves will now**
32   **serve dessert and coffee.** *(FROSTY exits Up Right.)*
33
34 *(Between scenes, the SHEPHERDSONS must leave their table and*
35   *prepare to enter Up Left platform area.)*

1	**Scene 6**
2	**Stan Sees the Light**
3	*(About 8:15 p.m. — This scene takes place toward the end of the*
4	*dessert course. House lights dim. The SHEPHERDSONS are just*
5	*coming "home." Stage lights come up on platform.)*
6	**BARB:** *(Removing her coat as she enters through Up Right kitchen*
7	*door.)* **Wasn't that a lovely banquet?**
8	**STAN:** *(Following her, he takes BARB's coat, places it on coat rack or*
9	*on his desk with his own.)* **You know, I can't remember when**
10	**I've come home with such a good feeling inside.**
11	**GARTH: Me too, Dad. I'm stuffed!** *(He sticks out his tummy and*
12	*flops on the sofa.)*
13	**EMILY:** *(Appalled as usual)* **Garth! Pul-eeze!** *(She sits on right arm*
14	*of sofa.)*
15	**STAN: No, I don't mean the food. I mean, well ... just a minute.**
16	*(He gets his Bible from under the end table to the right of the*
17	*sofa.)*
18	**GARTH: Uh-oh. Dad's gonna read the Christmas story again ...**
19	**BARB: Now, Garth ...** *(By desk Down Right)*
20	**STAN: No, not this time. I think we all know that story by now. It's**
21	**something else ...** *(Searching for a verse)* **Emily, would you**
22	**read this verse please?**
23	**EMILY:** *(Taking Bible and reading)* **"For God so loved the world,**
24	**that he gave his one and only Son, that whoever believes in**
25	**him shall not perish, but have eternal life"** (John 3:16).
26	**STAN: Thanks, honey.** *(He takes Bible again.)* **I have to confess ...**
27	**something happened when Fleckman gave me that light bulb.**
28	*(He turns a few pages, then hands the Bible to GARTH.)* **Read**
29	**here, son.**
30	**GARTH: "But God demonstrates his own love for us in this: While**
31	**we were still sinners, Christ died for us"** (Romans 5:8).
32	**STAN:** *(Retrieves Bible from GARTH.)* **Thank you.** *(Holds up the*
33	*bulb.)* **Somehow I let the light go out on Jesus, and Fleckman**
34	**noticed before I did. Then tonight, when I saw that baby come**
35	**by, it all made sense, right here.** *(Indicates his heart. Hands*

1   *Bible to BARB near desk.)* **One more verse ...** *(He points it out.)*
2   **BARB: "For the wages of sin is death, but the gift of God is eternal**
3   **life in Christ Jesus our Lord"** (Romans 6:23).
4   **STAN: Do you see? It took this one small gift, this light bulb, to**
5   **help me refocus on Jesus, God's greatest gift of all. That's why**
6   **I feel so good inside.**
7   **BARB:** *(Hugs him.)* **That's beautiful, dear.** *(A thoughtful pause)*
8   **EMILY: I guess you should go replace that bulb now, huh, Dad?**
9   **GARTH:** *(Jumping up)* **I'll do it!** *(Takes bulb from STAN and heads for*
10   *door. He stops short.)* **Hey, Dad ... who really needs a neon**
11   **manger scene anyway?** *(He exits. Lights go down on platform.)*
12
13   Dismissal
14
15   *(About 8:23 p.m. — This conclusion takes place just as dessert is*
16   *finished.)*
17   **PASTOR:** *(Shakes sleigh bells.)* **On behalf of Frosty, our Wait Elves,**
18   **the cast, crew, and kitchen staff, we sincerely thank you for**
19   **coming. It is our desire as a church to serve you by offering**
20   **our love, our support, and the truth that we have come to**
21   **learn from God's Word. We hope you have enjoyed your visit.**
22   **Please come again. God bless you, and good night.**
23
24   *Options to consider at this point: Carol-singing around the*
25   *piano, tree decorating, nighttime sledding party, kitchen clean up.*

Adaptations from Classics and Legends

A (Completely Condensed) Christmas Carol

By Charles Dickens

Adapted for Readers Theatre by Melvin R. White.

Cast of Characters

Narrator 1
Narrator 2
Voice (Man) — Mature voice.
Voice (Woman) — Perhaps an old woman.
Voice (Child) — Quite young.
Fred — Scrooge's nephew, a cheerful young man.
Scrooge — "A squeezing, wrenching, grasping, scraping, clutching, covetous old sinner."
Tiny Tim — A very small boy, ill and weak.

Production Notes

Although the full dramatic treatment of Dickens' *A Christmas Carol* is an unforgettable event, quite frankly, sometimes you just don't have the time, the antiquated costumes, and the energy to mount such a full-scale production. This brief overview may easily be worked into any program with ease — no props, no costumes, and no memorization!

1 NARRATOR 1: Hey, _____, *(Insert NARRATOR 2's name)*
2 only _____ more shopping days 'til Christmas! *(Insert*
3 *appropriate number.)*
4 NARRATOR 2: *(Big sigh)* Don't remind me! Gift-giving *is*
5 Christmas now. It's gotten so commercial in today's world.
6 NARRATOR 1: You say today? Nothing new, actually. Listen to
7 this: In 1897 an Episcopalian bishop wrote his wife, "The
8 Devil has stolen from us Christmas, the day of spiritual
9 redemption, and converted it into a day of worldly festivity,
10 shooting, and swearing!"
11 NARRATOR 2: I think the Christmas conflict between commercial
12 and humanitarian values is best expressed in the "Carol
13 philosophy" of Charles Dickens — remember Ebenezer
14 Scrooge? Tiny Tim? Bob Cratchit? "A Christmas Carol"
15 begins like this:
16 NARRATOR 1: Marley was dead, to begin with. There is no doubt
17 whatever about that. The register of his burial was signed by
18 the clergyman, the clerk, the undertaker, and the chief
19 mourner, Scrooge. Old Marley was as dead as a doornail.
20 Scrooge knew he was dead? Of course he did. How could it be
21 otherwise? Scrooge and he were partners — and Scrooge was
22 his sole executor, his sole administrator, his sole residuary
23 legatee, his sole friend, his sole mourner. Yes, Scrooge knew he
24 was dead, but he never painted out old Marley's name. There
25 it stood, years afterward, above the door — Scrooge and
26 Marley. *(SCROOGE moves to Down Center stool or chair.)*
27 NARRATOR 2: Oh, but he was a tightfisted hand at the
28 grindstone, was Scrooge! A squeezing, wrenching, grasping,
29 scraping, clutching, covetous old sinner! Nobody ever stopped
30 him in the street to say: *(Each VOICE moves Down Center*
31 *above SCROOGE for his line.)*
32 VOICE (MAN): My dear Scrooge, how are you? When will you
33 come to see me?
34 NARRATOR 2: No beggars implored him:
35 VOICE (WOMAN): Please, a farthing — or a crust of bread!

1   NARRATOR 2: No children asked him:
2   VOICE (CHILD): Do you have the time? Please, sir, what time is
3   it?
4   NARRATOR 2: No one ever once in all his life inquired:
5   VOICE (MAN): Can you tell me the way to the Exchange?
6   NARRATOR 1: But what did Scrooge care? It was the very thing
7   he liked — to edge his way along the crowded paths of life,
8   keeping all human sympathy at a distance. *(Transition)* Once
9   upon a time — of all the good days in the year, upon a
10   Christmas Eve — old Scrooge sat busy in his counting house.
11   It was cold, bleak, biting, foggy weather, and the city clocks
12   had only just struck three, although it was quite dark already.
13   The door of Scrooge's counting house was open so he could
14   keep an eye on his clerk, Bob Cratchit, who, in a dismal little
15   cell beyond, was copying letters. Suddenly the silence was
16   broken by a cheerful voice, the voice of Scrooge's nephew,
17   Fred.
18   FRED: *(Stands and comes Down Center to Right of SCROOGE who is*
19   *seated Down Center.)* A Merry Christmas, Uncle! God save
20   you!
21   SCROOGE: Bah! Humbug!
22   FRED: Christmas a humbug, Uncle? You don't mean that, I'm
23   sure!
24   SCROOGE: I do. Out upon merry Christmas! What's Christmas
25   time to you but a time for paying bills without money, a time
26   for finding yourself a year older and not an hour richer. What
27   right have you to be merry? What reason have you to be
28   merry? You're poor enough!
29   FRED: *(Determined to remain cheerful)* Well, then, what right have
30   you to be dismal? You're rich enough. Don't be cross, Uncle.
31   SCROOGE: What else can I be when I live in such a world of fools
32   as this? Merry Christmas! If I could work my will, every idiot
33   who goes about with "Merry Christmas" on his lips should be
34   boiled in his own pudding!
35   FRED: *(Pleading)* Uncle!

1   **SCROOGE:** *(Standing)* **Nephew, keep Christmas in your own way,**
2   **and let me keep it in mine.**
3   **FRED: Keep it! But you don't keep it!**
4   **SCROOGE: Let me leave it alone then! Much good it may do you!**
5   **Much good it has ever done you.**
6   **FRED:** *(Placatingly)* **Don't be angry, Uncle. Come! Dine with us**
7   **tomorrow!**
8   **SCROOGE: Good afternoon.**
9   **FRED: Uncle, I want nothing from you. I ask nothing of you. Why**
10   **can't we be friends?**
11   **SCROOGE: Good afternoon.**
12   **FRED: I'm sorry to find you so determined. We've never had any**
13   **quarrel to which I've been a party. I made this trial in homage**
14   **to Christmas, and I'll keep Christmas humor to the last. So —**
15   **a Merry Christmas, Uncle!**
16   **SCROOGE: Good afternoon!**
17   **FRED: And a happy New Year!** *(Returns to seat and freezes.)*
18   **SCROOGE: Good afternoon!** *(Returns to seat and freezes.)*
19   **NARRATOR 2: To this day, the world flocks to holiday**
20   **performances of Dickens' 1843 story, "A Christmas Carol," to**
21   **hear old Ebenezer Scrooge awake from his life-changing**
22   **encounters with the Ghosts of Christmas Past, Present, and**
23   **Future to declare:**
24   **SCROOGE: I will honor Christmas in my heart and try to keep it**
25   **all the year.**
26   **NARRATOR 1: And to hear Tiny Tim at the Cratchit Christmas**
27   **dinner cry out:**
28   **TINY TIM: God bless us, every one!**

The Fir Tree

By Hans Christian Andersen

Adapted for Readers Theatre by Melvin R. White

Cast of Characters

Narrator

Fir Tree — A boy who grows a bit older and taller during the play.

Others — Ten, twenty, or thirty readers of various ages, sizes, and voices to interpret a swallow (melodious voice), stork (tall and stately), sunbeam (bright and sunny), sparrows (quick of speech and movement), mice (high, thin, squeaky, sharp voices), and miscellaneous children including Alice, John, and Viola, and adults (woodchoppers, a mother, an uncle, etc.).

1   NARRATOR: Christmas is many different things to many
2   different people, but the evergreen tree — the Christmas
3   tree — has become a universal symbol of the holiday season.
4   A classic among Christmas stories, loved by old and young
5   alike, is Hans Christian Andersen's "The Fir Tree," written
6   over one hundred years ago. Out in the woods stood a sturdy
7   but little fir tree. It grew in a good place where it got lots of
8   sunshine and plenty of fresh air. Around it stood many tall fir
9   trees and pine trees. But the little fir tree was not happy. It
10   would sigh:
11 FIR TREE: I wish I were a grown-up tree like my comrades!
12 NARRATOR: Yes, the little fir tree was in a hurry to grow up. It
13   did not care a thing about the warm sunshine or the fresh air,
14   and took no interest in the children who ran about chattering
15   when they came to the woods to pick strawberries or
16   raspberries. Often when they had filled their pails, they would
17   sit down to rest near the little fir. They would say:
18 LITTLE BOY: Isn't that a nice little tree?
19 LITTLE GIRL: *(Giggling)* It's the baby of the woods.
20 NARRATOR: The little tree heard them, and said:
21 FIR TREE: I don't like your remarks at all!
22 NARRATOR: But of course the children did not hear it.
23   *(Transition)* The next year the little tree shot up a long joint of
24   new growth, and the following year, another joint, still longer.
25   You can always tell how old a fir tree is by counting the
26   number of joints it has. But the little tree was still unhappy.
27 FIR TREE: I wish I were a big tree like my comrades. Then I could
28   stretch out my branches and see from my top what the world is
29   like. Then birds would build their nests in me — and when the
30   winds blow, I could sway back and forth like the big trees do.
31 NARRATOR: Neither the sunbeams, nor the birds, nor the red and
32   gold sunsets gave the little tree any pleasure. In winter, when
33   the snow lay glistening white on the ground, a rabbit would
34   often come jumping along, sometimes jumping right over the
35   little tree.

1 FIR TREE: Oh, that makes me so furious! Why must I be so
2   small — so small that rabbits can jump over me?
3 NARRATOR: But two more winters passed, and a third, and in the
4   third the tree was so large that the rabbit had to go around it.
5 FIR TREE: To grow and grow, to get older and be tall, that, after
6   all, is the most delightful thing in the world! But here come
7   some men; they have hatchets and saws. I wonder what they
8   are here for? I must watch to see what they do.
9 NARRATOR: Yes, in the fall the woodcutters came each year to
10   cut down some of the largest trees. The fir tree, who had now
11   grown to quite a good size, trembled at the sight, for the
12   magnificent great trees fell to the ground with noise and
13   cracking. Their branches were lopped off, and the trees
14   looked long and bare. Then they were laid on wagons, and
15   horses dragged them away, out of the woods.
16 FIR TREE: I wonder where they are taking them. What becomes
17   of the trees after they cut them down and haul them away?
18   Swallows, do you know where they take the trees? Have you
19   seen them anywhere?
20 SWALLOW: No, I don't know anything about it. Maybe the stork
21   knows. Ask it.
22 FIR TREE: Stork, do you know where they take the trees after
23   they cut them and trim off their branches? Have you seen
24   them anywhere?
25 STORK: Yes, I think I know. I met many ships as I flew here from
26   Egypt, and each ship had high, high masts. I noticed they
27   smelled of fir. I think I should congratulate you, for the fir
28   masts held themselves on high most majestically!
29 FIR TREE: Oh, I wish I were old enough to be a mast and see the
30   sea. Tell me, how does the sea really look? What's it like?
31 STORK: That would take too long a time to tell.
32 NARRATOR: And with that, the stork flew away. The Sunbeams,
33   upset that the little fir tree was so unhappy, gave him their
34   advice.
35 SUNBEAM 1: Rejoice in thy growth!

1   SUNBEAM 2: Yes, rejoice in thy vigorous growth!

2   SUNBEAM 3: And in the fresh life that moveth within thee!

3   NARRATOR: And the sunbeams shone on the tree, and wind

4   kissed the tree, and the rain and dew wept tears over him, but

5   the little fir did not understand. *(Transition)* When Christmas

6   came, quite small trees were cut down, trees which often were

7   not even as large as the fir tree. These young trees — and they

8   were always the finest looking — kept their branches. They,

9   too, were loaded on carts and sleds, and the horses drew them

10   out of the woods.

11   FIR TREE: Why do they leave me? Where are they going? They

12   are no taller than I am! In fact, the men took one fir tree much

13   shorter than I! The woodcutters took the branches off the tall

14   trees. Where are they taking them?

15   SPARROW 1: I know! I know! I've peeked in the windows in the

16   town down in the valley.

17   SPARROW 2: I know, too! We sparrows all know where they take

18   the trees.

19   SPARROW 3: *(The SPARROWS tend to try to talk all at once,*

20   *overlapping and interrupting each other.)* You can't believe the

21   beauty, the splendor, the magnificence that awaits them!

22   FIR TREE: Beauty? Splendor? Magnificence? What do you mean?

23   SPARROW 2: Listen! The men plant the little trees, branches and

24   all, in the middle of big rooms.

25   FIR TREE: Plant them?

26   SPARROW 1: Well, sort of. And then they put splendid things on

27   them — strings of popcorn, and polished apples, and ...

28   SPARROW 3: And gingerbread men, and toys ...

29   SPARROW 2: And hundreds of tiny lights.

30   FIR TREE: Lights?

31   SPARROW 2: Yes. Candles, I think.

32   FIR TREE: And then? What happens then? *(Very excited)*

33   SPARROW 3: We did not see anything more, as a little boy saw us

34   and came to the window and chased us away.

35   SPARROW 2: But it was incomparably beautiful.

1   SPARROW 1: Exquisite!

2   FIR TREE: Oh, I hope I am destined for so glorious a career! That

3   is even better than being a mast on a ship! I wish I had been

4   taken to be a Christmas tree. I am now tall. My branches

5   spread like the ones the woodcutters just took. I wish I were

6   on the sled with the other fir trees, to be taken to a warm room

7   and made splendid with ornaments! Yes, and then, after that,

8   something even better, something even grander, will surely

9   follow. Don't you think so, sparrows?

10   SPARROW 1: Well, I don't know. Perhaps ...

11   FIR TREE: But why should they ornament the trees so unless

12   something better, something grander, is to follow? But what?

13   Oh, how I suffer! I don't know myself what's the matter with

14   me. I am so unhappy!

15   NARRATOR: Again the sunbeams, the wind, and the rain all

16   talked to him, but he did not heed them. The air and the

17   sunlight said:

18   AIR: Rejoice in our presence!

19   SUNBEAM: Rejoice in thy own fresh youth!

20   NARRATOR: But the fir tree did not rejoice at all. He grew and he

21   grew and was green both summer and winter. Finally it was

22   December again, and two men came to the woods with their

23   axes.

24   MAN 1: What a fine tree!

25   MAN 2: Yes, splendid!

26   MAN 1: Yes, that's the one, just the right height for our living

27   room, and well-shaped

28   NARRATOR: The fir tree was happy. He was the first tree to be

29   cut down! The axe cut deep into him, and he fell to the ground

30   with a sigh. And suddenly he found he was sorry to be leaving

31   his home, from the place where he had sprung up. He realized

32   he was leaving his old friends, the little bushes and flowers

33   around him, that he might not see them again — perhaps not

34   even the birds! The departure was not at all agreeable. But he

35   felt quite faint, and finally did not hear anything for quite

1   some time. When he came to, he found himself in a large and
2   splendid room — pictures on the walls, a porcelain stove with
3   two large Chinese vases beside it, easy chairs and sofas, and
4   tables filled with books and toys — lots and lots of children's
5   toys, everywhere.
6   FIR TREE: Where am I? I'm standing up again — oh, someone
7   has put me in this tub with sand in it, and laid a bright carpet
8   over the tub to hide the sand. But what are those people
9   doing?
10   MOTHER: Now be careful, but help me trim the tree. Alice, you
11   can put these strings of colored paper on the tree.
12   ALICE: Yes, Mother. *(All the trimming is done in pantomime.)*
13   MOTHER: Such a splendid tree! Just the right height — and so
14   green and fresh. I'm sure it'll last until after the holidays. I
15   hope so.
16   JOHN: What may I do, Mother?
17   MOTHER: Let me see. Why don't you hang those walnuts on the
18   tree — and Phoebe, try getting some of the apples hung.
19   VIOLA: May I put the little dolls on, Mother?
20   MOTHER: Of course. And here, I'll put this gold star on the very
21   top of the tree, just as we always do each year. We'll ask your
22   father to put the candles on, as we have to be so careful how
23   they are placed. We don't want a fire, you know. But I think
24   this is going to be the most beautiful tree we've ever had. How
25   it will shine this evening when we light all of the candles! *(The*
26   *FAMILY leaves.)*
27   FIR TREE: This evening! If only the evening were here. I can
28   hardly wait. To have my candles lit! But I wonder what
29   happens then. They've put so many packages under me, big
30   ones and little ones, and all wrapped in such splendidly
31   colored paper — and fancy, bright ribbons. I wonder ...
32   Maybe the other trees from the forest will come to look at me.
33   The sparrows were here to see last Christmas; maybe they'll
34   come to peek through the windows again. Maybe I'll take root
35   here in this tub and stand here, all winter and all summer,

1   covered with ornaments!
2   NARRATOR: He was so impatient. And he had a pain in his back
3   from all of the ornaments hanging on him. But soon, the
4   candles were carefully lighted. What brightness! What
5   splendor! The tree trembled so from his excitement that one
6   of the candles set fire to a branch. It blazed up splendidly, but
7   the fir tree was frightened.
8   MOTHER: Help! Help!
9   CHILDREN: The tree's on fire. Father, help put out the fire!
10   MOTHER: *(Throwing water on the tree)* Thank goodness your
11   father had this pail of water handy. I think the fire is out. Oh,
12   dear. Candles are so dangerous on a tree. Oh, dear. Oh, dear!
13   NARRATOR: After the accident with the fire, the tree did not even
14   tremble anymore. What a state he was in. He was afraid he
15   might lose some of his handsomeness if he caught fire again —
16   and he was quite bewildered amidst the glare and the
17   brightness. Then, suddenly, doors opened and in rushed the
18   children. They shouted so the whole place echoed with sound.
19   They danced around the tree, and one present after another
20   was pulled off the tree or taken from underneath it. The tree
21   was plundered, some of his branches broken, and the candles
22   all put out. No one looked at the tree, as they were opening
23   presents and playing with the new toys — until an uncle *(Or*
24   *aunt)* said:
25   UNCLE/AUNT: Anyone want to hear a story?
26   CHILDREN: *(Ad lib)* Yes, yes! A story. We want a story. *(Etc.)*
27   UNCLE/AUNT: All right, a story — but just one story, as it is
28   getting late. Which one will you have? The one about Ivedy-
29   Avedy, or the one about Klumpy-Dumpy who tumbled
30   downstairs, and yet, after all, married the princess and came
31   to the throne?
32   CHILDREN: *(Ad lib, some wanting one story, some the other.)*
33   UNCLE/AUNT: I think more of you want to hear about Klumpy-
34   Dumpy. So, once upon a time ...
35   NARRATOR: And the storyteller told about Klumpy-Dumpy who

1 tumbled down, and notwithstanding, came to the throne, and
2 at last married the princess. When the story was over the
3 children cried:
4 CHILDREN: Go on! Tell another story! Please, another story!
5 *(Etc.)*
6 NARRATOR: But it was late, so there were no more stories. The fir
7 tree stood quite still in his tub, absorbed in thought.
8 FIR TREE: The birds in the wood had never related things like
9 this: Klumpy-Dumpy fell downstairs, and yet he married the
10 princess. Yes, yes! That's the way of the world! Who knows,
11 perhaps I'll fall downstairs, too, and get a princess as a wife!
12 I can hardly wait until tomorrow, because then I expect they'll
13 deck me out again with playthings, fruits, tinsel, and lights. I
14 won't be frightened tomorrow. I won't tremble. I will enjoy to
15 the full my splendor! Tomorrow I shall hear again the story of
16 Klumpy-Dumpy, and maybe the story about Ivedy-Avedy, too.
17 Now, I'll just think about it until morning.
18 NARRATOR: In the morning the men who first found the fir tree
19 in the woods came in. The fir tree thought:
20 FIR TREE: Now, then, the splendor will begin again.
21 NARRATOR: But the men dragged him from the room, took him
22 up some long, dark stairs to the attic, and left him in a dark
23 corner where no daylight entered.
24 FIR TREE: What's the meaning of this? What am I to do here?
25 What is to happen next? I wonder. It's winter out of doors
26 now. The earth is frozen, covered with snow. They can't plant
27 me now, so I guess they put me here until spring comes. How
28 thoughtful of them! But I wish it were not so lonely here — so
29 dark. Not even a rabbit. Out in the woods, it was so pleasant,
30 especially when the snow was on the ground, and the rabbit
31 leaped by; yes — even when he jumped over me, although I
32 did not like it then. It is so terribly lonely and dark here!
33 *(Hears a squeak.)* What's that? Oh, a mouse, peeping out of his
34 hole. Hello, little mouse.
35 MOUSE 1: Squeak! Squeak! It is terribly cold up here, old fir. But

1   for that, it would be a nice place up here, wouldn't it?

2   FIR TREE: I am not old, not by any means. There are many much

3   older than I.

4   MOUSE 2: Where do you come from? And what can you do?

5   MOUSE 1: Tell us about the most beautiful place on the earth.

6   MOUSE 2: Have you been there?

7   MOUSE 1: Have you ever been in the larder?

8   MOUSE 2: The pantry? Where there's lots of cheese and bread

9   and such?

10   MOUSE 1: And tallow candles?

11   MOUSE 2: That place where one enters lean and comes out again

12   fat?

13   FIR TREE: I know of no such place. But I know my woods where

14   the sun shines and the little birds sing.

15   MOUSE 2: How great! You have seen so much. You must have

16   been very happy there.

17   FIR TREE: I? happy? Well, yes, I guess those were happy times.

18   But let me tell you about when I was the Christmas tree

19   downstairs.

20   NARRATOR: And then he told all about Christmas Eve, when he

21   was decked out with cakes and candies and candles.

22   MOUSE 1: How lucky you have been, old fir tree!

23   FIR TREE: I am not at all old. I came from the woods just this

24   winter; I am in my prime, and am only rather short for my

25   age.

26   MOUSE 1: You know such delightful stories!

27   MOUSE 2: Yes, yes!

28   NARRATOR: The next night the two little mice came with four

29   other little mice to hear what the tree recounted. The more he

30   told, the more plainly he remembered all himself — and the

31   more he realized that those times had really been happy times.

32   He told this to the little mice:

33   FIR TREE: Yes, those were good times — and I did not realize it.

34   But they may still come again. Klumpy-Dumpy fell

35   downstairs, and yet he got a princess.

1 MOUSE 1: Who is Klumpy-Dumpy?

2 NARRATOR: So then the fir tree told the fairy tale he had heard

3   on Christmas Eve, for he could remember every single word

4   of it. The little mice jumped for joy, they enjoyed it so much,

5   and each night they brought other mice to hear the fir tree.

6   But after a while, they began to think that the fir tree's stories

7   were not so interesting.

8 MOUSE 2: Do you know only that one story?

9 FIR TREE: Only that one. I heard it on my happiest evening — but

10   I did not know then how happy I really was.

11 MOUSE 2: It's a very stupid story.

12 MOUSE 3: Don't you know a story about bacon?

13 MOUSE 1: Or tallow candles?

14 MOUSE 3: Can't you tell any pantry stories?

15 FIR TREE: No.

16 MOUSE 2: Well, good-bye. *(The other two MICE ad lib their good-*

17   *byes, too.)*

18 FIR TREE: Good-bye. I shall miss you. *(Sighing)* It was very

19   pleasant when the little mice sat around and listened to what

20   I told them. I liked their company — even the rats, when they

21   came. Now that, too, is over. But if I ever get brought out

22   again, I'll take good care to enjoy myself.

23 NARRATOR: A few days later one of the men who had brought

24   him to the attic came, dragged him from his dark corner,

25   down the stairs, and way out into the yard, through beds of

26   beautiful flowers, rows of roses in bloom, past large green

27   trees — and dumped him onto the ground around a corner

28   behind a garage. He spread out his branches, but they were

29   withered and yellow. Only one ornament remained; the golden

30   star of tinsel. It was still on the top of the tree, and it glittered

31   in the sunshine. One of the children saw it, ran over, and tore

32   it off.

33 CHILD: Look what is still on this ugly old Christmas tree. The

34   star! I'll take it to Mother; she'll want it for next year's tree.

35 FIR TREE: Look at me. I wish I had been left in the corner of the

1   attic where no one could see me.

2   NARRATOR: He thought of his youth in the woods, of the merry

3   Christmas Eve, and of the little mice who had at first listened

4   with so much pleasure to the story of Klumpy-Dumpy.

5   FIR TREE: It's all over for me, all past. If only I had been happy

6   when I had reason to be happy. Now it is all gone, all gone!

7   But perhaps not. Here comes the lady, the Mother of the

8   children. Perhaps she'll help me!

9   MOTHER: *(Enters with JOHN.)* John, I want you to do something

10   for me. Your father must have forgotten he put this dead

11   Christmas tree here behind the garage. Get your father's axe

12   and cut it into short pieces — oh, about ten or twelve inches

13   long. It'll make good wood for the fire on a chilly evening this

14   fall.

15   JOHN: Yes, Mother. I'll do it right away.

16   NARRATOR: So John chopped the tree into small pieces. When he

17   had finished, there was a whole heap lying there. Then he

18   returned to the yard to play with his younger brothers and

19   sisters. The youngest wore the gold star on his chest, the one

20   the fir tree had had at his top on the happiest evening of his

21   life. However, that was over now. The tree was gone. All, all

22   was over. The tree was no more, and there's no more to my

23   story. No more, nothing more. All stories come to an end. Well,

24   no, not all stories come to an end. For some two thousand

25   years there has been one story that has been told and re-told,

26   written and re-written, hundreds of times — and told,

27   perhaps millions of times. It is the story of the real meaning of

28   Christmas: the beginning of Christianity. True, changes are

29   everywhere. Our world seems increasingly distraught,

30   chaotic. At Christmas, stores are jammed, shopping is a trial,

31   traffic is hopeless, parking spaces scarce. But Christmas is not

32   in the stores. Christmas is in the knowledge that Jesus came

33   into the world. *Merry Christmas!*

Scripts Based on
Christmas Carols

Here We Come A-Caroling
By Arthur L. Zapel

Production Notes

This script need not be presented as written. The right sequence of songs and stories depends largely on when the program is presented. If, for example, this presentation is scheduled for Christmas Eve, you may find it more appropriate to end the service with "Silent Night" or "O Little Town of Bethlehem" and candlelight. Or if the program is to be given on the Sunday morning before Christmas, you may want the final carol to be "Hark, the Herald Angels Sing" to give a rousing lift to the concept of Christmas soon-to-be.

We have staged the program for a non-liturgical occasion, though it can be part of a worship service.

We have indicated throughout the script places where both the choir and congregation may sing together and where descants may be used to heighten the joy of the music. These are choices for the choir director according to his or her own evaluations of the opportunity.

The script should also be edited as needed, for length. The choir director may choose to add or subtract choruses or entire selections to accommodate the time available for the presentation. It was designed as an hour-long program or service, but no time was allowed for the free-will offering or any special comments by the pastor.

The Wise Men should be costumed in royal-looking robes and carry gifts such as a decorated bottle, a fancy box, and a dish of gold coins (play money).

1   *(CHOIR OF CAROLERS sings four verses and refrains to the*
2   *traditional old English melody "Here We Come A-Wassailing," as*
3   *the choir enters down the center aisle.)*
4   **PASTOR/NARRATOR: Welcome! In the spirit of the most joyful**
5   **season on earth, we are here to entertain you with a program**
6   **of carol music. Featured today** *(Tonight)* **are the carolers from**
7   **our adult** *(Or women's or children's)* **choir and their director,**
8   *(Name)* **_____. The instrumental accompaniment will be**
9   **provided by** *(Name(s))* **_____.**
10   **In addition to stirring renditions of the world's most**
11   **famous Christmas carols, we will tell you something of the**
12   **history of the carols themselves — how they came to be**
13   **written, who composed them, and why they have become so**
14   **popular.**
15   **Our introductory song, "Here We Come A-Wassailing," is**
16   **one of the top twenty of the best-loved carols, especially for**
17   **strolling carolers who find this bright carol to be a great door-**
18   **opener as they sing their way along residential streets during**
19   **the evenings of Christmas.**
20   **It is a very old song dating back to the Middle Ages or**
21   **before. The carol in its present form may have helped the**
22   **early Christians in the British Isles displace the pagan Yule**
23   **custom of wassailing. The** *wassail* **comes from the ancient**
24   **Anglo-Saxon word** *Wase- hael*, *(Pronounced WAZ-HAYEEL)*
25   **which translated means "Be in health." At the pagan Saxon**
26   **festivals, it was the custom to drink from the wassail to the**
27   **honor of the lord and leader. The tradition was adopted by the**
28   **Christian community, and to this day, the wassail bowl is to be**
29   **seen in all of the great country houses of England during the**
30   **Christmas holidays, from Christmas Eve to Twelfth Night.**
31   **The original wassail drink was made of mulled ale, eggs,**
32   **curdled cream, roasted apples, nuts, and spices. The mixture**
33   **would seem to be a heavy brew compared to our lighter tastes**
34   **of today.**
35   **As we proceed with our program of carols today** *(Tonight)*,

we will ask both you and the choir to participate in the singing of the carols we have selected. As I relate the stories and facts about each carol, you may enjoy trying to guess the title before I announce it. Your trivia knowledge about carols may place you in the upper percentile of hymnologists. Let us then begin.

Perhaps it was David, the young psalm writer and singer from Old Testament days, who first conceived the mood of the first carol we shall sing. Do you have any idea what famous carol found its beginnings in these words from Psalm 98, verse 4?

Make a joyful noise to the Lord, all the earth;
Break forth into joyous song and sing praises!

And Psalm 98 verses 8 and 9:

Let the floods clap their hands;
let the hills sing for joy together
Before the *Lord*, for he comes
to judge the earth.
He will judge the world with righteousness,
and the peoples with equity.

Do these words sound similar in content?

He rules the world with truth and grace
And makes the nations prove
The glories of his righteousness,
And wonders of his love.

Psalm 98 was a joyful expression that said, "O sing to the Lord a new song, for he has done marvelous things!" (Psalm 98:1). Isaac Watts, some eighteen centuries later in the year 1719, rediscovered the zest of this cry of praise to God and redirected it to celebrate the birth of the Savior from the house of David. His exuberant words were:

Joy to the world! The Lord is come:
Let earth receive her King.

Though the verses to this carol were written more than fifty years before our Revolutionary War of Independence, they are as fresh and meaningful today as they were over 250 years ago.

1   It is believed that the melody to this carol derived from the
2   tune "Antioch" from Handel's *Messiah*, but many say that the
3   arranger Lowell Mason borrowed musical phrase from other
4   works of Handel.

5   Let us sing the stanzas to this carol antiphonally, which
6   means both you and the choir will share the joy of singing. You,
7   of the congregation, will sing the first and second lines of each
8   stanza; the choir will sing the third and fourth; and we will all
9   join together in the refrain. *(CHOIR and congregation sing "Joy*
10   *to the World," verses 1, 2, 3, and 4. Consider use of a descant for*
11   *the last verse.)*

12   It was in the year 1223 that Saint Francis of Assisi created
13   the first Christmas crèche or manger scene to enact the
14   beautiful images of the Nativity. Though the scene is very
15   familiar to all of us today, the Bible gives us very little detail
16   about the traditional picture of the Nativity. The entire story is
17   told in but one sentence in Luke 2:7.

18   And she gave birth to her first-born son and
19   Wrapped him in swaddling cloths, and laid
20   him in a manger, because there was no
21   place for them in the inn.

22   All of the beautiful visions we have of the stable, the animals,
23   and the manger-crib stem from that first St. Francis crèche
24   dramatization in the Italian city of Assisi, together with the
25   added creative expressions of artists, musicians, poets, and the
26   clergy over the centuries.

27   Our next carol has probably done as much as any other
28   works of art to dramatize and humanize that most holy event.
29   Some hymn books refer to this carol as Martin Luther's
30   "Cradle Hymn," but there is no verifiable evidence that he
31   wrote it. In fact, until relatively recent years, it was unknown in
32   Germany. Had Luther been the author, it certainly would have
33   been used through the centuries along with his other songs.

34   Investigations of recent years seem to indicate that the
35   carol originated in a colony of German Lutherans in

1   Pennsylvania. The Luther association to the song was most
2   likely the result of a picture of Luther and his family at
3   Christmas painted by Gustave F.L. Koenig which was
4   included with the carol in a book called *Luther's Christbaum*
5   by T.B. Stork, published in Philadelphia in 1855.
6   Whether the original lines were written in English or
7   German is unknown, but the earliest publications are in
8   English. Several German translations followed and it has
9   become as popular in Germany as in America.
10 The composer of the original melody is also not definitely
11 known. Some credit a man named Carl Mueller. Others list
12 William J. Kirkpatrick. The most popular musical setting is
13 traceable to J.R. Murray in 1887.
14 All of this demonstrates that many of the most beautiful
15 attributes of our Christmas holiday traditions stem from
16 many sources.
17 Many devout and creative people like yourselves have been
18 instrumental over the years in nurturing and enhancing the
19 finest moments of our Christmas worship.
20 Our choir will now sing the carol whose history I have told
21 you — "Away in a Manger." *(CHOIR sings all three stanzas of*
22 *"Away in a Manger." Consider having the congregation sing one*
23 *stanza or a choir soloist. The slow tempo would also permit a*
24 *second song as a counter melody.)*
25 Almost every carol or hymn is a combination of works by
26 at least two talented and inspired creative people — a poet-
27 writer and a musician-composer. If you will take the time to
28 read carols, you will find that the words to many of our
29 favorites, taken alone, represent very fine poetry that is
30 inspirational and a joy to read. Without music, let me read
31 some of the words to our next carol:
32 Angels, from the realms of glory,
33 Wing your flight o'er all the earth;
34 Ye who sang creation's story
35 Now proclaim Messiah's birth:

1   Come and worship, come and worship,

2   Worship Christ, the newborn King.

3

4   Shepherds, in the fields abiding,

5   Watching o'er your flocks by night,

6   God with man is now residing;

7   Yonder shines the infant Light:

8   Come and worship, come and worship,

9   Worship Christ, the newborn King.

10

11   Saints, before the altar bending,

12   Watching long in hope and fear,

13   Suddenly the Lord, descending,

14   In his temple shall appear:

15   Come and worship, come and worship,

16   Worship Christ, the newborn King.

17   The writer of these lines was James Montgomery, who lived

18 from 1771 to 1854. He is considered the greatest of the

19 Moravian hymn writers. He authored over four hundred

20 hymns, one hundred of which are still in steady use. He came

21 from a devout peasant family in Ayrshire, Scotland. He

22 studied for the ministry in a Moravian school near Leeds,

23 England, but he was a dropout. His greater love for poetry

24 consumed all his energy, and after several irregular jobs, he

25 became editor of *The Sheffield Iris*, a liberal journal. His

26 liberal statements, which by standards of today would be

27 conservative, caused him to be imprisoned twice. But nothing

28 could dim his enthusiasm for hymnology. So widely is his work

29 accepted that he is considered to be one of the threesome of the

30 greatest hymn writers: James Wesley, Isaac Watts, and James

31 Montgomery.

32   But who was it that wrote the music to this beautifully

33 written carol? His name was Henry Smart. He gave up his

34 position in the legal profession to devote his life to music.

35 Thirteen years after the death of Montgomery, in the year

1   1867, he composed this melody even though he was unable to
2   transcribe the musical notes to paper. He had lost his sight
3   some years before and could only dictate the tune to another
4   musician. He named the melody "Regent Square" after the
5   most prominent Presbyterian church in London at that time.
6   Our choir will now sing all four verses of this beautiful
7   carol, "Angels, from the Realms of Glory." *(CHOIR sings all*
8   *four verses of "Angels from the Realms of Glory.")*
9   During a Christmas worship celebration in Berlin,
10   Germany, in the year 1854, the entire choir of the Imperial
11   Church sang a quiet song. A breathless hush followed the
12   performance. So beautiful was the melody and its
13   presentation that everyone present was lost in its
14   enchantment. Among those present was the King of Prussia,
15   Frederick William the fourth. Soon afterward he declared
16   that this song should be given first place in all Christmas
17   concerts thereafter.
18   The song had begun to gain some popularity before this
19   time, but no one knew its source. Many thought it was a folk
20   song or a composition by Michael Hayden, a well-known
21   musician of the time. The court musicians in Berlin, needing
22   the musical score for the royal Christmas service, wrote to
23   Salzburg for a copy of the manuscript. They thought it might
24   be found there at Saint Peter's Church. By a wondrous stroke
25   of fate, Felix Gruber, the youngest son of the song's composer,
26   Franz Gruber, was a choir boy at the church. He heard of the
27   request and told his father, who was an unknown town parish
28   choir director and organist in Hallein, Germany.
29   You may be sure that Franz Gruber was thrilled to learn
30   that his music was to be performed before the King of Prussia
31   in Berlin. Along with his musical manuscript and the
32   complete words, he sent a letter authenticating the
33   circumstances of the song's creation. In translation to English,
34   this is what he wrote:
35   It was on December twenty-fourth of the year 1818 when

1	Joseph Mohr, then assistant pastor of the newly
2	established St. Nicholas' parish church in
3	Oberndorf, handed to Franz Gruber, who was
4	attending to the duties of organist (and was at
5	the same time a schoolmaster in Arnsdorf) a poem,
6	with the request that he write for it a suitable
7	melody arranged for two solo voices, chorus, and
8	a guitar accompaniment. On that very same evening
9	the latter, in fulfillment of this request made to him
10	as a music expert, handed to the pastor his simple
11	composition, which was thereupon immediately
12	performed on that holy night of Christmas Eve
13	and received with all acclaim. As this Christmas
14	song has come into the Tyrol through the
15	well-known Zillerthaler, and since it has also
16	appeared in a somewhat altered form in a collection
17	of songs in Leipzig, the composer has the honor to
18	dare to place beside it the original.
19	Signed,
20	Franz Gruber

21 As you know, this song, "Silent Night," has become the most
22 famous of all Christmas carols, having been translated into
23 more than ninety languages and dialects. It has become the
24 subject of endless articles, Christmas cards, stories, plays,
25 novels, and even a motion picture.

26   Popular legends are told of its origin. Some say that it was
27 created because of an emergency. Mice had eaten into the
28 bellows of the church organ at the St. Nicholas Parish in
29 Oberndorf, rendering the instrument useless for the
30 Christmas Eve worship celebration. The assistant Catholic
31 priest, Father Joseph Mohr, decided to write a new hymn to
32 substitute for the organ music. Late in the evening as he
33 climbed a small mountain, returning home, the quiet darkness
34 and the snow-covered beauty of the village below inspired
35 him. The words came to him almost as a gift from God, who

1   wished for the Nativity story to be told as quietly and simply
2   as the holy birth itself that glorious night in Bethlehem.
3   Father Mohr gave his poem to the organist and teacher of
4   the village school, hoping he would be able to set it to music.
5   The inexperienced composer, Franz Gruber, must have also
6   been moved by the Holy Spirit, for the melody came to him
7   surprisingly quickly — almost as if his hand was being
8   directed by a greater force. He wrote the arrangement for two
9   voices and a guitar. Some say that he also arranged to have a
10   choir of girls from the village join in the melody. Father Mohr
11   did his best to sing the tenor lead as Franz Gruber sang bass
12   harmony and did the guitar accompaniment. So reads the
13   legend.
14   Certainly there is no fiction in the unique beauty of this
15   carol that so greatly portrays all the key events of the Nativity.
16   Now our choir will sing the first three stanzas, with soloist
17   *(Name)* _____ singing the third verse. We ask that
18   everyone join with us to sing the final stanza. *(CHOIR and*
19   *congregation sing "Silent Night." CHOIR and SOLOIST sing*
20   *first three stanzas; CHOIR and congregation sing the fourth.*
21   *There are many wonderful descants available for CHOIR's use*
22   *over congregational singing.)*
23   If you were to study any collection of the world's most
24   famous carols, you would find very few that are indisputably
25   American in origin. Earlier I told you that it is believed that
26   "Away in a Manger" was created by the German Lutherans
27   in Pennsylvania.
28   The source of another popular carol that found its
29   beginning in the state of Pennsylvania has never been
30   challenged for either the words or the music. It is
31   unquestionably American. John H. Hopkins, Jr., whose life
32   spanned most of the nineteenth century, was born in
33   Pittsburgh, received his higher education at the University of
34   Vermont, and became the rector of Christ Church in
35   Williamsport, Pennsylvania. It was during his years at

1   Williamsport that he wrote both the words and melody to this

2   next carol. It is considered a masterpiece of its kind because

3   the tune has the quality of a folk song, and yet there are no

4   known folk songs that carry the same melodic line.

5   It is a song that adapts beautifully to simple dramatic

6   presentation. Perhaps it was written for use within a pageant

7   in the author's own church. There is no account of this, but we

8   would like to demonstrate how this carol might have been

9   staged. It is comprised of five stanzas and refrains. Three

10   soloists from our choir will portray the three wise men who

11   came to Bethlehem to pay homage to the newborn King.

12   Matthew 2:1-12 tells of their visit, but the Scripture does not

13   specify that there were three visitors from the Orient. The

14   number is assumed because of the three gifts of gold,

15   frankincense, and myrrh. Legend has given these wise men

16   names. They were Melchior, Caspar, and Balthazar. How the

17   tradition began that they were kings themselves is unknown.

18   It is said that they arrived at Bethlehem twelve days after

19   Jesus' birth to present their gifts. That is why gifts are

20   exchanged on Twelfth Night in many countries.

21   With the enchantment of the music that we shall now

22   present, we ask that you free your imagination to believe that

23   this is the twelfth night in Bethlehem, and the wise men are

24   standing beside the holy manger.

25   Our next carol is "We Three Kings of Orient Are." *(Three*

26   *soloists and CHOIR sing "We Three Kings of Orient Are." Stanza*

27   *1 — all WISEMEN, Stanza 2 — Melchior, Stanza 3 — Caspar,*

28   *Stanza 4 — Balthazar, Stanza 5 — all WISEMEN and CHOIR. The*

29   *CHOIR sings the refrain to each stanza.)*

30 KINGS: We three kings of Orient are,

31   Bearing gifts we traverse afar,

32   Field and fountain, moor and mountain,

33   Following yonder star.

34   O star of wonder, star of night,

35   Star with royal beauty bright,

1	Westward leading, still proceeding,
2	Guide us to thy perfect light.
3	MELCHIOR: Born a King on Bethlehem's plain,
4	Gold I bring to crown him again,
5	King forever, ceasing never
6	Over us all to reign.
7	CASPAR: Frankincense to offer have I;
8	Incense owns a Deity nigh,
9	Prayer and praising all men raising;
10	Worship him, God on high.
11	BALTHAZAR: Myrrh is mine: its bitter perfume
12	Breathes a life of gathering gloom:
13	Sorrowing, sighing, bleeding, dying,
14	Sealed in the stone-cold tomb.
15	ALL: Glorious now behold him arise,
16	King and God and sacrifice;
17	Alleluia, alleluia!
18	Sounds through the earth skies.
19	PASTOR/NARRATOR: There are stately carols, there are quiet
20	carols, and there are exuberant carols. Our next carol is of the
21	joyful type that celebrates, with a steady beat, the birth of
22	Christ who came to save us all.
23	The first words to this carol were written in a dialect of
24	Latin, later translated to German, and then into English by a
25	scholar of Cambridge University in England. His name was
26	John Mason Neale and he was the son of an evangelical
27	clergyman. He had a superb talent for beautiful translations.
28	"Good King Wenceslas" and "Art Thou Weary, Art Thou
29	Languid?" are other popular hymns that he gave to the
30	English language.
31	The melody to this next carol came from an unknown
32	source in Germany during the fourteenth century. Neale
33	wrote his translation in 1853 and the melody was harmonized
34	by Sir John Stainer in 1867.
35	Christian fellowship characterizes this carol. Through

1   Christ's birth it affirms a marvelous sense of worldwide unity
2   among men and women of our faith. Please join with us to
3   sing, "Good Christian Men, Rejoice." *(Congregation and*
4   *CHOIR alternately sing four stanzas and the refrain of "Good*
5   *Christian Men Rejoice.")*
6   I doubt that you could guess from the words and melody of our
7   next carol that it is another all-American composition. Though the
8   words were written by an American clergyman of some renown,
9   the music was written by a man whose name could easily have
10   been forever lost in the halls of clerical music.
11   The composer of the melody, Lewis Radner, was a successful
12   businessman dealing in real estate in Philadelphia. He was at
13   the same time the organist and Sunday school superintendent
14   at the Holy Trinity Church during the period that Phillips
15   Brooks presided as the pastor. The dynamic Pastor Brooks,
16   who later became a bishop of the Episcopal Church, was called
17   the "prince among preachers." Without advance notice, he
18   called a meeting with his church organist, Radner, and
19   requested that the part-time musician/businessman compose a
20   melody for some verses he had written. He had promised the
21   children of the church he would have a special song for their
22   Christmas program next week.
23   The request was presumptuous and typical of the proud and
24   mighty who expect others to do the impossible for them on short
25   notice. Lewis Radner took the words and said he would do his
26   best. A week passed and the melody was still unwritten. It was
27   Saturday and the music was needed the next day. Radner had
28   tried again and again, but nothing came to him. In despair he
29   retired for the evening. During the night he was awakened by an
30   "angel strain singing in his ears." (These were his own words.) He
31   quickly wrote out the musical phrases, as if in a dream, and went
32   back to sleep. On rising the next morning he reviewed his jottings
33   with considerable delight. It all worked so beautifully. He added
34   the harmony parts with magical ease. He felt that the tune had
35   been a gift from heaven.

1   Later, when the tune was to be titled, the humble Radner
2   suggested that it be called "Saint Phillips" in honor of the
3   inspired words of the Reverend Doctor Brooks. But the famous
4   clergyman responded generously saying that he thought,
5   instead, it should be called "Saint Louis" for Lewis Radner.
6   Neither title was used, but the words and melody were
7   printed on leaflets and sung by six teachers and thirty-six
8   Sunday school children. It was later published in *The Church*
9   *Porch* in 1874, but went unnoticed and was almost forgotten
10   until someone included it in the hymnal of the Episcopal
11   Church. Each year it became better known, and today it
12   ranks among the most popular carols of the English language.
13   Have you guessed the name of this all-American carol? It is
14   "O Little Town of Bethlehem," composed in 1868. Our choir
15   will now perform it for you. *(CHOIR sings three or four stanzas*
16   *of "O Little Town of Bethlehem.")*
17   We would be terribly remiss if we were not to include in
18   this program of church music at least one hymn or carol by
19   the most famous hymn-writer of all — Charles Wesley.
20   Authorities differ about whether it was he or Isaac Watts who
21   contributed the most to the world of hymns. Wesley published
22   some four thousand hymns and left two thousand more
23   unpublished in waiting manuscripts.
24   The hymn/carol of Wesley's that we have selected to
25   conclude our program was written in his early years, within a
26   year of his conversion. He was full of zeal, beginning a career
27   of hymn-writing after a trip to America in 1736. In the
28   colonies, he had been inspired by a group of Moravians that
29   sang their hymns so beautifully. Their dedication and
30   interpretation stirred him deeply. He knew then that he must
31   try to do as well in the service of the Lord, and you know the
32   rest of the story.
33   The original title of this next carol was "Hymn for
34   Christmas Day." It was included in the English *Book of*
35   *Common Prayer*. This was a distinction in itself, since the

Wesleys were in disfavor with the Anglican Church at the time of this publication.

In its later publications over the years, some of Wesley's original lines were revised. Two lines of the present first stanza were changed from:

Universal nature say

Christ the Lord is born today

To this more familiar verse:

With the angelic hosts proclaim

Christ is born in Bethlehem

Another change in the first stanza was:

Hark! How all the welkin rings

Glory to the King of Kings

Those original Wesley lines were changed, by George Whitefield or the Rev. Martin Madan, to:

Hark! the herald angels sing,

Glory to the newborn King.

These revised words had been in use for one hundred twenty years or more before the present music was selected the best musical setting.

The current melody was adapted in 1856 by Hayman Cummings from Mendelssohn's "Festgesang, No. 7, Lied 2." This Mendelssohn music had been composed to celebrate the anniversary of the discovery of printing. Mendelssohn himself had said, "It will never do to sacred words."

The Lord's work surprises the best of us, doesn't it? Let us now sing together this carol refined by so many great talents and the Holy Spirit — "Hark! the Herald Angels Sing."

(Congregation and CHOIR sing three stanzas of "Hark! the Herald Angels Sing." A descant with high soprano voices or trumpets would add an especially beautiful uplifting ending. PASTOR gives benediction and closing. As a bright note, the CHOIR may repeat "Here We Come A-Wassailing" as they exit through the congregation down the center aisle and the congregation leaves.)

The Story of "Silent Night"
by Michael C. Vigilant

A small cast play with music

Cast of Characters

Narrator
Franz Gruber
Joseph Mohr
Church Choir
Strasser Family

Production Notes

This Christmas play is easy to stage. Its short length means it may easily be incorporated into a worship service any time during the holiday season. The small cast is conducive to easy rehearsals. The actors playing Franz Gruber and Joseph Mohr should have strong singing voices. It is preferred that the person playing the part of Franz Gruber knows how to play guitar. If this isn't possible, a guitar-playing member of the congregation may accompany the singers. Guitar chords are included with the lyrics to "Silent Night" on page 219. The Strasser Family may be comprised of a sub-group from the choir (three to six persons) or by an actual family with singing ability from your congregation.

Time

Christmas Eve, 1818.

Setting

The opening scene takes place in Franz Gruber's music room at the church. The room is furnished with a desk Stage Right which has manuscript paper and a quill pen upon it. A guitar is set on a stand next to the desk in plain sight of the audience. In addition, a Christmas tree is located at Right Center, a coat rack is at Left Center, and a small table with two chairs on either side is at Center Stage. Extra touches should include some book shelves, at least one cross, and miscellaneous greenery or a wreath for decoration. A podium for the Narrator should be placed at an extreme side of the stage.

Costumes

Franz Gruber is dressed in 19th-century formal attire. Dark coat with tails, an ascot, ruffled shirt, and vest. Joseph Mohr is dressed in a monk's robe with a rope belt. Upon entering Franz Gruber's room, he wears a wide-brimmed hat and coat.

The Choir and Strasser Family are attired in choir robes. The Choir and Strasser Family, however, should wear different colored robes with the latter's being more elaborate (mult-colored and/or additional embroidery).

The Narrator need only be well-dressed by present-day standards.

ChristmasCarolMusic.org - free Christmas carol sheet music

Silent Night

words by Joseph Mohr
trans. John F.Young

tune by Franz Gruber, alt.

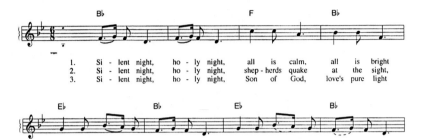

1. Si - lent night, ho - ly night, all is calm, all is bright
2. Si - lent night, ho - ly night, shep - herds quake at the sight,
3. Si - lent night, ho - ly night, Son of God, love's pure light

round yon vir - gin moth-er and child. Ho - ly in - fant so ten - der and mild,
glo - ries stream from heav-en a - far, heav'n-ly hosts sing al - le - lu - ia.
ra - diant beams from thy ho - ly face with the dawn of re - deem - ing grace,

sleep in heav - en - ly peace, sleep in heav - en - ly peace.
Christ the Sav - iour is born, Christ the Sav - iour is born!
Je - sus, Lord at thy birth, Je - sus, Lord at thy birth.

Bibliography

Fuld, James J. *The Book of World-Famous Music.* Crown Publishers, Inc., New York, 1966.

Blom, Eric (ed.). *Grove's Dictionary of Music and Musicians.* 5th ed., St. Martin's Press, New York, 1954.

Simon, William L. (ed.). *Reader's Digest Merry Christmas Song Book.* Reader's Digest Association, Pleasantville, NY, 1981.

1 NARRATOR: Every Christmas is special. But sometimes
2   something happens on a particular Christmas which makes it
3   stand out from the rest. One such Christmas occurred over a
4   century and a half ago in a small village in the Austrian Alps.
5   That's where circumstances inspired two friends — Franz
6   Gruber, a church organist and composer, and Joseph Mohr, a
7   priest and poet — to create one of the most beautiful carols
8   ever written. *(Lights rise on FRANZ GRUBER. He is pacing*
9   *anxiously as NARRATOR continues.)* The story of "Silent Night"
10   begins on Christmas Eve in the year 1818. Franz Gruber was
11   in a state of near despair because the church organ was
12   broken. With midnight services only hours away, he did not
13   know what to do.
14 FRANZ: *(Knock on door)* I can't believe it! *(Knock on door)* How
15   can this happen? *(Knock becomes louder.)* And on Christmas
16   Eve, no less. *(Knock becomes even louder.)* What a disaster!
17   *(Knock becomes a bang.)* Oh, come in!
18 JOSEPH: *(Enter JOSEPH MOHR. As he speaks, he hangs up his hat*
19   *and coat. His mood is very jovial.)* What a glorious day! The
20   snow is falling, children are laughing, feasts are cooking — I
21   *love* this time of year. *(Throwing his arms around FRANZ)*
22   Merry Christmas, Franz!
23 FRANZ: It might be Christmas, Joseph, but it's not so merry.
24 JOSEPH: My goodness, Franz. Why so glum? Wait a minute ...
25   Are you upset because you forgot to get me a present again
26   this year? You poor man. You must be absolutely guilt-ridden.
27   Well, don't worry, I forgive you. Just don't let it happen again.
28 FRANZ: I wish my problem was so simple.
29 JOSEPH: What could be worse than forgetting my present?
30 FRANZ: *(With great concern)* The church organ is broken.
31 JOSEPH: *(Taken aback)* What?! It can't be broken It's Christmas
32   Eve. You have music to play. The choir has carols to sing.
33 FRANZ: I know, I know.
34 JOSEPH: Well, maybe that organ just has a loose part or two. How
35   about I go out there and give it a whack with the ol' iron fist?

1   I'll put that organ in line. *(Heading for the door)* **Breakdown**
2   on Christmas Eve — how inconsiderate.
3   FRANZ: Joseph, don't touch that organ! I've already called the
4   repairman.
5   JOSEPH: Great. When will he get here?
6   FRANZ: Unfortunately, not until sometime after Christmas.
7   JOSEPH: After Christmas! What good will that do?
8   FRANZ: Not much, I'm afraid.
9   JOSEPH: *(Raising fist)* Are you sure you don't want me to use my
10   iron fist?
11   FRANZ: Put that hand away. You might hurt yourself.
12   JOSEPH: *(Putting hand in pocket)* Just trying to help.
13   FRANZ: *(After a short pause)* Well, we can't just sit here. Let's do
14   something.
15   JOSEPH: You're right. Let me see ... *(Thinking for a moment)* Ah-
16   ha! Let's pray. Let's pray for — a *miracle.*
17   FRANZ: *(Unconvinced)* A miracle? Great idea. Why didn't I think
18   of that?
19   JOSEPH: Because I'm a priest and you're not, my friend. Now
20   let's get to it. *(FRANZ and JOSEPH begin to pray, silently.*
21   *Suddenly)* I've got it!
22   FRANZ: What?
23   JOSEPH: *(Moving over to his coat)* Your Christmas present!
24   FRANZ: *(Puzzled)* My Christmas present? Joseph, it would be a
25   miracle if I remembered to get you a Christmas present — not
26   vice versa. Besides, this is no time —
27   JOSEPH: It's a poem — a gift from me to you.
28   FRANZ: *(Touched but confused)* Why, thank you, Joseph. You know
29   I love your poems and I appreciate the thought ... But don't
30   you think we have other pressing concerns right now?
31   JOSEPH: Go ahead and read it.
32   FRANZ: But —
33   JOSEPH: Please?
34   FRANZ: All right, my friend. *(FRANZ begins to read, silently. A look*
35   *of great concentration overtakes his face. While he reads,*

1   *JOSEPH paces like an expectant father as he waits for a*
2   *reaction.)*
3   **JOSEPH:** *(Circling FRANZ, nervously)* **I hope you like it. I honestly**
4   **think it's the nicest piece I've ever written. But, of course,**
5   **that's not up to me to decide.** *(Losing confidence)* **Well, maybe**
6   **it's not the best thing I've ever written. Maybe it's the second**
7   **or third ... You know, I should probably flip-flop the second**
8   **and third stanzas. But I'll wait and see what you think.**
9   *(Becoming upset)* **I really think this thing needs some major**
10   **repair work.** *(Exasperatedly)* **You hate it, don't you?**
11   **FRANZ: Joseph?**
12   **JOSEPH:** *(Anxiously)* **Yes?**
13   **FRANZ: This is absolutely** — *(Searching for the right word)* —
14   **glorious.**
15   **JOSEPH: Glorious? Glorious!** *(Thrilled)* **He thinks it's** *glorious!*
16   **FRANZ: You've truly outdone yourself, my friend. Thank you. It's**
17   **a beautiful gift. But how can I possibly reciprocate?**
18   **JOSEPH:** *(Inspired)* **Put music to it.**
19   **FRANZ: Put music to it. I can do that. As soon as the organ is fixed,**
20   **I'll** —
21   **JOSEPH: Put music to it today — so it can be sung tonight.**
22   **FRANZ:** *(Searching for an excuse)* **But how? The organ** —
23   **JOSEPH: Use your guitar.**
24   **FRANZ: Joseph, I don't know. There's so little time.**
25   **JOSEPH: Start now.**
26   **FRANZ: I — I —**
27   **JOSEPH: Franz, let's turn this into our gift to Jesus.**
28   **FRANZ: I don't know** —
29   **JOSEPH: Listen, if the little drummer boy could do it** —
30   **FRANZ:** *(Picking up his guitar and taking up the challenge)* **Little**
31   **drummer boy, huh? You know, I think I feel a melody coming on.**
32   **NARRATOR: Franz and Joseph spent the rest of the afternoon**
33   **composing, rewriting, and anguishing until finally — their**
34   **song was complete.** *(Music begins.)* **That evening, it was**
35   **debuted by the creators themselves, accompanied by a guitar**

1   and church choir.

2   FRANZ: Silent night,

3   Holy night,

4   All is calm,

5   All is bright.

6   JOSEPH: Round yon virgin

7   Mother and child.

8   Holy infant

9   So tender and mild,

10   FRANZ and JOSEPH: Sleep in heavenly peace,

11   Sleep in heavenly peace.

12   NARRATOR: *(As instrumental continues in background with CHOIR*

13   *humming softly)* "Silent Night" was received with great

14   adulation. And it no doubt would have remained a part of the

15   tiny parish of Oberndorf's Christmas pageant for years to

16   come. But this song had a greater destiny. Remember that

17   organ repairman? Well, he came a few days later, heard this

18   new carol, and was so impressed that he proceeded to share it

19   with every church organist on his route. Eventually, the song

20   fell into the hands of The Strasser Family, one of the day's

21   best-known singing troupes. It would be through their voices

22   that Gruber and Mohr's little miracle of a song would become

23   one of the most beloved in the Christian world.

24   THE STRASSER FAMILY: *(With JOSEPH and FRANZ)*

25   Silent night,

26   Holy night,

27   Shepherds quake

28   At the sight!

29   Glories stream

30   From heaven afar,

31   Heavenly hosts

32   Sing alleluia

33   Christ the Savior is born!

34   Christ the Savior is born!

35   Silent night,

1	**Holy night,**
2	**Son of God,**
3	**Love's pure light**
4	**Radiant beams**
5	**From thy holy face,**
6	**With the dawn**
7	**Of redeeming grace,**
8	**Jesus, Lord at thy birth.**
9	**Jesus, Lord at thy birth.**
10	*(FRANZ, JOSEPH, and STRASSER FAMILY encourage audience*
11	*to participate in reprise of first verse. CHOIR also sings. Big*
12	*finish!)*
13	**Silent night,**
14	**Holy night,**
15	**All is calm,**
16	**All is bright,**
17	**Round yon virgin**
18	**Mother and child.**
19	**Holy infant**
20	**So tender and mild,**
21	**Sleep in heavenly peace,**
22	**Sleep in heavenly peace.**

Plays and Programs
for Teens and Adults

Heavenly Committee Plans Christmas
By Kenneth L. Gibble

Cast of Characters

Ariel — A soft-spoken angel who just returned from an earthly assignment.
Fred — Friendly, enthusiastic fellow.
Betty Sue — Energetic and loves to write music.
J.D. — A firm, feminist type, not unfriendly.
Nick — An insensitive, brash, dominating type.

Production Notes

"Heavenly Committee Plans Christmas" was originally staged as a chancel drama. No curtain is needed.

The play takes place in a committee room in heaven. The only essential set pieces are a large table that will seat the entire cast around it and five chairs. Props will add a touch of authenticity: pictures on the wall, notebooks, paper, pencil, a gavel for J.D., etc. You can let your imagination dictate what a committee room in heaven would contain.

Costuming should be appropriate to the characters. Ariel, naturally, should be dressed in white — shirt, slacks, and shoes. Nick might be wearing whatever "macho" clothing is in style, e.g., tight pants, shirt with top buttons unbuttoned, etc. Betty Sue should wear clothing which reflects her image of herself as an artistic person. J.D. could wear a business suit or some other professional, no-nonsense style of clothing. Fred should be dressed neatly but casually.

A fairly fast pace seems best for this play, except when Ariel is raising his questions and trying to interpret what Christmas ought to be. Have fun with the interchange between Betty Sue and Nick. Towards the end of the play, it's a good idea to have Betty Sue doing some mild flirting with Ariel. Special attention must be given to the character of J.D. She must run the meetings with a take-charge attitude; the other characters treat her with the proper amount of respect.

Above all, let the characters enjoy each other. If they do, so will the audience.

1 **Scene 1**
2
3 *At Rise: FRED is standing, looking out a window. ARIEL enters,*
4 *dressed in white.*
5 **ARIEL: Ahem. Ah, excuse me, but ...**
6 **FRED: Yes?**
7 **ARIEL: Uh, I must have gotten lost. I'm looking for the meeting of**
8 **the Planning Committee ... ?**
9 **FRED: No mistake. The rest will be along soon.**
10 **ARIEL: You ... you mean, you are on ... I mean, this is the room**
11 **where the Planning Committee meets?**
12 **FRED: Yes.**
13 **ARIEL: Oh.**
14 **FRED: You seem a little disappointed.**
15 **ARIEL: No, no. No. Not disappointed, just a little** *(Laughs*
16 *nervously)* **... well, surprised, I guess. But then, it's been so**
17 **long ...**
18 **FRED: I'm sorry; I should have introduced myself. I'm Fred.**
19 *(They shake hands.)* **And you ... ?**
20 **ARIEL:** *(Stares at him.)* **Fred.** *(Pause)* **Hello ... Fred. Uh ... My**
21 **name is Ariel.**
22 **FRED: Ariel. How quaint. I'm curious. You were saying, "It's been**
23 **so long."**
24 **ARIEL: Yes. Well, you see, for a long time — a long, long time —**
25 **I've been out on assignment — on earth, that is. And ...**
26 **well ... It's been a very long time since I've been back, and ...**
27 **there have been a lot of changes, haven't there?**
28 **FRED: Maybe so. Although to an angel like myself who has been**
29 **here all along, the changes have been so gradual, I've hardly**
30 **noticed them.**
31 **ARIEL: You are an angel, then?**
32 **FRED:** *(Slightly miffed)* **Well, certainly! What made you think**
33 **otherwise?**
34 **ARIEL: Oh, nothing, nothing. I guess I'm still used to white robes**
35 **and all that.**

1   FRED: Oh, the white robes went out ages ago, about the same time
2   halos became old-fashioned.
3   ARIEL: I see.
4   FRED: But, tell me, have you been assigned to the Christmas
5   Planning committee?
6   ARIEL: Yes. In fact, I think maybe that's one of the reasons I was
7   recalled. Although I can't imagine why the Almighty wanted
8   me. You heavenly angels have so much more experience in
9   these things.
10   FRED: Well, yes, we have all served on committees before. But
11   never anything as big as this. Imagine, it's up to us to make
12   arrangements for the birth of the Christ child.
13   ARIEL: Who else is on the committee?
14   FRED: Well, J.D. chairs the committee. Then there's Nick and
15   Betty Sue.
16   ARIEL: Betty Sue? You mean there are women angels now?
17   FRED: Boy, you have been gone a long time. Things have really
18   changed up here since the women's angel movement got
19   started.
20   ARIEL: I'll bet they have. *(Noises outside)*
21   FRED: Sounds like the rest are here now. *(J.D., NICK, and BETTY*
22   *SUE enter.)*
23   BETTY SUE: Oh, what a gorgeous day it is. It reminds me of the
24   poem I wrote last week: "When bright the brilliance of the
25   sky, when ..."
26   J.D.: Yes, well, it's time to get started. We've got a lot of work to do.
27   *(To ARIEL)* You're the new one, right? I'm J.D., chairperson of
28   this committee. You've met Fred, I see. That's Nick and that's
29   Betty Sue.
30   BETTY SUE: *(To ARIEL)* What's your name?
31   ARIEL: Ariel.
32   NICK: Ariel? What kind of sissy name is that?
33   J.D.: Don't mind Nick. He talks that way to everybody.
34   NICK: *(To J.D.)* I beg your pardon; I was asking a perfectly
35   reasonable —

1   **J.D.:** Yes, yes. OK, this meeting will come to order. As you know,
2   I've been appointed to be in charge of this committee's work.
3   Headquarters is expecting a preliminary report from us ...
4   **FRED:** *(Raises hand.)* **Uh, J.D.?**
5   **J.D.:** The chair recognizes Fred. Yeah, Fred?
6   **FRED:** Shouldn't we appoint a secretary?
7   **J.D.:** Good idea, Fred. All right, who wants to be secretary?
8   **NICK:** I nominate Betty Sue. It's a woman's job, and she's the only
9   woman. Uh ... except you, of course, J.D., but ... but you
10   couldn't be ...
11   **J.D.:** So, it's a woman's job, is it? Well, Nick, I nominate you to be
12   secretary. All in favor say "Aye."
13   **BETTY SUE:** Aye.
14   **J.D.:** *(Very rapidly)* **All opposed, like sign, the "Ayes" have it.**
15   *(Sweetly)* **Need some paper, Nick?** *(FRED passes paper and a*
16   *pen to NICK.)* **All right, let's get started. Now, we know that**
17   Headquarters wants the birth to take place in Palestine. And
18   the child must have Jewish parents. As long as we operate
19   within those guidelines, we can suggest whatever we think
20   best. Any ideas?
21   **NICK:** Why must Palestine be the place? Why not Rome? The only
22   logical place for the Savior of the world to be born is in the
23   capital city of the Roman Empire. Or, if not there, then at
24   least Athens, for heaven's sake.
25   **BETTY SUE:** Athens! Of course! The home of music and art and
26   drama. Think what a grand, artistic occasion could be made
27   of Christmas. There could be a contest to find the poet who
28   could write the most exquisite verse in honor of the Child.
29   Musicians could create lovely choruses to be sung.
30   **FRED:** But the point is, the child isn't going to be born in either
31   Rome or Athens. Let's be practical. We've got to decide on a
32   place in Palestine.
33   **NICK:** There is no important place in Palestine. It's a wretched
34   country from top to bottom.
35   **ARIEL:** There's always Jerusalem.

1   J.D.: What's Jerusalem?

2   ARIEL: The capital city of Palestine. Where King Herod has his

3   palace.

4   NICK: Did you say palace?

5   ARIEL: Yes.

6   NICK: Well, that's a start, anyway.

7   BETTY SUE: What about art? Are there beautiful paintings and

8   statuary in this place?

9   ARIEL: I should think so.

10   NICK: And the king — you say his name is Herod. Is he an

11   important king?

12   ARIEL: Important? Oh, yes. He's also a bloodthirsty brute.

13   J.D.: Doesn't sound like a very good father for the Prince of Peace.

14   NICK: But look, the child has to have royalty for parents. Isn't it

15   part of the plan for him to be a descendant of King David?

16   ARIEL: Yes, I believe so.

17   NICK: It's settled then. Herod will be the father. But ... what about

18   the mother?

19   J.D.: The queen, naturally.

20   ARIEL: A bit of a problem there.

21   FRED: Oh?

22   ARIEL: Herod has had quite a few wives. He's even had a few of

23   them murdered when they displeased him.

24   BETTY SUE: Oh, dear.

25   ARIEL: It's anybody's guess who is queen right now.

26   NICK: OK. Whoever the queen is, she'll be the mother.

27   FRED: Just a minute. You're all forgetting something. Timing is of

28   the utmost importance. After all, we want the whole world to

29   know about this birth the moment it happens. Now Palestine

30   is a terribly remote part of the world. But if that's what we've

31   got to work with, we'll have to make the best of it. At least

32   Jerusalem is a capital city, so we will be able to arrange for

33   important people to be on hand. Naturally, we'll want to have

34   messengers ready to spread the word back to Rome, to

35   Greece, to Egypt, to India ...

1 J.D.: Good thinking, Fred. What else can we do to publicize
2   Christmas?
3 BETTY SUE: How about a fireworks display?
4 J.D.: What?
5 BETTY SUE: You know, meteors, shooting stars, maybe an eclipse
6   in there somewhere. That way, everyone in the world will
7   know some momentous event is about to take place. And
8   shooting stars are so romantic. It reminds me of a song I once
9   wrote: *(Sings)* "When you wish upon a star ..."
10 J.D.: OK, shooting stars. What other details can we arrange?
11 NICK: Well, the birth itself ought to take place in the palace, in the
12   royal bedchamber. As soon as the child is born, he can be
13   wrapped in silk and ermine and carried out to the head of the
14   giant winding staircase. *(To ARIEL)* Does the palace have a
15   staircase?
16 ARIEL: I don't know.
17 NICK: It must. All palaces have winding staircases. So the King
18   will carry his son out to the top of the staircase, and —
19 BETTY SUE: And then the trumpets will sound a fanfare and a
20   choir, made up of the best singers and brought all the way
21   from Athens, will sing an anthem.
22 NICK: Then an address from Caesar Augustus. A sort of
23   welcoming speech. And then he can proclaim a festival — a
24   real celebration with parties and dancing and all the rest. Of
25   course, Caesar will bring expensive gifts to honor the new
26   King.
27 FRED: Good idea. And each year after that, Christmas will be a
28   big extravaganza in celebration of the Child's birth. We can
29   have a tradition of everyone buying lots of gifts and having a
30   wonderful time!
31 BETTY SUE: And there can be lovely decorations. Lots of reds
32   and greens. They're my favorite colors, you know.
33 J.D.: Well, we've had a lot of good ideas. Let's see. The Child will
34   be born in Jerusalem, in the King's palace, lots of celebrities
35   there, music, dancing, a proclamation by Caesar ... Sounds

1   good to me. You getting all this down, Nick?

2 NICK: *(Writing furiously)* Right, J.D.

3 ARIEL: *(Hesitatingly)* I don't know.

4 J.D.: What do you mean?

5 ARIEL: I'm not so sure the people on earth need this kind of
6   Christmas. Maybe we ought to think this through a little
7   more.

8 BETTY SUE: I know what you mean. I don't think we've given
9   enough attention to the artistic side of things.

10 NICK: Aw, I'm sick and tired of all your talk about art. I don't
11   think you know an ode from a sonnet. And if you start singing
12   one more of your drippy songs, I'll scream.

13 BETTY SUE: How dare you? Just because you've read a few books
14   on political science, you think you're some kind of expert.
15   Well, let me tell you —

16 J.D.: Quiet, you two. I'm interested in what our new friend here is
17   driving at.

18 ARIEL: Well, I can see why you all are thinking in terms of a
19   spectacular approach. After all, this is the Savior of all men
20   who will be born.

21 J.D.: All persons.

22 ARIEL: Right. Everybody. So it is something to get excited about.

23 NICK: So what's the problem?

24 ARIEL: Somehow I don't think the Almighty will approve.

25 ALL: *(In unison)* Not approve? Come on! What do you mean?

26 J.D.: Quiet! *(To ARIEL)* Look, you're entitled to your opinion, but
27   we are the ones with the experience in these matters. *(To*
28   *GROUP)* OK, do I hear a motion for adjournment?

29 FRED: So moved.

30 J.D.: Meeting adjourned. We meet tomorrow at the same time
31   when I'll have a report for you from Headquarters. *(Exit J.D.*
32   *and NICK and BETTY SUE, still arguing.)*

33 FRED: Well, what did you think?

34 ARIEL: A very interesting collection of angels. Tell me, what does
35   the J.D. in J.D.'s name stand for?

1 FRED: No one knows. And, by the way, don't ever ask her. *(They*
2   *exit.)*
3
4   **Scene 2**
5
6   *At Rise: J.D. enters first. Sits down wearily at the table. FRED*
7   *enters.*
8 FRED: Good morning, J.D. *(No response)* Uh-oh. *(NICK and BETTY*
9   *SUE enter, still arguing.)*
10 NICK: I don't care what you say. I'd a thousand times rather
11   watch a chariot race in the Coliseum than sit through a poetry
12   reading.
13 FRED: Don't you two ever get tired of arguing? *(ARIEL enters.)*
14 ARIEL: Good morning, everyone. *(Everyone greets him except J.D.)*
15 FRED: Uh, J.D., isn't it time to start the meeting?
16 J.D.: *(Comes out of her daze.)* Oh yes, of course. *(Without enthusiasm)*
17   The meeting will come to order. *(Pause)*
18 NICK: Well?
19 J.D.: To get right to the point, Headquarters rejected every one of
20   our proposals.
21 BETTY SUE and FRED: *(Ad lib together.)* What? What do you
22   mean? Are you serious?
23 NICK: But why?
24 J.D.: The only explanation given was that we were on the wrong
25   track.
26 BETTY SUE: But what does that mean?
27 FRED: Maybe it means we should have listened to Ariel.
28 NICK: That's right. *(To ARIEL)* You said we were going about
29   things the wrong way, didn't you?
30 ARIEL: Let's just say I had some questions about our approach.
31 J.D.: What do you suggest we do?
32 ARIEL: I don't have the answers. But why don't I describe the
33   way things are on earth these days? Maybe once you
34   understand what people's needs are, you'll be able to plan for
35   the kind of Christmas the Almighty prefers.

1   FRED: Sounds good to me.

2   OTHERS: Me, too. Sure. Tell us.

3   ARIEL: OK. To begin with, there is a lot of unrest in the world. In

4   Palestine, for example, the Jewish people are oppressed by

5   their rulers. King Herod is a tyrant, although he keeps his

6   throne only because he is friendly with Augustus Caesar. The

7   Roman legions are conspicuous throughout Palestine, and

8   they don't tolerate any funny business. All the Jews hate

9   Herod because he has sold out to Rome and has desecrated his

10   faith. Herod is also politically corrupt and personally

11   immoral.

12   FRED: Well, that explains why the Messiah simply couldn't be

13   Herod's son.

14   NICK: But who else is of royal blood in Palestine? Someone rich

15   and famous and powerful?

16   ARIEL: Nick, I think the world has seen enough of wealth and

17   power. Rulers appear and become heroes for a time, but

18   inevitably their power makes them cruel and fearful. No king

19   or general will ever save the world.

20   J.D.: What kind of Savior does the world need?

21   ARIEL: The world needs someone who can heal. There is so much

22   pain and fear and loneliness on earth. People are selfish.

23   Instead of caring for each other, they grab everything they can

24   for themselves. And so the world is filled with anger and

25   bitterness, even fighting and killing.

26   BETTY SUE: I had no idea the world was such an ... ugly place.

27   ARIEL: Oh, but it's not ugly. Not really. And neither are the men

28   and women who live there. If only they could see what they are

29   doing to themselves — how their self-centeredness makes

30   everything go bad when life could be beautiful, just the way

31   the Almighty planned it.

32   BETTY SUE: Do art and music teach them about beauty?

33   ARIEL: Oh yes, it helps a great deal. But it's not enough. There's

34   got to be someone who can show the way, who can live out in

35   his own life the kind of love and integrity and truth that came

1   from the Almighty himself.

2   J.D.: And that's what the Child will do, won't he?

3   ARIEL: I think so.

4   NICK: So what you're saying is that we shouldn't try to make
5   Christmas such a big celebration.

6   ARIEL: It will be a joyous event, but if the Child is born in a
7   palace or even in Jerusalem, everyone will expect him to be
8   famous and powerful.

9   FRED: So the Child should come from simple, humble parents.

10   J.D.: From a family that nobody would expect a Messiah to come
11   from.

12   NICK: *(Enthusiasm begins to catch everyone.)* Maybe the father
13   could be a farmer, or a fisherman, or a carpenter.

14   J.D.: Carpenter. I like that.

15   FRED: And the Child could be born in just an ordinary house.

16   NICK: I've got it. If the Child comes from the lineage of David,
17   why not have him born in David's home village, Bethlehem?

18   J.D.: Great idea, Nick! But how will we get the parents to
19   Bethlehem?

20   ARIEL: Augustus is planning a new tax that will require everyone
21   to return to his home village to register.

22   BETTY SUE: That's perfect! It's all beginning to fit together!

23   FRED: The Child can be born in the village inn. At least that way,
24   the village people will know about the Child's birth.

25   ARIEL: Just so the inn isn't too crowded.

26   J.D.: We'll have to arrange for it not to be. Nick, are you getting all
27   this down?

28   NICK: *(Writing)* Yeah, yeah. I'm getting it … I think.

29   BETTY SUE: *(Wistfully)* I still wish we could have a Greek chorus
30   do an anthem.

31   ARIEL: How about an angel choir?

32   J.D.: *(Incredulously)* What? You're the one who said Christmas
33   shouldn't be a big show. Now you want a choir of angels.

34   BETTY SUE: Oh, please, J.D. It's a wonderful idea!

35   ARIEL: But this choir would only be seen by a few people —

1   maybe some travelers on the road, or something like that.
2   Betty Sue, wouldn't you like to write an appropriate anthem?
3   BETTY SUE: Oh, Ariel, would I ever!
4   NICK: *(To ARIEL)* You're making a big mistake.
5   ARIEL: In fact, maybe I'll try out for the choir myself. I used to do
6   quite a bit of singing up here ages ago.
7   FRED: I guess the big fireworks display is out.
8   BETTY SUE: Oh, no.
9   J.D.: Ariel, how do you think the Almighty would feel if we had just
10   one meteor or maybe a very bright star for the occasion?
11   ARIEL: *(Smiling)* I'd say it would be worth a try.
12   BETTY SUE: That would be lovely.
13   NICK: Of course, Caesar won't be able to be present. What about
14   King Herod?
15   ARIEL: If I know Herod, he's not going to find the birth of the
16   Christ child an event to celebrate. He might even be upset
17   about the whole thing. Anyway, we don't want his kind on
18   hand for this holy occasion.
19   FRED: What about the idea of gifts? The Child will be the
20   Almighty's best gift to the world. Wouldn't it be fitting to
21   symbolize that in some way?
22   BETTY SUE: I love symbolic things.
23   ARIEL: Well, there is a Scripture reference to foreigners bringing
24   rare gifts in homage to a king, son of the Almighty.
25   J.D.: Why not have some foreign dignitaries bring gifts? Nick, you
26   are the expert on these things. I'm assigning you to take care
27   of this — just make sure there aren't any Romans involved in
28   it. By the way, it wouldn't hurt to have a few of these
29   dignitaries be women. No reason they all have to be men. Got
30   that, Nick?
31   NICK: I ... uh ... I'll do my best, J.D. My very best.
32   BETTY SUE: I'm so excited. This is going to be a beautiful
33   Christmas.
34   FRED: Do you really think Headquarters will approve these plans,
35   Ariel? Some of our ideas seem pretty far-out to me.

1   ARIEL: Well, I can't be sure, but I have a good feeling about what
2   we've come up with.
3   BETTY SUE: Are we done? I'm anxious to get started on my
4   anthem. How about something like this: "God rest ye merry,
5   gentlemen ..."
6   FRED: Watch the sexist language, Betty Sue!
7   NICK: Must I listen to this?
8   J.D.: No. Meeting adjourned. *(Exit NICK. Exit BETTY SUE, singing*
9   *"Glory to God ... Peace on earth, good will to ... persons.")*
10 FRED: Thanks for everything, Ariel. You really got us on the right
11   track.
12 J.D.: You're right, Fred. Ariel, I'd like to hear more about your
13   duty on earth. And maybe I can bring you up to date on
14   what's been happening up here. *(They begin moving toward*
15   *exit.)*
16 ARIEL: Great.
17 J.D.: Anything you'd like to ask about especially?
18 ARIEL: Well, I was curious about one thing.
19 J.D.: Yes?
20 ARIEL: *(As they exit)* Well, J.D. is a kind of unusual name for a
21   female ... and ...
22 FRED: Uh-oh. I warned him about that. Ariel, oh Ariel. *(Exit*
23   *FRED.)*

Jesus Lives!
(If We Give Him Half a Chance)
By Douglas Grudzina

*To the Setauket United Methodist Church School,
who first believed and encouraged.*

Cast of Characters

Businessman
Housewife
Boy
Angel
Girl
Mary
Joseph
Innkeeper
Sunday School Teacher
Three Shepherds
Three Wise Men
Choir

Production Notes
Characters

10 males, 5 females, choir.

Playing time

30-35 minutes with music.

Costumes

Lower level characters wear modern clothes. Housewife has hair in curlers, boy wears overalls, etc. Upper level characters wear traditional Christmas pageant costumes.

Props

Christmas tree, gift box, wrapping paper, tape, ribbon, etc., Christmas tree ornaments, two metal folding chairs, three shepherds' staffs, play money, Wise Men gifts.

Setting

Typical church chancel area. On the upper level is a rude frame which could suggest the stable of Bethlehem. The lower level is bare.

Music

All songs are traditional songs which can be found in most hymnals and many song books. The choir should sing the hymn versions, preferably in four parts.

1 **Scene 1**
2 *The stage is empty. Lower level, Stage Left is the Christmas tree,*
3 *lying unassembled on the floor. Lower level, Center, is the box*
4 *with wrapping paper, tape, ribbons, etc. While a medley of*
5 *traditional Christmas carols is either played or sung, the*
6 *BUSINESSMAN enters from the left and assembles the tree, with*
7 *great difficulty, and exits. The HOUSEWIFE enters from the left*
8 *with a box of Christmas tree ornaments. She puts a few token*
9 *decorations on the tree and exits. The BOY enters from the right*
10 *and attempts to wrap the gift. The result is a mess, but he appears*
11 *quite proud of it. He places it under the tree and exits. The ANGEL*
12 *enters on the upper level.*
13 **CHOIR:** *(Singing)* **Angels we have heard on high,**
14 **sweetly singing o'er the plains.**
15 **And the mountains in reply,**
16 **echoing their joyous strains.**
17 **Gloria in excelsis deo.**
18 **Gloria in excelsis deo.**
19 **ANGEL: For God so loved the world that he gave his only begotten**
20 **son —** *(BUSINESSMAN enters on the lower level.)*
21 **BUSINESSMAN: Of course we celebrate Christmas. We put up a**
22 **tree, we give gifts, and we usually put up lights outside.**
23 **ANGEL: ... that whoever believes in him should not perish, but**
24 **have —** *(HOUSEWIFE enters on the lower level.)*
25 **HOUSEWIFE: I used to love Christmas when I was a child. The**
26 **whole house would be filled with the smell of cookies baking**
27 **in the oven, Father would go out and cut down a tree from our**
28 **very own backyard, and my brother and I would string**
29 **popcorn. It was plain and simple then, but an awful lot of fun.**
30 **Christmas is too commercial nowadays.**
31 **ANGEL: ... everlasting life. For God didn't send his son into the**
32 **world to condemn the world —** *(BOY and GIRL enter on the*
33 *lower level.)*
34 **BOY: I'll tell you, last year I asked for a BB gun, and do you know**
35 **what I got?**

1   GIRL: What?
2   BOY: A lecture about violence. I didn't ask for a lecture, I asked
3   for a gun.
4   GIRL: That's too bad. I got everything I wanted.
5   BOY: Well, If I don't get what I want this year, I'm going to run
6   away from home.
7   GIRL: What do you want?
8   BOY: A motorbike.
9   ANGEL: ... but that the world through him could be saved.
10 HOUSEWIFE: I like to go to church on Christmas Eve. I used to
11   go when I was younger, but now I just don't have enough
12   time. What with all the running around trying to find Uncle
13   Joe a tie he'll like and Aunt Mae a sweater that won't make
14   her itch, I'm exhausted. There's just too much going on.
15 *(MARY and JOSEPH enter on the upper level.)*
16 MARY: Won't we come to an inn soon? I'm so tired.
17 JOSEPH: Everybody and his brother is in Bethlehem. It must be
18   the census.
19 MARY: But surely someplace in this city there must be a room for
20   two tired bodies.
21 JOSEPH: I'm sure we'll find a place soon. I'm positive.
22 ANGEL: Caesar Augustus had sent out a decree that the whole
23   world should be taxed. All of the Hebrews had to travel to
24   their ancestral city to pay these taxes. Joseph, a son of the
25   house of David, had to travel with his wife, Mary, who was
26   going to have a baby soon, to the city of Bethlehem.
27 CHOIR: *(Singing)* O little town of Bethlehem,
28   How still we see thee lie.
29   Above thy deep and dreamless sleep,
30   The silent stars go by.
31   Yet in thy dark streets shineth
32   The everlasting light.
33   The hopes and fears of all the years
34   Are met in thee tonight.
35 BUSINESSMAN: *(To HOUSEWIFE)* I'm sorry, dear, but I've got to

1 work late tonight.
2 HOUSEWIFE: Again? This is the third time this week.
3 BUSINESSMAN: I know. It's the Christmas rush. *(To audience)*
4 We're always extra busy around Christmas. All of the stores
5 are selling toys like crazy and, of course, we have to supply
6 them. *(He laughs.)* You wouldn't believe what people will
7 spend their money on. This year we've designed a doll that
8 rocks its cradle, wets, cries, and throws its food on the floor.
9 *(Shrugs.)* Oh, well, people are buying them.
10 JOSEPH: I think I see an inn ahead.
11 MARY: I hope so. I don't think I can go any farther. *(INNKEEPER*
12 *enters.)*
13 INNKEEPER: You might as well go back where you came from. I
14 don't have a single room left.
15 JOSEPH: But —
16 INNKEEPER: I hate to do this, but I just can't squeeze anyone else
17 in.
18 JOSEPH: Sir, my wife is about to have a baby. Isn't there any place
19 you can put us? A cellar? A corner? A stable?
20 INNKEEPER: A stable? Are you serious?
21 JOSEPH: Yes, we're serious. We'd be grateful for any place that
22 will shelter us from the night.
23 INNKEEPER: Well, I do have a stable. I guess it's clean as far as
24 stables go. If you really don't mind ...
25 ANGEL: And so Joseph and his wife, Mary, stayed in a stable, for
26 there was no room for them in the inn.
27 BUSINESSMAN: I realize that I don't spend nearly enough time at
28 home with my kids, but what am I supposed to do? I work a
29 forty-hour week, have the Elks on Wednesday, golf on
30 Saturday, and I like to sleep late on Sunday. The kids are
31 always running around here and there. It's just impossible to
32 stop everything. But at Christmas, I make it all up to them.
33 One night on my way home from work, I stop to buy their
34 gifts. I buy whatever they want. Money is no object. It's the
35 least I can do for them.

1   HOUSEWIFE: Last year I thought the kids were a little ridiculous
2   with their Christmas lists. When I was a child, I was happy
3   with just a rag doll, but that was all there was. Now my
4   daughter wants a doll that rocks its cradle, wets, cries, and
5   throws its food on the floor. *(MARY, JOSEPH, and the*
6   *INNKEEPER approach the stable.)*
7   INNKEEPER: Well, here it is. It's not the most comfortable place
8   in the world, but at least it will give you a chance to rest.
9   MARY: We can't thank you enough. We'll remember you forever
10   for your kindness. *(SUNDAY SCHOOL TEACHER enters on the*
11   *lower level, bringing two folding chairs which the BOY and GIRL*
12   *set up and sit in. We are now in a Sunday school classroom.)*
13 TEACHER: What is Christmas?
14 GIRL: Oh, I know, I know.
15 BOY: Let me answer, please.
16 GIRL: I had my hand up first. I get to answer.
17 TEACHER: All right, Laurie, you may answer.
18 BOY: That's not fair.
19 GIRL: I had my hand up first. Christmas is the birthday of Jesus.
20 TEACHER: Very good. Why was Jesus born? You may answer
21   this, John.
22 BOY: I don't know this answer. You should have asked me the easy
23   one.
24 GIRL: I know, I know.
25 BOY: Some people, I won't mention names or anything, but some
26   people think they're smart.
27 TEACHER: You're not being Christian, John. Now I want you to
28   apologize to Laurie.
29 BOY: I'm sorry.
30 TEACHER: That's good. We must remember, especially at
31   Christmas, to be kind to one another. Now, Laurie, what's the
32   answer?
33 GIRL: I forgot the question.
34 TEACHER: I asked why Jesus was born.
35 GIRL: Oh, that's easy. Jesus was born so they could write the Bible

1   about him.

2   BOY: What a stupid answer. I could even come up with a better one

3   than that.

4   GIRL: Oh, yeah? What answer do you think is right?

5   TEACHER: Yes, John, what do you think?

6   BOY: Jesus was born because God loved us and he was sad to see

7   that we were being sinful.

8   GIRL: Oh, you silly thing. That's the story of Noah's Ark. That's a

9   whole different thing. You really are dumb.

10   CHOIR: *(Singing)* God rest ye, merry gentlemen, let nothing you

11   dismay.

12   Remember Christ our Savior was born on Christmas day,

13   To save us all from Satan's power when we were gone astray.

14   O tidings of comfort and joy ... *(HOUSEWIFE re-enters. The*

15   *SUNDAY SCHOOL TEACHER exits, taking the chairs with her.)*

16   GIRL: Oh, Mother, Mother, you would have been so proud of me

17   in Sunday school.

18   HOUSEWIFE: Shhhh. Your father's still asleep.

19   GIRL: But you would have been so proud. The teacher asked me

20   two questions, and I answered them both right. At first, John

21   said he didn't know the answer and then he said he did, but he

22   said the most stupid thing. The whole class was laughing at

23   him. I was so embarrassed.

24   BOY: It wasn't stupid. You're all missing the whole point.

25   GIRL: Missing the point? Ha! We'll see who's missing the point on

26   Christmas morning when I wake up and find lots of presents

27   on my side of the tree and you wake up and find nothing.

28   BOY: You just don't understand.

29   GIRL: You don't understand. You have to be good to get presents,

30   and that's the truth.

31   ANGEL: And while they were in Bethlehem, the time came for

32   Mary's baby to be born. She had a son, whose name was

33   Jesus. There was no cradle in the stable, so Mary wrapped her

34   son in ragged cloth bands and laid him in the manger, which

35   was filled with hay for the animals to eat.

1 CHOIR: *(Singing)* **Away in a manger, no crib for a bed**
2   **The little Lord Jesus laid down his sweet head.**
3   **The stars in the sky looked down where He lay,**
4   **The little Lord Jesus, asleep on the hay.** *(All CHARACTERS on*
5   *both the upper and lower levels exit as the lights fade.)*
6
7   **Scene 2**
8   *(The stage is empty.)*
9 CHOIR: *(Singing)* **There's a song in the air!**
10   **There's a star in the sky!**
11   **There's a mother's deep prayer and a baby's low cry!**
12   **And the star rains its fire while the beautiful sing,**
13   **For the manger of Bethlehem cradles a King!**
14   *(HOUSEWIFE enters.)*
15 HOUSEWIFE: **Last night I had the strangest dream. I dreamed**
16   **that I was mysteriously taken back to Bethlehem. I saw Mary,**
17   **Joseph, and the baby Jesus.** *(MARY and JOSEPH enter on the*
18   *upper level. MARY is carrying the baby Jesus. They position*
19   *themselves inside the "stable" as in a traditional manger scene.)*
20   **Then I heard choirs of angels singing.** *(The ANGEL enters on*
21   *the upper level.)* **It was all so beautiful. I wonder what it could**
22   **mean.**
23 CHOIR: *(Singing)* **It came upon the midnight clear,**
24   **That glorious song of old,**
25   **From angels bending near the earth,**
26   **To touch their harps of gold:**
27   **"Peace on the earth, good will to men, from heaven's all-**
28   **gracious King."**
29   **The world in solemn stillness lay,**
30   **To hear the angels sing."** *(BOY enters.)*
31 BOY: **At Sunday school they laughed at me. In school they laughed**
32   **at me. I just don't know. My mind tells me I'm wrong, but I**
33   **can feel that I'm right. I can just feel it.**
34 GIRL: **The older you get, the less there is to ask for. The less you**
35   **ask for, the less you get. It's sort of taken a lot of the magic out**

1   of Christmas. It just doesn't mean anything anymore.

2   ANGEL: And there were shepherds in the same area, keeping

3   watch over their flocks by night. *(Three SHEPHERDS enter on*

4   *the upper level.)* And an angel of the Lord appeared to them

5   and they were afraid. The angel said to them *(the*

6   *SHEPHERDS)*, "Don't be afraid, for I bring you great news

7   that will make you very happy. Today, in the city of

8   Bethlehem, a child was born. That child is Christ the Lord.

9   You will know this child because he is sleeping in a manger in

10   Bethlehem's stable. He is wrapped in ragged cloth bands."

11   1st SHEPHERD: Let's go to Bethlehem and see this Christ child.

12   2nd SHEPHERD: We have to tell the whole world about the angel

13   who appeared to us.

14   3rd SHEPHERD: Well, let's hurry before it's too late. *(They*

15   *position themselves before the "stable" again in the manner of a*

16   *traditional manger scene.)*

17   CHOIR: *(Singing)* The first Noel, the angel did say,

18   Was to certain poor shepherds in fields as they lay;

19   In fields where they lay keeping their sheep,

20   On a cold winter's night that was so deep.

21   Noel, Noel, Noel, Noel,

22   Born is the King of Israel.

23   GIRL: What do shepherds have to do with anything?

24   BOY: The shepherds took a great risk by leaving their sheep to go

25   all the way to Bethlehem. They could have lost their jobs.

26   GIRL: They shouldn't have left their sheep then.

27   BOY: You just don't understand. You'll never understand.

28   *(BUSINESSMAN enters.)*

29   BUSINESSMAN: This is going to be a very prosperous year. The

30   toys are getting more and more complicated and more and

31   more expensive. In January I'm going to take that trip to

32   Bermuda that I've been promising myself. I really deserve it.

33   *(Takes a big wad of money from his pocket.)* This is what

34   Christmas is all about.

35   ANGEL: In a distant land there were wise men, kings, who had

1   seen the star shining brightly over Bethlehem. They
2   remembered the writings about the birth of the Savior, and
3   they knew the time had come. They packed all of their
4   belongings and started on a journey to see the newborn
5   Savior. They had no idea where he was, but they knew to
6   follow the star. This is what they did. *(Three WISE MEN enter*
7   *on upper level.)*
8   CHOIR: *(Singing)* We three kings of Orient are,
9   Bearing gifts we traverse afar,
10   Field and fountain, moor and mountain,
11   Following yonder star.
12   O, star of wonder, star of night,
13   Star with royal beauty bright,
14   Westward leading, still proceeding,
15   Guide us to thy perfect light.
16   1st WISE MAN: I bring him gold. Gold is a proper gift for a king.
17   2nd WISE MAN: I have frankincense, a fragrance very rare and
18   expensive.
19   3rd WISE MAN: I have myrrh to anoint his holy body.
20   BUSINESSMAN: Gold?
21   ANGEL: And myrrh and frankincense.
22   BUSINESSMAN: Yes, but gold?
23   BOY: Why are you so thrilled about gold? What good is it?
24   BUSINESSMAN: What good is it? I don't hear you complain on
25   Christmas morning when you see hundreds of dollars in toys
26   and things under the tree, all for you.
27   HOUSEWIFE: I remember the excitement of waking up on
28   Christmas morning and going to see all of the presents that
29   Santa Claus had left. There never was a lot because Mom and
30   Dad weren't rich, but I really loved everything I got. I don't
31   feel that now. Something is missing, but I don't quite know
32   what.
33   CHOIR: *(Singing)* What child is this, who, laid to rest, on Mary's
34   lap is sleeping?
35   Whom angels greet with anthems sweet while shepherds

1   watch are keeping?

2   This, this is Christ the King, whom shepherds guard and

3   angels sing;

4   Haste, haste, to bring him laud, the babe, the son of Mary.

5   ANGEL: *(To BUSINESSMAN)* Think back to the days when you

6   were in high school. Did you join any of the teams?

7   BUSINESSMAN: Well, yes. I was on the hockey team.

8   ANGEL: Didn't you have trouble joining? You didn't have any of

9   the equipment, did you?

10   BUSINESSMAN: No. We searched and searched until we finally

11   put together a second-hand uniform. And Dad gave me the

12   stick for Christmas. Boy, was that a good hockey stick.

13   ANGEL: You liked it?

14   BUSINESSMAN: I loved it. I used it in college, too.

15   ANGEL: Do you know where your father got that stick?

16   BUSINESSMAN: *(Proudly)* He made it himself. It took him weeks

17   of filing and sanding to get it right. It wasn't perfect, but it

18   sure was good.

19   ANGEL: And it cost your father practically nothing. He spent

20   almost no money on it at all.

21   BUSINESSMAN: What's the point of all this?

22   BOY: Your father spent a lot of time making it for you. Money

23   wasn't important as long as there was love.

24   BUSINESSMAN: So what? Are you saying that I'm showing less

25   love by buying a gift? Dad had time to make things. I don't.

26   BOY: But why do you buy the gift? Why do you even bother giving

27   a gift?

28   BUSINESSMAN: I give gifts because everyone would hate me if I

29   didn't.

30   HOUSEWIFE: That's the most ridiculous thing I've ever heard.

31   Don't you remember that little story about Saint Florentin

32   and the first Christmas tree?

33   BUSINESSMAN: No.

34   GIRL: I know it. There was a good old man who lived all alone in

35   a mountain hut. Every day the children would come to visit

1 him. He wanted to give them a Christmas gift very badly, but
2 he had no money. Then one day, he saw a little fir tree
3 sparkling with ice and snow on its branches, so he cut it down,
4 decorated it with candy and cookies, and put candles on it to
5 make it light up. When the children saw it, they were very
6 happy. It was the best Christmas present they could have
7 hoped for.
8 BUSINESSMAN: So?
9 HOUSEWIFE: So that's what made my childhood Christmases so
10 different. There was so much that we had to do ourselves; we
11 didn't have packaged decorations and automatic dolls. We
12 had to do it all ourselves, and we never got a chance to forget
13 why we were doing it.
14 CHOIR: *(Singing)* Joy to the world, the Lord is come!
15 Let earth receive her King.
16 Let every heart prepare him room,
17 And heaven and nature sing,
18 And heaven and nature sing,
19 And heaven, and heaven, and nature sing.
20 GIRL: I don't understand. What does Christmas have to do with
21 all this? What's the point of the tree? Why do we have a
22 manger scene? Christmas is Jesus' birthday, and yet everyone
23 gets gifts but him. I don't understand.
24 BOY: I told you that you were missing the whole point, didn't I?
25 Now, let's start all over again. What is Christmas?
26 GIRL: Christmas is Jesus' birthday.
27 BOY: And why was Jesus born? Don't tell me he was born so they
28 could write the Bible about him. That's stupid.
29 GIRL: I don't know why Jesus was born.
30 BOY: You have no idea? Why did Saint Florentin make a
31 Christmas tree for the children?
32 GIRL: Because he loved the children and wanted to make them
33 happy.
34 BOY: Why was Jesus born?
35 GIRL: Oh!

1 ANGEL: For God so loved the world that he gave his only begotten
2 son, that whoever believes in him should not perish but have
3 everlasting life.
4 GIRL: God loved the world, and he gave us Jesus. We love each
5 other, and we give each other gifts. I think I've got it.
6 CHOIR: *(Singing)* Hark! The herald angels sing,
7 "Glory to the newborn king; peace on earth, and mercy mild,
8 God and sinners reconciled!"
9 Joyful, all ye nations rise,
10 Join the triumph of the skies:
11 With th' angelic host proclaim,
12 "Christ is born in Bethlehem!"
13 Hark! The herald angels sing,
14 "Glory to the newborn king!"
15 BOY: When you know all that, how can you say that Christmas has
16 lost its meaning?
17 HOUSEWIFE: All of the pushing and shoving of the holiday
18 crowds is worth the joy of my family on Christmas morning.
19 BUSINESSMAN: All year long I miss the chance to tell those
20 around me exactly how much I love them. Now at Christmas,
21 I've almost missed the chance again. We're all so busy with
22 what we do and how well we do it that we totally forget *why*
23 we do it.
24 GIRL: God has given us so much. We should give him something in
25 return. What does he want for Christmas?
26 ANGEL: We can give him our lives. We can serve him and help his
27 kingdom on earth. *(To audience)* We must adore and worship
28 the Lord. Come, all who are faithful, worship Christ the Lord.
29 CHOIR: *(Singing)* O come, all ye faithful, joyful, and triumphant.
30 O come ye, O come ye to Bethlehem.
31 Come and behold him, born the king of angels.
32 O come, let us adore him.
33 O come, let us adore him.
34 O come, let us adore him, Christ the Lord.

O Little Town of Bennington
By Daniel Wray

Cast of Characters

Gabby — The angel who visits Mary. This is the lead role, as Gabby also serves as the Narrator. She is a little offbeat but always sincere. (Could also be played by a man.)

Mary — A student at Divinity Junior College who is at first unsure, then accepting, and finally joyful about her new role.

Joe — A carpenter and Mary's fiancé; an average guy thrust into a decidedly unaverage situation.

Gossips 1 and 2 — Mary's girlfriends. They are chatterboxes. Every little tidbit of news is sensational and melodramatic.

Homeless — A man (an ex-sheep farmer) living on the street. He is a colorful character who appears to be crazy and is prone to spontaneous prophetic outbursts.

Hot Dog Vendor — Just trying to make a buck in the park. May be male or female.

Lawyers 1, 2, and 3 — All business in their demeanor. They may be male or female.

Production Notes

This play is designed to be performed by youth groups, and was inspired by a desire on the part of the youth in our church to make people smile, as well as to think about some of the more practical complications of the Christ child's birth. It is intended as a look into what *might* have happened had Christ been born 2,000 years later, and to make us look at the event in a very non-traditional light. I hope your audience enjoys it as much as ours did.

Costumes

Modern dress. Mary and Joe wear jeans and sweatshirts. Gossips 1 and 2 also dress casually. Angel Gabby should wear white jeans with a white T-shirt and cardboard wings. Her sunglasses should be in her pocket, ready to whip out and put on to make a fashion statement at a moment's notice. Lawyers 1, 2, and 3 may be male or female. They should wear suits and carry briefcases. Homeless should wear tattered clothing — check your local thrift shop for old flannel shirts, a stocking cap, old jeans, etc. The Hot Dog Vendor should wear a box like the vendors that work the crowds at athletic events. This may be as simple as a cardboard box with "Hot Dogs" painted on the front and string attached, worn around the neck.

Props

A remote control; two telephones, cell or regular; a jacket, pen, and note pad for Joe; a bowl of popcorn, a textbook, and a baby doll wrapped in a blanket for Mary; a flashlight for Homeless; a "reservation list" (just a piece of paper is fine) and a self-standing sign saying "Welcome to Bennington Inn — Check in Here" for Gabby; and briefcases, business cards, and a lighter for the Lawyers.

Sound Effects

Tape a slap and a baby's cry to be played during the "birth" scene.

Set

The set requirements are very basic: A cardboard box painted to resemble a TV (this will also function as Homeless' box), a desk (or small table) and chair, an additional chair, small potted trees (optional), various signs for the parking garage saying "No Parking," "Sub-Compacts Only," etc., and an old tire (or two stacked tires) for the "manger."

Even though the scenes actually change, the changes are so minimal that they may easily be achieved without a curtain. No stage or special lighting is necessary; the play may easily be performed in the chancel area of a church. If a spotlight is used, it should be focused on the narrator Gabby during scene alterations, and other lights should be faded as needed for transitions.

Designate one or more stagehands to make the two scene transitions quickly and smoothly. The play opens in Mary's apartment, which may be as simple as a chair at Center Stage and a television placed off to one side. The desk is far Stage Right with a telephone, note pad, and pen on top. The desk remains in place throughout the play. The action then moves to Joe's apartment, which is not remarkably different. No changes are required, but if desired, the scene may be altered somewhat by simply moving the television. No changes are needed for the "gossip" scene either. Next is the park scene. The stagehand simply takes the cardboard box TV and turns it upside down for Homeless' abode, adds some potted trees, if desired, for an outdoor effect, and removes the chair from Center Stage. No changes are needed in the Bennington Inn scene. Gabby merely sits at the desk Stage Right and carries in the hotel sign and places it on the desk to establish the setting. For the final parking garage scene, the stagehand removes the box and trees, posts the parking garage signs, and places the tire(s) Center Stage.

1   *(The scene is MARY's apartment. When the play begins, the TV and*
2   *a chair should be Center Stage and the desk and chair with*
3   *telephone, note pad, and pen on top should be Stage Right.)*
4
5   *(Optional: GABBY or extra narrator reads the Christmas story*
6   *from combined verses in Matthew and Luke, then:)*
7
8   GABBY: OK. I guess I should probably explain a few things first. I
9   mean, it's not really a strength of mine, understand — I think
10   that's why things worked out the way they did. Oh, I'm doing
11   it again — getting ahead of myself! Well, anyway, I'm sure most
12   of you are familiar with the Christmas story, right? It all turned
13   out OK, as I'm sure you've heard. But what you probably don't
14   know is that God considered doing things differently — a "Plan
15   B" if you will. Yes, before he settled on Bethlehem 2,000 years
16   ago as the perfect choice, he considered another time, another
17   place. Jesus would have just now been coming onto the scene.
18   And instead of Bethlehem, he would have been born in the town
19   of Bennington — Bennington, Indiana.
20   *(MARY enters carrying a bowl of popcorn, a textbook, and a remote*
21   *control. She plops down on the floor Center Stage. She points at the*
22   *TV with the remote, as if turning it on. She tries to study, but her*
23   *attention is divided.)*
24   GABBY: You see, Mary was an English major at Divinity Junior
25   College, living alone in a studio apartment in a small
26   Midwestern town. She was engaged to be married in September
27   to Joe, who did drywalling and finish carpentry and lived a few
28   miles away. I came into their lives in early March, as Mary was
29   relaxing and enjoying an evening snack with her studies.
30   *(GABBY tiptoes into the scene and watches MARY for a moment,*
31   *smiling adoringly, before speaking her name.)* **Mary?** *(MARY bolts*
32   *upright, but doesn't turn around. Instead, her eyes move from side*
33   *to side slowly, then she shrugs and resumes eating.)* **Mary?** *(This*
34   *time MARY does turn slowly around, and catching sight of the*
35   *angel, spits popcorn and tries to scream.)* **Relax, Mary.**

1   MARY: Who are you? How did you get in here?
2   GABBY: I was sent by God, Mary. Uh, it *is* Mary, isn't it? The
3   directions I got weren't all that hot.
4   MARY: I'm not kidding! You better tell me who you are or I'm
5   calling the cops!
6   GABBY: I'm an angel, Mary. I was sent here to let you in on
7   something that will change the course of history. Your name *is*
8   Mary, isn't it? Because this is a special delivery and I don't
9   want to ...
10   MARY: An angel? *(Looks as though she should do something, but after*
11   *looking in vain for something to throw at the apparition, boldly*
12   *points the TV remote control in her hand at GABBY and tries to*
13   *make her disappear.)*
14   GABBY: Look, are you Mary or not?
15   MARY: *(Pauses.)* I guess that depends. Who wants to know?
16   GABBY: Just call me "Gabby."
17   MARY: Gabby who?
18   GABBY: Just Gabby. Actually, you and me are good friends, Mary.
19   MARY: You and *I* are good friends. And we're not. Who are you and
20   why are you in my apartment?
21   GABBY: I told you, Mary. I'm an angel of God with a message for
22   you.
23   MARY: Sure you are. How come I've never seen you before?
24   GABBY: Well, you may not have seen me, in the sense of seeing, but
25   you could have seen me if you saw the way I see. You see?
26   MARY: What are you talking about?
27   GABBY: *(Thinking back)* Actually, you would have seen me ...
28   several years back, when you fell off that swing set ... except I
29   got lost and didn't get there until you were in the ambulance.
30   So then I thought, what's the point?
31   MARY: What? *(Then remembering)* Oh, yeah! *(Pause)* Hey, thanks a
32   lot — I spent three days in the hospital!
33   GABBY: *(Changing the subject)* Anyway, I'm not real good at
34   introductions.
35   MARY: You mean *really* good.

1   GABBY: Huh, oh sure, *really* good. Can I sit down? My wings are
2   killing me!
3   MARY: Sure, I guess.
4   GABBY: *(Sitting)* **Thanks.** *(Looks around to make certain they are*
5   *alone. MARY does the same, instinctively, then rolls her eyes.)*
6   **OK. Maybe if I just come out with it direct.**
7   MARY: Directly.
8   GABBY: Yeah, OK, directly. I was sent *directly* here with a special
9   purpose.
10   MARY: What are you talking about? Is this some kind of a joke?
11   GABBY: *(Laughing at the comment, then abruptly serious)* **No. Mary,**
12   you've heard of miracles, haven't you?
13   MARY: Well ... sure. In the Bible. They were inexplicable events
14   that happened a long time ago.
15   GABBY: Right. They are wh ... whatever you said. *But,* they can
16   still happen today. You remember the little girl who was hit by
17   a car and went into a coma?
18   MARY: Yes.
19   GABBY: Things didn't look so good. But a lot of people prayed for
20   her, and she eventually came out of it. The doctors couldn't
21   explain it. Remember how surprised everyone was when she
22   woke up?
23   MARY: Yeah, I guess that was pretty amazing. So that was a
24   miracle, huh?
25   GABBY: Sure was.
26   MARY: So there are a lot of miracles still happening today?
27   GABBY: Well, not many. But some.
28   MARY: What was another?
29   GABBY: Well ... *(Looking around)* Do you really think the
30   _____ *(Insert your favorite local sports team)* would
31   have made the playoffs last year on their own?
32   MARY: Now that you mention it, that was pretty weird.
33   GABBY: What was my point? *(Pause)* Oh, yes. God is aware of
34   your positive spirit, Mary. That's like the reason I came to talk
35   with you.

1   MARY: That *is* the reason. It's not *like* the reason.

2   GABBY: You're an English major, right?

3   MARY: Yes. Why?

4   GABBY: 'Cause you're driving me up the wall! My point is, God

5   has chosen you.

6   MARY: Why me? I mean, I don't think I'm so special.

7   GABBY: *(Putting hands of MARY's shoulders and smiling sweetly)*

8   And neither do I, Mary. But God has a pretty good sense of

9   things. Maybe we should learn to trust his choices.

10 MARY: Well ... OK. But what could God possibly want me to

11   know?

12 GABBY: *(Getting excited)* OK, OK, OK! This is the good part! Are

13   you ready? OK. *(Pauses.)* You're going to have a baby!

14 MARY: *(Laughing)* Yeah, right. Now, come on. What does God

15   want me to know?

16 GABBY: That's it! You're going to carry God's child!

17 MARY: *(Still disbelieving)* Oh, you should be a comedian! Now

18   seriously ...

19 GABBY: Mary, you are pregnant with God's baby!

20 MARY: *(Stunned, she pauses.)* What? But that's impossible!

21 GABBY: Now, Mary ...

22 MARY: I mean, it is *really, really, really* impossible! Do you

23   understand what I'm telling you?

24 GABBY: Mary, nothing is impossible with God.

25 MARY: But I mean ... *(Whispers into GABBY's ear.)*

26 GABBY: I know, Mary. But that's what I was trying to tell you

27   about miracles. God has chosen you for that very reason.

28 MARY: *(Still disbelieving)* You mean to tell me I'm pregnant?

29 GABBY: God moves in mysterious ways, Mary. Who are we to

30   question them?

31 MARY: Well, right now I'll tell you who! I'm one upset nineteen-

32   year-old, that's who!

33 GABBY: Remember, it's a miracle, Mary.

34 MARY: Pregnant? *(Pause)* Me? *(Sits unbelieving on top of the desk.)*

35 GABBY: It will take a little bit of explaining to some people. And

1   some won't understand anyway; they'll just make you
2   miserable. But you have to trust God through every minute.
3   MARY: But what will I do with a baby? A *baby! (Pause)* I'm
4   supposed to be married in September! Joe's going to think
5   I've been, uh … I mean, how can I just suddenly be pregnant
6   and explain that to him? He's never going to believe that!
7   GABBY: Mary, it will all work out.
8   MARY: Oh, sure! Easy for you to say! You're not the one who'll go
9   through morning sickness. *You* won't gain twenty-five
10   pounds!
11   GABBY: *(Gently, shaking her head)* Mary …
12   MARY: I'm the one who won't fit into her wedding dress! I'm the
13   one who'll get booties instead of nighties at my wedding
14   shower!
15   GABBY: *(More seriously)* Mary?
16   MARY: I'm the one who'll be the laughingstock of everyone. I'm
17   the one who'll be God's pack mule for nine months!
18   GABBY: *(Firmly) Mary!* Hey! Pull yourself together! *(Gently)* God
19   will work it out.
20   MARY: *(Getting a grip, breaks away slowly from GABBY and walks*
21   *toward the audience.)* A baby. *(Pause)* God's baby? And God
22   chose me, huh?
23   GABBY: Yes, Mary.
24   MARY: I mean, God chose me out of the millions … out of the
25   thousands … well, out of all the virgins in the world?
26   GABBY: That's right.
27   MARY: I mean, it's not like he's narrowed it down to three or four
28   until he finds out how they react or anything, is it?
29   GABBY: *(Not smiling)* No, Mary, it's not. You're it. *(MARY looks*
30   *visibly disappointed.)*
31   MARY: Well … I guess if God chose me, he must know what he's
32   doing. *(Pause)* Wow. A baby. God's baby. Do you know what
33   the baby will grow up to be?
34   GABBY: Well, if tonight is any indication, pretty strong-spirited,
35   I'd guess. *(Pause)* And one who will lead a lot of people to

1 **God's light.** *(MARY exits. GABBY moves to Center Stage. JOE*
2 *enters and picks up the telephone and paces a bit as he*
3 *pantomimes having a telephone conversation as GABBY speaks.*
4 *To audience)* **Well, the scene with Joe didn't go a whole lot**
5 **more smooth — uh, smoothly. Mary couldn't wait to let him**
6 **know that something was up, so I wasn't left with much time**
7 **to fill him in before she did. Plus, I got stuck in traffic ...**
8 *(GABBY exits.)*
9 JOE: *(In the middle of his telephone conversation with MARY)* **Mary,**
10 **can't you give me a hint about what's bothering you? You**
11 **sound upset.** *(Pause)* **OK. Yeah, I'll come right over. Are you**
12 **all right?** *(Pause)* **OK. Look, it's uh ...** *(Glancing at watch)*
13 **about eight o'clock. I'll be there by eight-thirty. I'll see you**
14 **in ... What?** *(Pause)* **Sure. Let me get a pen.** *(He picks up a pen*
15 *and note pad.)* **Sure, no problem — it's right on my way. Uh-**
16 **huh.** *(Writing)* **Pickles, ice cream, soda crackers,** *(Pause)* **box of**
17 **Pampers ... What? OK.** *(Pause)* **Honey, are you OK?** *(Pause)*
18 **All right. I'll be right over to talk. See you in half an hour.**
19 **Kiss, kiss. Bye.** *(Hangs up.)* **Gee! What's with her?**
20 *(GABBY enters with jacket, unseen by JOE. He starts to exit, and*
21 *GABBY hands his jacket to him as he passes.)*
22 JOE: **Thank you.** *(He keeps walking, but then realizes that GABBY is*
23 *standing there.)*
24 GABBY: **Hi, Joe.**
25 JOE: **Hi.** *(Pause)* **Uh, who are you?**
26 GABBY: **Just call me Gabby.**
27 JOE: **Hi, Gabby.** *(Pause)* **Uh, could I ask what you're doing in my**
28 **apartment?**
29 GABBY: *(Cheerily)* **Sure!**
30 JOE: **Well?**
31 GABBY: **Oh! You're asking! Well, this may take a while ... may I**
32 **sit down?**
33 JOE: **I don't know that I could stop you.**
34 GABBY: *(Sitting)* **Thanks.**
35 JOE: **You were saying?**

1   **GABBY:** I was? Oh, yeah! I was about to tell you that I'd been sent
2   from God to talk to you about fatherhood.
3   **JOE:** Oh, I get it. My mom sent you, didn't she?
4   **GABBY:** No, Joe. I was sent by God.
5   **JOE:** Yeah, well — she tells people that's who she is sometimes.
6   **GABBY:** Joe, I need for you to understand something. God has great
7   plans for you and Mary, but you have to trust his timing.
8   **JOE:** Oh, I get it! This is one of those hidden camera gags, isn't it?
9   *(Looking around for the camera)* Nice try, Mom, but there is no
10   way I'm postponing this wedding!
11   **GABBY:** Joe, you aren't listening! *(Grabs him by the shoulders.)* I am
12   an angel of God, and I was sent to tell you that you are going to
13   be a father very soon.
14   **JOE:** You're serious.
15   **GABBY:** Very serious.
16   **JOE:** Well, I *am* getting married in a couple of months. I guess that's
17   not too highly irregular, except that we were going to wait until
18   we could better afford it.
19   **GABBY:** God will work that out. But there's one tiny little detail that
20   I haven't mentioned yet ...
21   **JOE:** *(Pauses)* Yeah?
22   **GABBY:** Well, you know how Mary wanted you to come over to her
23   place? To talk about something?
24   **JOE:** Yeah?
25   **GABBY:** Well, you may be experiencing fatherhood a little earlier
26   than you might think.
27   **JOE:** *(Pauses)* Like how early?
28   **GABBY:** Like nine months from now.
29   **JOE:** *(Stunned)* What are you telling me?
30   **GABBY:** Joe, Mary is going to have a baby.
31   **JOE:** *(Long pause, then JOE starts chuckling and looking around for the*
32   *camera again.)* All right, Mom, the joke is up! I have told you over
33   and over that we are being good, but you just keep pushing ... !
34   **GABBY:** Joe, I have never even met your mother!
35   **JOE:** Look. Mary is a wonderful girl and we're going to get

1   married. There is no way that she could be pregnant!

2   GABBY: God has chosen her to be the mother of his son.

3   JOE: But how?

4   GABBY: It's a miracle, Joe.

5   JOE: You mean Mary's pregnant and we didn't even ... ? *(More*

6   *solemnly)* Mary's pregnant and we didn't even ... *(Now angry)*

7   *Hey!* Mary's pregnant and we didn't even ... !

8   GABBY: Now Joe ...

9   JOE: Oh, come on! This is all too weird ...

10   GABBY: I understand that this is going to take some getting used

11   to. *(Puts sunglasses on.)* But hey, everything's cool. God is

12   going to work things out.

13   JOE: *(Pauses.)* A baby, huh? But if this is true, why did God choose

14   us? We're certainly nothing special.

15   GABBY: Apparently God thinks otherwise.

16   JOE: Well, what do we do now?

17   GABBY: Well, there's going to be a convention in Bennington in

18   December. You'll need to apply as one of the temporaries.

19   That's about all I can tell you.

20   JOE: Why?

21   GABBY: Mostly because that's all I know.

22   JOE: No, I mean why Bennington?

23   GABBY: Trust, Joe. That's all I can say. *(Pause as JOE tries to sort*

24   *everything out.)* Does everything I've told you make sense?

25   JOE: None of it makes sense. But somehow I believe you. There's

26   only one thing about what you said that bothers me.

27   GABBY: What?

28   JOE: You said you'd never met my mother?

29   GABBY: That's right.

30   JOE: Well, how would you like to? She'll never believe *me*! *(JOE*

31   *exits. GABBY moves to Center Stage.)*

32   GABBY: And I don't think she ever really did, although I let Joe

33   take care of that one on his own. In fact, not a lot of people

34   believed either of them — not that they told many. They

35   didn't have to ... *(GABBY exits. GOSSIPS 1 and 2 enter*

1   *simultaneously. GOSSIP 1 enters from Stage Right and plops*

2   *down on the desk, her feet up in the air, and picks up the phone.*

3   *GOSSIP 2 enters from Stage Left, carrying her phone. She may*

4   *pace back and forth as she talks.)*

5   **GOSSIP 1: No! Not Mary!**

6   **GOSSIP 2: She told me herself! Provided, of course, that I kept it a**

7   **secret. Poor girl!**

8   **GOSSIP 1: I can't believe it. How embarrassing!**

9   **GOSSIP 2: Oh, that's not the half of it. She's so upset that she's**

10   **convinced herself it's ... are you ready? She's convinced**

11   **herself that it's *God's* baby!**

12   **GOSSIP 1: What?!**

13   **GOSSIP 2: Yep. She claims that *God* made her pregnant.**

14   **GOSSIP 1: Oh, how sad.**

15   **GOSSIP 2: I tried to help her.**

16   **GOSSIP 1: Oh?**

17   **GOSSIP 2: Yeah, I sent over some literature about alternatives, but**

18   **she just threw it away.**

19   **GOSSIP 1: Some people just can't see the impact their actions**

20   **might have on future generations.**

21   **GOSSIP 2: Nope. Well, listen, it's about time for my soap to come**

22   **on, so I've gotta go.**

23   **GOSSIP 1: So are you going to call Sue or should I?**

24   **GOSSIP 2: You call Sue. I'll catch Tess and Lisa.**

25   **GOSSIP 1: OK. See ya later!**

26   **GOSSIP 2: Bye!** *(GOSSIPS 1 and 2 hang up and exit. Stagehand sets*

27   *up potted trees if desired for the park scene, then takes the*

28   *cardboard box TV and turns it upside down. Stagehand exits,*

29   *taking the chair.)*

30   **GABBY:** *(As Stagehand is setting up)* **And so the news got around ...**

31   **sort of. But they weren't all skeptics. In fact, some of the most**

32   **unusual people are chosen to play important parts in these**

33   **kinds of things. I mean, shepherds and wise men? It sounds**

34   **unbelievable, but God had a similar idea in "Plan B" too.**

35   **Some very interesting characters hang out in Bennington's**

1   park. Well, you'll see what I mean ... *(GABBY exits. HOT DOG*
2   *VENDOR and HOMELESS enter. HOMELESS climbs into*
3   *cardboard box. HOMELESS appears to be somewhat crazy, often*
4   *prophesying between panhandling and making benign*
5   *conversation.)*
6   HOMELESS: *(Standing up in box)* **It's gonna rain tomorrow! Yes**
7   **sir, it's gonna rain cats and dogs!** *(Holds out his hand to*
8   *imaginary passerby.)* **Got any change, sir?**
9   VENDOR: **Hot dogs! Get your Red Hots here!** *(Pause)* **Man! I**
10   **don't think I could sell these things today even if they were**
11   **real meat. Want one, Homeless?**
12   HOMELESS: **Are you kidding? You forget I used to be a sheep**
13   **farmer. I know what's in those things.** *(Then, getting a vision)*
14   **I see a plague of leeches descending on the city!**
15   VENDOR: **Give it a rest, Homeless. Everybody knows about the**
16   **Bar Association Convention being in town. It's in all the**
17   **papers.** *(HOMELESS shrugs, then ducks into box. LAWYERS 1,*
18   *2, and 3 enter carrying briefcases. They are discussing a recent*
19   *court case.)*
20   LAWYER 1: **It's all right here, Simpson. I'll have the briefs back**
21   **to you by Tuesday.**
22   VENDOR: **Hot dogs!** *(LAWYER 1 reaches for his wallet to get money*
23   *for a hot dog.)*
24   HOMELESS: *(Peeks head out of box and says to LAWYER 2)* **Got**
25   **any change, sir?** *(LAWYER 2 takes a card out of his pocket and*
26   *hands it to HOMELESS.)*
27   LAWYER 2: **Give me a call. You probably don't know who to**
28   **blame, but together we could come up with something.**
29   *(HOMELESS ducks back down.)*
30   LAWYER 3: **Say, you know how my air conditioning was out in my**
31   **suite?**
32   LAWYER 1: **Yeah?**
33   LAWYER 3: **The hotel manager said it would take him three days**
34   **to get to it! So I threatened to go elsewhere, and he just**
35   **laughed at me. "Good luck," he says. "Every hotel in town is**

1 booked." Think I can get him on a failure to keep a contract
2 in small claims?
3 **LAWYER 2:** Not if he offers any kind of compensation. Besides,
4 you should be thankful you got a room to yourself. Old
5 windbag here snores so loud that the deaf guy staying in the
6 suite next to ours complained.
7 **LAWYER 1:** *(Sarcastically)* **Ha ha.**
8 **HOMELESS:** *(Climbs out of box and yells out to no one in particular,*
9 *having a vision.)* **A blackout! I see every light in the city going**
10 **out! Every ... last ... light ... black!** *(Pause)* **But in one**
11 **garage ... one place ... the lights will shine to light the world!**
12 *(HOMELESS, looking up toward the stars, spins slowly Off-*
13 *stage.)* **Bright ... shining ... light!** *(There is a long pause as the*
14 *VENDOR and LAWYERS 1, 2, and 3 stare at each other, then*
15 *shrug. LAWYERS 1, 2, and 3 exit.)*
16 **VENDOR: Hot dogs! Piping hot!** *(He ad libs his sales pitch as he*
17 *exits. Stagehand removes trees and box and adds "No Parking"*
18 *and "Sub-Compact Only" signs and the tire manger Center Stage.*
19 *GABBY enters with reservation list and "Welcome to Bennington*
20 *Inn — Check in Here" sign and sits behind the desk, placing the*
21 *sign on top.)*
22 **GABBY:** *(May speak while Stagehand is still setting up.)* **So**
23 **everything was in place. But I thought I would keep an eye on**
24 **things just to make sure. I mean, when something's important,**
25 **you can't be too careful ...** *(MARY and JOE approach the desk*
26 *to inquire about their reservation.)*
27 **JOE: Hi. Do you have a room for Brown?**
28 **GABBY:** *(Looks down, checking her list.)* **Brown ... Brown ...**
29 **Brown. Nope, I'm sorry. No Brown at this hotel. Next!**
30 **JOE: There must be some mistake. I'm here to work at the**
31 **convention. They need help with repairs when the lawyers**
32 **leave. Perhaps it's under the company that hires me. Starlight**
33 **Construction?**
34 **GABBY: Starlight ... Starlight ... Starlight. Nope. Nothing under**
35 **Starlight. Next!**

1   JOE: Wait a minute. Is this the only Bennington Inn in town?
2   GABBY: Yes, sir. This is the only one.
3   JOE: Well ... I guess we'll have to get another room. *(Turning to*
4   *MARY)* I'll just put it on a credit card and get reimbursed.
5   GABBY: Excuse me. *(Turning around and laughing hysterically, then*
6   *back to face JOE, straight-faced)* I'm sorry, sir, but I'm afraid
7   there aren't any rooms available.
8   JOE: What?
9   GABBY: Which word didn't you understand? I'll try and speak
10   more slowly. There ... aren't ...
11 JOE: Listen. My company reserved a room for us, we're very tired
12   from the drive, and as you can see, my wife is going to have a
13   baby.
14 GABBY: Congratulations! Now, if you'll excuse me ... *next* !
15 MARY: Joe? *(MARY is starting to go into labor. She should make*
16   *obvious signs to the audience, but JOE doesn't notice.)*
17 JOE: Just a minute, honey. *(Turning back to GABBY)* Now listen, I
18   want to speak to the manage ... hey! *(Leaning closer)* Hey! You
19   look awfully familiar. Have we met?
20 MARY: *(Slumping down)* Joe ...
21 GABBY: I don't think so.
22 JOE: *(Still oblivious)* Honey, doesn't she look a lot like ...
23 GABBY: *(Putting on sunglasses)* I must just have one of those
24   angelic faces ...
25 MARY: *(Distressed)* Joe!
26 JOE: Hey! What's the big ...
27 MARY: Joe, I'm going to have the baby!
28 JOE: Well, of course you are, dear. *(Turning around)* What are you
29   doing down there?
30 MARY: I mean *now*, Joe!
31 JOE: What?! You can't!
32 MARY: Watch me! *(Sanctuary lights dim.)*
33 JOE: *(Thoughtfully)* Hmmmm, ironic timing.
34 MARY: Uh-oh! Joe, do something! *(HOMELESS enters silently,*
35   *carrying a flashlight.)*

1   **JOE:** *(Turning back to GABBY)* **Hurry! Call a baby! My wife's going**
2   **to have a doctor!**
3   **GABBY:** *(Very calmly)* **That doesn't make any sense.** *(Picks up*
4   *telephone, listens, then hangs it up.)* **But it also doesn't matter.**
5   **Whatever knocked the power out also got the phones.**
6   *(Cheerily)* **Sorry!**
7   **JOE: Sorry! What good is that …**
8   **HOMELESS:** *(Interrupting)* **Follow me. I know of a place that is**
9   **private and safe.**
10   **JOE: Who are you?**
11   **HOMELESS: I'm someone who can help you. Come with me.**
12   *(GABBY exits. JOE and MARY follow HOMELESS to Center*
13   *Stage. In transit, she passes behind any obstacle that shields her*
14   *from the audience, pulls the pillow from her clothes and "has" the*
15   *baby. While behind the obstacle, the sound effect tape of a slap*
16   *and a baby crying are heard. Only the lights directly overhead*
17   *come up as MARY crosses to Center Stage carrying the baby,*
18   *followed by JOE and HOMELESS. The whole transaction should*
19   *take five seconds or less.)*
20   **HOMELESS: Here … lay down.** *(Points to a place.)*
21   **JOE: Are you sure you're feeling all right?**
22   **MARY:** *(Smiling, looking at the baby)* **I'm better now.** *(She pauses to*
23   *look at baby.)* **Oh, Joe, isn't he beautiful?**
24   **JOE: Of course he is. He has his mother's eyes.**
25   **MARY: And he certainly has your …** *(pause)* **Well, isn't he**
26   **beautiful?!**
27   **JOE:** *(Looking sarcastically Off-stage)* **Yeah.** *(LAWYERS 1, 2, and 3*
28   *enter. They are stumbling around in the dark with a lighter.)*
29   **LAWYER 1: Man, oh man! That was close!**
30   **LAWYER 2: No kidding! And to think we almost got into that**
31   **elevator!**
32   **LAWYER 3: Can you imagine being stuck on an elevator during a**
33   **power outage in this city?**
34   **LAWYER 1: Yeah. We'd all be representing each other!**
35   **LAWYER 2:** *(Glances in the direction of MARY and JOE and does a*

1   *double take.)* **Hey, what's going on?** *(LAWYERS 1 and 2 take*
2   *notice of the trio. MARY has laid the baby in the center of an old*
3   *tire Center Stage.)*
4   **LAWYER 1: Think we should get involved?**
5   **LAWYER 2: You two go ahead. I'll defend you if something goes**
6   **wrong.**
7   **LAWYER 3: Oh, come on!** *(Then, seeing the baby)* **Oh no. Oh yes!**
8   **A baby! A newborn baby!**
9   **LAWYER 2:** *(To MARY)* **What happened? Are you OK?**
10   **LAWYER 1:** *(Taking off his jacket)* **Please take this. It's freezing out**
11   **here!**
12   **LAWYER 2:** *(Taking his off as well)* **You must be in shock!**
13   **LAWYER 3:** *(Takes his off also and HOMELESS takes it from him and*
14   *admires it before putting it on.)* **What are you doing in the**
15   **middle of a parking garage?**
16   **JOE: Well, we were in the hotel lobby when the lights went out,**
17   **and the phones were out ...**
18   **HOMELESS: I knew this was going to happen. All the lights in the**
19   **city ...** *black!* **But plenty of light here in this garage!**
20   **LAWYER 3: Why didn't you just go to your room?**
21   **JOE: Well, the hotel sort of lost our reservation ...**
22   **LAWYER 1: What? You mean to tell me there was no room in the**
23   **inn and they sent you away?** *(Pause)* **Does this sound familiar**
24   **to anybody else?**
25   **LAWYER 2: It sure does!** *(Pause)* **Barker vs. Ramada Inn, 1999!**
26   **LAWYER 3: Of course! What did that settle for?**
27   **LAWYER 1: A quarter of a million, I think. But we can get twice**
28   **that!**
29   **MARY: What are you talking about?**
30   **LAWYER 3: Why, a wrongful endangerment case. On contingency,**
31   **of course!**
32   **ALL 3 LAWYERS:** *(Simultaneously handing her their cards)* **My**
33   **card!**
34   **MARY: No, thank you, really. This was meant to happen.**
35   **LAWYER 2: Quick! More coats! She's delirious!**

1   JOE: No! My wife is right. This baby is a miracle.

2   LAWYER 1: Of course he is. But under these conditions, he's also
3   a gold mine!

4   MARY: Don't you understand? This baby was sent by God for a
5   special purpose. He is meant to bring joy to all the world.

6   LAWYER 3: You bet! Beginning with you and your husband. At
7   least $300,000 worth, I'd guess.

8   JOE: You can't put a price on the kind of love he will bring into the
9   world!

10   LAWYER 2: Of course you can't. That would be the judge's
11   responsibility.

12   HOMELESS: *Light!* (*LAWYERS scatter as HOMELESS yells and*
13   *flails arms. They retreat farther and farther back until they run*
14   *Off-stage.*) Light the world has never known! A baby who will
15   grow to be the answer to the question! Death will be powerless
16   against such light! Light! Wonderful, warming light! The
17   Light of the World. (*The lights come up.*) Born in a parking
18   garage!

19   MARY: Thank you again for helping us find this place.

20   JOE: And for scaring those wise guys off. Who are you, anyway?

21   HOMELESS: Just a homeless old sheep farmer who listens to
22   every voice.

23   MARY: I guess we're lucky that some people still do.

24   JOE: We certainly are.

25   HOMELESS: *Listen!* (*Pause*) Do you hear that?

26   JOE: Hear what? I don't hear anything.

27   HOMELESS: To the untrained ear, maybe not. But I'll tell you
28   what. That nothing is peace. (*Pause*) In the darkness there is
29   no peace. But in the light ... just listen!

30   MARY: (*After a pause*) It does seem different. Like no silence I've
31   ever heard.

32   HOMELESS: May I hold this child of peace? (*MARY nods*
33   *cautiously and HOMELESS picks up the child.*) Ohhhh! From
34   this night on, life will never be the same. From now on, man
35   will feel the peace of forgiveness ... the light of grace.

1   *(HOMELESS walks to Center Stage.)* **No more must man**
2   **wander in the darkness of sin, but in the light of his wonderful**
3   **gift. The Son of God has come, born to set the world free!**
4   *(Spins two or three times back toward the tires, setting the baby*
5   *down gently.)* **Happy birthday, Baby!** *(Turning around to the*
6   *audience)* **Happy birthday, world!** *(HOMELESS, MARY, and*
7   *JOE turn and kneel before the baby as GABBY enters and speaks,*
8   *Center Stage.)*
9 GABBY: **And that's the way it would have happened, too, if there**
10   **was a "Plan B." But God's "Plan A" was the right choice. It**
11   **wouldn't have been right to make people wait 2,000 years**
12   **without the hope of the risen Messiah. And besides, with all of**
13   **the craziness of these times, we figured there wouldn't have**
14   **been many believers, anyway.** *(She starts to walk Off-stage, then*
15   *turns.)* **Or would there have been?** *(Shrugs and shakes head*
16   *while walking Off-stage.)*

And the Child Was Born

By Arthur L. Zapel

Cast of Characters

For the slides:
Joseph (Same Joseph as in program)
Mary (Same Mary as in program)
Man
Two women
Innkeeper (May be played by Man)
Angel
Young Girl
Infant
Shepherd

For the program:
Joseph
Mary

PowerPoint Projector Operator

Production Notes

This play is best presented as an audiovisual presentation. Twenty slides may be created in advance to heighten the spoken words. Properly used, these visual scenes will stimulate the viewer to create within his imagination visions of the events as they actually occurred. Careful blending of narration, music, and visuals will, within moments, transport the audience across the barrier of years and distance. The following will assist in achieving this mood: Position Mary at a lectern at Stage Right and Joseph at Stage Left. The scripts from which they read should be illuminated with a small light unseen by the audience. Small pen flashlights will suffice if other equipment is not available. You will also need a PowerPoint projector. A screen is set up between them in the altar area.

The projection of slides occur as the narrators speak their lines. We recommend that only one narrator at a time be spotlighted, the other kept in darkness. As Joseph speaks, a spotlight illuminates him. When he finishes, his light is snapped off and the light spotlighting Mary is snapped on. For the smoothest professional touch, you can plug the spotlights into a simple control panel made with mercury switches. This will avoid any distracting snapping sound of switches. Of course, this can be more easily done by not using a switch at all, but simply plugging the light in and out of the plug as required. No special spotlights are necessary. Standard photo spots from the photo store are ideal. Mount them low on the floor in front of the lecterns, clamped to a chair or placed directly on the floor, and they cast dramatic, mystic shadows.

Music

Your church pianist or organist can add another important dimension of artistic impact to this presentation. Creative bridging of the events of the narration together with selection of appropriate carols and hymns as a background to the narration will do as much for the total effect as costumes, visuals, or story. Let your pianist or organist study the script and be a creative part of the rehearsals and performance.

(Don't let all of these instructions scare you. Staging this play is not difficult at all. If you're confused on first reading, read these instructions again and you'll find that you have several easy alternatives in each instance.)

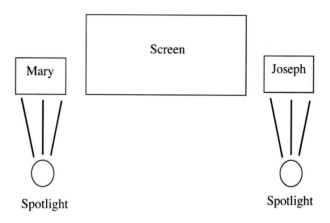

Props

(For slides) Sword (may be child's toy sword), pottery jug, scroll, carpentry tools, basket.

Other Items Needed: Cross (a rough-hewn wooden one works nicely), and a well. A well may be suggested by curving a large piece of cardboard (such as an appliance box) into a circular shape and painting "stones" on it. Papier mâché on a circular chicken wire frame would also work.

If you're lucky enough to have access to a farm, you can shoot slides 13 (Joseph leading donkey carrying Mary) and 17 (stable with cow) there. Although a real donkey is preferable, a horse will do just fine if you zoom in a bit closer. If you do not have access to a farm, you may simply look for a stock photo of a stable scene on the Internet, and suggest Mary riding on a donkey by having her sit riding-style on a sawhorse covered by a blanket, zooming in so the sawhorse does not show. Joseph may hold reins or a rope as if leading "donkey."

Costumes

(For the slides) Biblical robes for Joseph, Mary, and the other biblical characters. The women should have a length of cloth draped loosely over their heads. The men's headpieces should be tied with a strip of fabric around the circumference of their heads. The shepherd, too, should dress this way, with the addition of a shepherd's crook. The angel should wear a white robe. Wings and halo are optional. All should wear sandals.

(For the performance) Since the two participants in this presentation are not players in a pageant, but rather narrators in a reading, simple dress is more appropriate. White church robes are recommended for both Mary and Joseph. These provide a proper church mood and also are in keeping with the light and dark effect of the screen visuals that dramatize the reading.

Slide Descriptions

The following slides may be photographed weeks, or even months, in advance of the performance.

SLIDE 1 — A single star of the east (There are many to choose from on stock photo sites on the Internet).

SLIDE 2 — A MAN with a sword.

SLIDE 3 — MARY carrying a jug.

SLIDE 4 — MARY at a well with two WOMEN in background talking suspiciously about her.

SLIDE 5 — JOSEPH studying a scroll.

SLIDE 6 — MARY and JOSEPH talking at the well.

SLIDE 7 — MARY and JOSEPH talking to each other intently (close-up).

SLIDE 8 — MARY walking down a path.

SLIDE 9 — MARY looking up at a brilliant ANGEL.

SLIDE 10 — MARY and JOSEPH in carpenter shop.

SLIDE 11 — ANGEL talking to surprised JOSEPH.

SLIDE 12 — MARY and JOSEPH, arm in arm and looking happy.

SLIDE 13 — JOSEPH leading donkey carrying MARY.

SLIDE 14 — Biblical buildings (Available from a stock photo site on the Internet).

SLIDE 15 — INNKEEPER pointing, directing JOSEPH to another place to stay.

SLIDE 16 — YOUNG GIRL with basket.

SLIDE 17 — Stable with cow (Shot on location at a farm, or use one of the stock photo sites on the Internet).

SLIDE 18 — MARY with BABY (close-up).
SLIDE 19 — Star (May be same as SLIDE #1).
SLIDE 20 — SHEPHERD looking up at a brilliant light in the night sky.
SLIDE 21 — Star (May be same as SLIDE #1).
SLIDE 22 — Cross.

Music

It is recommended that music be used to reinforce the mood of the entire presentation. It should be used preceding, following, and behind the spoken words, and for bridging transitions as indicated in the script. Because this is a Nativity story, primarily Christmas music is used. Some of the selections that seem most appropriate to the subject matter include:

"Oh Come, All Ye Faithful"
"Away in a Manger"
"Fairest Lord Jesus"
"Hark! the Herald Angels Sing"
"It Came upon the Midnight Clear"
"Joy to the World"
"O Come, O Come, Emmanuel"
"O, Holy Night"
"O Little Town of Bethlehem"
"Silent Night"

Each music minister and each church may prefer their own selections. See page 277 for the song "And the Child Was Born," which may be used to bridge slide or mood changes throughout the play.

AND THE CHILD WAS BORN

by JAMES C. HUFFSTUTLER

1   *(The PowerPoint Operator projects the proper photos at the*
2   *places indicated in the script. MARY and JOSEPH are in place*
3   *behind their lecterns, at Stage Right and Stage Left respectively.)*
4 **SLIDE 1:** *(A star appears on center screen. After a pause, a light falls*
5   *on JOSEPH, Stage Left. He narrates.)*
6 **JOSEPH:** It would be better, my friends, if you would ask me to
7   repair a broken plow, or carve a yoke to fit your oxen, or
8   fashion you a sturdy chest for your garments. At these things
9   I am skilled, for I am a carpenter. *(Start fading out star slide.)*
10   But at words I am a poor builder. Still, I will try to tell you
11   something of my foster son and how he came to be born in
12   Bethlehem.
13
14 **SLIDE 2:** *(Shot of a man with sword.)*
15   You must first understand that despair, hate, and fear were
16   everywhere in Judea in the days before the birth. Tortures,
17   executions, and murder were common. Sadly, it was not only
18   the Romans who slaughtered the innocent and the loyal. Our
19   own people, too, chose to forget the seventh commandment of
20   Moses and killed in hate and rebellion. My own boyhood
21   friends spit on me when I refused to hide in the hills of Galilee
22   with them to strike down the Romans from ambush. They
23   believed me a fool to be waiting for the promised Messiah as
24   foretold in the prophecy of Isaiah. *(Start fading out man with*
25   *sword slide.)* They could not understand how I could wait
26   when they knew that I, with them, dreamed of justice and
27   freedom. Why the strength of peace and patience was given
28   me, I began to understand after I saw Mary for the first time.
29
30 **SLIDE 3:** *(MARY carrying jug appears.)*
31   She was carrying an earthen jug on her head as she passed my
32   carpenter shop on the way to the well at the bottom of the hill.
33   *(Start slow fade away of slide of Mary.)* I saw in this girl, now
34   just becoming a woman, a serenity and peace, as in the music
35   of my highest thoughts. I wondered then if she could be mine
36   to wed.

1 **SLIDE 4:** *(Mary at well as two women in background talk suspiciously*
2   *about her.)*
3 **MARY:** Joseph never knew how many times I thought of him
4   before he noticed me. He never guessed that I carried much
5   more water up the hillside than was ever needed by my
6   mother, Anna. *(Pause)* It was hard to become acquainted in
7   Nazareth. Newcomers like us were suspiciously avoided. *(Start*
8   *fading out slide of women.)* It was only when our nearest
9   neighbors came to trust us that I learned anything about
10   Joseph.
11
12 **SLIDE 5:** *(Joseph studying scroll.)*
13   They were critical of his quiet, independent ways. They
14   could not understand why he would rather spend his idle time
15   carving animal figures from mountain briar for the children
16   than gambling with the men of the passing caravans. Seldom
17   did he attend the village festivals, they said, saying also that he
18   seemed to prefer studying his holy books like *(Fade Joseph*
19   *slide)* an elderly patriarch than to live with an eye to joy and
20   devil-may-care as a young man in his twenties should. All of
21   this made me want to know more about Joseph.
22
23 **SLIDE 6:** *(Mary and Joseph, as they talk at the well.)*
24 **JOSEPH:** It was hard for me to talk to Mary at first, but my
25   confidence grew quickly. Before six weeks had passed, I
26   became certain that Mary felt about me as I felt about her. I
27   made an appointment to talk with her father, Joachim. *(Fade*
28   *Mary and Joseph slide.)* After many questions by her father ...
29   many tears from her mother ... then three anxious days of
30   deliberation, we were espoused.
31
32 **SLIDE 7:** *(Shot of two profiles, Mary and Joseph, looking at each*
33   *other intently.)*
34 **MARY:** Our engagement was to be a half-year, and how much the
35   more I came to love Joseph in that time. He was gentle, wise,

1   and strong. My silly moments — my little-girl moods and
2   angers — never seemed to disturb him.
3 JOSEPH: Mary's laughter took away my shyness, and I talked as
4   endlessly about our marriage as she did. *(Fade slide of*
5   *profiles.)* Time passed quickly until it was the month we were
6   to be betrothed, and then *(Pause)* Mary disappeared.
7
8 SLIDE 8: *(Silhouette of Mary walking down a path, alone.)*
9 MARY: Without thinking — without wanting to think, I left to be
10   with my cousin Elizabeth. Elizabeth, who now in her forty-
11   fifth year was great with child after the miraculous vision of
12   her husband, Zachariah. Zachariah, who disbelieved the
13   angel Gabriel when the messenger of God told him his prayer
14   for a child would be answered. Zachariah, who had been
15   struck dumb for questioning. I wanted to be with Elizabeth,
16   who herself was experiencing a miracle. I knew that she was
17   the only one I could talk with after what had happened that
18   mysterious *(Fade slide of Mary)* April night.
19
20 MUSIC
21   My parents were sleeping and after thoughts of Joseph, I
22   was about to loosen my hair for bed when I heard a voice
23   saying:
24
25 SLIDE 9: *(Silhouette of Mary looking up at brilliant angel figure)*
26   "Hail, thou that are highly favoured, the Lord is with thee:
27   blessed are thou among women" (Luke 1:28). I turned and saw
28   a brilliant figure standing in the far corner of the room. I was
29   afraid, and to calm me, the figure spoke again, saying softly:
30   "Fear not, Mary; for thou hast found favor with God. And
31   behold, thou shalt ... bring forth a son, and shall call his name
32   Jesus. He shall be great, and shall be called the Son of the
33   Highest ... and of his kingdom there shall be no end" (Luke
34   1:30-33). I could not understand and I asked, "How shall this
35   be?" The angel answered and said unto me: "The Holy Ghost

1   shall come upon thee, and the … Highest shall overshadow
2   thee; therefore also that holy thing which shall be born of thee
3   shall be called the Son of God" (Luke 1:35). I fell to my knees.
4   I prayed. I said, "Behold the handmaiden of the Lord; be it
5   unto me according to thy word" (Luke 1:38). *(Fade out angel*
6   *slide.)* And then — the brilliant figure disappeared.
7
8   SLIDE 10: *(Shot of Mary and Joseph in carpenter shop.)*
9   JOSEPH: Three months later, as I was working in my shop, Mary
10   stopped in, unexpectedly — quietly. Our eyes met, but neither
11   of us spoke. Mary, sensing my hurt at her long disappearance,
12   finally broke the awkward silence. Slowly — serenely —
13   quietly — and speaking now as a woman for the first time,
14   Mary told me everything that had happened. She ended with
15   a soft question: Would I be her husband still? I would not
16   answer, for I did not believe her story. *(Fade slide of Mary and*
17   *Joseph.)* I would not even look at her, and saying no more, she
18   left. *(Pause)* That night I wept.
19
20   SLIDE 11: *(Shot of an angel figure in Joseph's dream.)*
21   And then at last sleep came to me, and I had a vivid dream.
22   An angel appeared and said: "Joseph, thou son of David, fear
23   not to take unto thee Mary thy wife; for that which is
24   conceived in her is of the Holy Ghost" (Matthew 1:20). I awoke
25   and then the words from Isaiah returned to my mind:
26   "Therefore the Lord himself shall give you a sign. *(Fade angel*
27   *slide.)* Behold, a virgin shall conceive, and bear a son" (Isaiah
28   7:14).
29
30   MUSIC: *(A short bridge transition)*
31
32   SLIDE 12: *(Shot of two figures arm in arm — Mary and Joseph.)*
33   MARY: Joseph and I were married. I cooked, I mended, I helped
34   Joseph keep his shop clean and ready for new business. Five
35   months passed. Joseph and I were wonderfully happy — then

1	we were told of the decree from Caesar Augustus himself in
2	Rome — that every one of his subjects must be counted and
3	taxed. Even those of us in faraway Palestine were not to be
4	overlooked. The tax officials in Rome would not trust King
5	Herod, so they appointed Cyrenius, Governor of Syria, as
6	administrator of the court. He decided that each person must
7	register at the city headquarters where his tribe was founded.
8	Both Joseph and I were of the House of David, and so were
9	required to go to Bethlehem. Joseph did not want me to travel,
10	for my child was soon to be born. He talked with the officials,
11	but they would not *(Fade slide of Mary and Joseph.)* be
12	bothered with exceptions. I must go to Bethlehem, and that
13	was final.
14	
15	SLIDE 13: *(Shot of Joseph leading donkey carrying Mary.)*
16	JOSEPH: The trip was seventy-five miles. That would be three
17	days on a balky donkey for our Mary, large with child. But as
18	we traveled, she did not complain. Indeed, she found
19	inspiration in the places we came to along the way. Shiloh,
20	where Samuel came to pray for the gift of a child. Gilgal,
21	where Samuel judged our people more than eleven hundred
22	years before. Then we approached Bethlehem, and as we
23	passed through the *(Fade slide of donkey.)* tall defile of rocks
24	known in legend as the Valley of Tears, a feeling of foreboding
25	came over us.
26	
27	SLIDE 14: *(Shot of biblical buildings)*
28	MARY: When I saw the buildings of Bethlehem in the distance, the
29	first pains of delivery came upon me. I remembered then
30	another part of the prophecy I had forgotten. It was said that
31	the promised one would be born in Bethlehem. It would be as
32	written. *(Fade slide of buildings.)* My time was near. I was
33	afraid, but I said nothing to Joseph or my parents.

SLIDE 15: *(INNKEEPER directing Joseph to another place where lodging may be found.)*

JOSEPH: I knew Mary was soon to be delivered, and I was desperate to find her a room. Every place of lodging had been taken by the early comers. We had traveled too slowly. After a while I noticed that Mary was trying to conceal surges of pain, and I knew we had no further to travel. The inn we were approaching would have to be the place — it had to be. Drunken songs and laughter spilled toward us from the open windows. Mary and the others waited in the evening shadows of a heavily fruited fig tree near the back entrance as I went inside the inn. The mixed humid smells of spiced wine, unleavened bread, and perspiration sickened me as I entered. As I looked upon the clustered men and women numbed by drink, overfeeding, and noise, I felt a sudden loathing toward them. *(Fade slide of figure.)* Why should Mary have to suffer in a place like this? I thought — but still, she could go no further.

SLIDE 16: *(Shot of young girl with kitchen basket.)*

A hand touched my arm. I turned. It was a young girl, thin and sallow-faced. She was carrying a basket of kitchen garbage. She knew my thoughts. "You seek lodging, but you do not like this place." I shook my head. "There is no room in any inn in all of Bethlehem," she said, "not even here."

I said, "It is not for me that I ask, but for my wife. Very soon she is to be delivered." A sad inner thought moved across her face and with its going came a smile of tenderness. "Come," she said softly. "There is a warm place. I will show you where your wife may have her child." *(Fade slide of young girl.)* The ragged-robed girl led us to a cave that extended under the inn building itself.

SLIDE 17: *(Shot of stable with cow.)*

It was where they kept their cattle. It was warm with the

good sweet smell of animals and straw and grain. "I will tell my mistress, the innkeeper's wife, that you are here," said the girl. "After the baby comes she will let you stay, no matter what the master says. I am only the kitchen girl, but I know you will be all right if you stay quiet and say nothing. I will bring you water and some bread." She paused a moment. Her eyes looked at ours, but they were not seeing us, *(Fade stable slide.)* but some others long ago. Then with a stiff-lipped smile, she left us.

SLIDE 18: *(Close-up of Mary with baby.)*

MARY: My mother, Anna, cared for me, and before the night had passed, I was delivered. Joseph squeezed my hand gently. "Your son Jesus is born healthy and strong," he whispered, and kissed my forehead. I asked then that the Lord be with Joseph always for his gentleness and understanding. Then the baby was wrapped in swaddling clothes and placed in a makeshift cradle made from a manger — the feeding box of the cows and donkeys. *(Fade slide of Mary with baby.)* I smiled and rested, for I knew my resourceful, kindly Joseph would keep him well.

JOSEPH: There came no sign from the Lord when Jesus was born. None, at least, for my eyes to see,

SLIDE 19: *(Repeated — the single star of the east.)*

But before the morning's dawning, a group of shepherds walked into the courtyard of the inn. "Is this the place where a baby was born and placed in a manger?" they asked. I was astounded at their question, and I asked them how they knew of this. *(Fade slide of star.)* Then they told me of the miraculous incident in the hills which they had all witnessed together.

SLIDE 20: *(Silhouette figure of a shepherd looking up at the brilliance above.)*

They told me that as they were keeping watch over their

1   flock by night, an angel of the Lord came upon them, and they
2   were afraid. Then the angel said to them, "Fear not: for,
3   behold, I bring you good tidings of great joy, which shall be to
4   all people. For unto you is born this day in the city of David a
5   Savior, which is Christ the Lord" (Luke 2:10-11). They asked
6   then if they might see the child. I showed them where he lay.
7   Then, as they looked upon him, they repeated what the angel
8   spoke: "Glory to God in the highest, and on earth peace, good
9   will toward men" (Luke 2:14). *(Pause. Fade slide of shepherd.)*
10   Now it was done.
11
12 **SLIDE 21:** *(Repeated again. The star fades in again, slowly becoming*
13   *brighter and brighter.)*
14   Everything had happened as it had been promised, but
15   neither Mary nor I knew what was destined to happen. Jesus,
16   the Son of God, had been born. *(Pause. Fade slide of star.)*
17
18 **SLIDE 22:** *(Fade on the cross slowly.)*
19   All we came to understand in our lifetime was that Jesus
20   was born of the Virgin Mary and that he was, indeed, the Son
21   of God. The rest has yet to be written.

Kept in Her Heart
by Jon McCauley Smith

Cast of Characters

Mary
Zachariah
Elizabeth
Herdsman
Shepherd
Caspar
Melchior
Balthazar

Production Notes

Setting

A bare platform with sound equipment at both sides and in the center. Perhaps some stools or rough boxes at various levels could be placed for interest. In the center there should be a simple ladder-backed chair for Mary. The characters come in and sit around the stage area. They stand when they are speaking. This may be done in Readers Theatre style with the characters reading their parts.

Costumes

They should have some suggestive costuming on, although full period costume is not needed. Choir robes can be used for all if it is desired with perhaps a band around the heads of the shepherds, a headdress for Mary, and fancy stoles for the Magi.

Lighting

Spots on the speaking groups will enhance the effect, but is not necessary. Mary remains standing throughout, looking into space ahead of her as if she is seeing the action behind her in "her mind's eye." If spots are used, a dim spot (blue) should always be on Mary, adding a full white or pink spot when she speaks. The lights should dim slowly after the characters finish so that they are off when the characters sit.

1   **MARY: My name is Mary. I am a simple girl, not used to speaking**
2   **in front of people. In my day, I wouldn't have even been**
3   **allowed to stand in front of you — much less speak to the**
4   **whole assembly. Women were not thought worthy. So, forgive**
5   **me for being a little shy.**
6   **I wanted to tell you about my son, Jesus.** *(Brightening up)*
7   **You know him, don't you! I can always tell by the smiles and**
8   **the glimmer in people's eyes when they know my son — and**
9   **you know him!** *(Looking down, the smile gone)* **Oh, but I can**
10   **also see some empty eyes out there. I do hope you get to know**
11   **him someday. He already loves you.**
12   **I wanted to come tonight to tell you all about my son's birth**
13   **— how he came to be born on this earth. Maybe it will help**
14   **you as you get ready to celebrate his birthday.**
15   **It began on a night like this. It was during the changing of**
16   **the seasons — when you are either too warm or too cold a**
17   **hundred times a day. I had just been promised to Joseph — we**
18   **had joined our hands as one before our families and before**
19   **our God, and that was almost the same thing as being married**
20   **in my day. I was saying my evening prayers alone in my room,**
21   **and I heard the wind blowing — it seemed to be blowing all**
22   **around me, but I wasn't cold. It was beside me. It was inside**
23   **my soul. And then I heard a voice ... Gabriel's voice ... "Hail,**
24   **O favored one, the Lord is with you." I was afraid, but I**
25   **listened as the angel told me that I was to be the mother of**
26   **God's child. How is that possible, since I am yet a virgin? But**
27   **he told me that with God, nothing is impossible. And I said:**
28   **"Let it be according to your word"** (Luke 1:28, 34, 37-38,
29   author's paraphrase).
30   **In those days there were no homes for unwed mothers. It**
31   **was death and family shame when a woman who was**
32   **unmarried found herself with child. Since I had been**
33   **promised to Joseph, the law said it was up to him whether I**
34   **was stoned to death or not. I knew Joseph would choose to**
35   **silently divorce me rather than to see me die. Joseph loved me,**

1   but he didn't believe my story about Gabriel at first. So I

2   knew I had to go. Sadly, I left to stay with my cousin Elizabeth

3   and her husband Zachariah. *(ZACHARIAH and ELIZABETH*

4   *walk in from Stage Left to Center Stage as MARY steps aside to*

5   *Upstage Right.)*

6   ZACHARIAH: I'm Zachariah. I'm one of the temple priests at

7   Jerusalem.

8   ELIZABETH: And I'm his wife.

9   ZACHARIAH: My good wife of many, many years.

10   ELIZABETH: A good wife in some ways maybe, but still I could

11   not give you a child. It was my greatest shame. In our land, it

12   is grounds for divorce.

13   ZACHARIAH: *(Condescendingly)* But we remained married. I was

14   happy with you.

15   ELIZABETH: Then came that special day when out of the

16   thousands of priests, the lot fell to you to lead the morning and

17   evening sacrifice.

18   ZACHARIAH: Only those born of Aaron are allowed to go into the

19   innermost court of the temple — right up to the curtains that

20   enclose the Holy of Holies — the place of the Ark of the

21   Covenant — the place where God's presence dwells. Some live

22   their whole lives never having the lot fall to them. I was

23   blessed. I was chosen.

24   ELIZABETH: Before he went to the temple, I asked him to pray

25   for us to have a child. It would be a miracle only God could

26   give. Zachariah said he wouldn't do it.

27   ZACHARIAH: I couldn't. I was chosen out of all the other priests

28   to pray for the sins of Israel. Morning and evening I was the

29   one who took the special sacrifice and prayed the special

30   prayers for all the people — not just for one couple. This was

31   not a time to be selfish.

32   ELIZABETH: But I had put it into his mind.

33   ZACHARIAH: As she said, it was in my mind. When I entered the

34   court, I prepared the lamb — without spot or blemish — as

35   the sacrifice for the whole nation. There was also a meal

1　　　offering and a drink offering. Then I lit the sweet-smelling
2　　　incense burners and prayed.
3　ELIZABETH: It's a frightening day for a priest's wife, let me tell
4　　　you. To be so close to the curtain — so close to the very spot
5　　　where God dwelt. God can be a dove, but he can also be a
6　　　blazing fire or an earthquake. For your husband to be
7　　　there — well, it's just a frightening day. Especially when you
8　　　put a selfish thought in his head. Oh, I wished I hadn't done
9　　　it. What would happen to all of us if God was displeased with
10　　　the chosen priest for the sacrifice? Oh, what if God got angry?
11　ZACHARIAH: I did think about it. And I must have prayed too,
12　　　for an angel appeared to me. Gabriel appeared to me. In the
13　　　stillness of that court, my mind had wandered from my holy
14　　　purpose and I thought about our childlessness. I thought
15　　　about what I shouldn't have been thinking about. My wife
16　　　may have planted the seed, but I let it grow. But Gabriel
17　　　wasn't angry with me. He spoke to me and told me that my
18　　　wife would bear me a son and that we would call him John —
19　　　and that he would have the Spirit of Elijah, making a path
20　　　ready for the coming of the Messiah to the world.
21　ELIZABETH: My husband is an educated man — a logical man —
22　　　with a wall full of theological diplomas. Only such a one as he
23　　　would argue with an angel. "That can't be," he said.
24　　　"Elizabeth is too old!"
25　ZACHARIAH: I have paid for my stupidity already.
26　ELIZABETH: "Elizabeth is too old." As if you were such a spring
27　　　chicken.
28　ZACHARIAH: The angel struck me silent — I couldn't say a word
29　　　until the baby was born.
30　ELIZABETH: Of course, what the angel said came to pass. And I
31　　　stayed inside — ashamed to have anyone see me lest they
32　　　think I was pretending or crazy or something. The worst thing
33　　　was I felt no movement inside. The child was still — I feared
34　　　dead within me. But then my cousin Mary came to see me, and
35　　　she too was with child. And when she came close to hug me,

1   my baby leapt up within me — he came to life — and oh, the
2   joy I felt. Only a mother can know such joy. I knew that the
3   angel's word was true. And my cousin was carrying the proof
4   — the King — the Messiah — the Lord come to earth that we
5   had been waiting for — for generations!
6 ZACHARIAH: Three months later when our child was born, my
7   tongue was loosed. I praised God and prophesied in his name
8   of the salvation, mercy, and forgiveness coming as a light in
9   our darkness through Mary's son that our own John would
10   prepare the way for.
11 ELIZABETH: And our children grew in the ways of God.
12   *(ELIZABETH and ZACHARIAH exit Stage Right and MARY*
13   *moves up to Center Stage again.)*
14 MARY: And I kept all these things in my heart, for I knew my child
15   would need to grow, learn, and discover and be loved by his
16   mother before that secret would be told. My son would bring
17   life to people. He would make them leap up. He would bring
18   the Light. He would lead the way to God. But first, a mother's
19   love. And I kept all these things in my heart.
20   Before John was born, Joseph sent for me. Gabriel had
21   come to him in a dream and told him to believe me — that
22   truly I was carrying God's own son. So, Joseph brought me
23   home and claimed me as his wife. He believed that the
24   prophecies were true — that a virgin did conceive, and would
25   bring forth God's own son, the Savior, the Messiah.
26   Just a little while before my time to deliver, we were told
27   that we had to return to our homeland. We were both from the
28   lineage of David, so we traveled to Bethlehem, the City of
29   David, to be counted. When we arrived, there was no place to
30   stay. All the inns and houses were full. Joseph begged for a
31   place for our baby to be born. Finally one innkeeper offered
32   his stable — carved in the side of a mountain. We gratefully
33   went there to have our child. *(HERDSMAN and SHEPHERD*
34   *enter from Stage Left and move to Center Stage as MARY again*
35   *steps back to Upstage Right.)*

1   HERDSMAN: As Zachariah and Elizabeth told you, there were
2   morning and evening sacrifices in the temple for the sins of Israel,
3   and that meant two perfect lambs had to be supplied to the priests
4   every day. The priests have their own private flocks near
5   Bethlehem, and we were the shepherds of the temple sheep.
6   SHEPHERD: The cool, gentle hills around Bethlehem and the still
7   waters and the green pastures — all these things made
8   Bethlehem the best place for keeping sheep — and of course,
9   the priests wanted only the best sheep to sacrifice to God.
10   HERDMAN: We were two of the shepherds there that night,
11   watching the temple sheep.
12   SHEPHERD: It was late, and we were gathered around the fire
13   trying to keep warm, and telling the stories we had told a
14   hundred times before.
15   HERDSMAN: Suddenly the whole sky opened up, and there was a
16   tremendous light that bathed us in its warmth and brilliance.
17   We were scared to death!
18   SHEPHERD: But an angel told us not to be afraid. God's Son had been
19   born — the Messiah — the Lord. And then a host of angels sang
20   about peace and good will all over the whole world.
21   HERDSMAN: It was odd — a paradox. The words "A Savior,
22   Christ the Lord" put alongside of the words "A babe wrapped
23   in swaddling cloths and lying in a manger." It seems
24   impossible. Was a manger the place for God? Were swaddling
25   rags the raiment of a King?
26   SHEPHERD: But we went — all of us went.
27   HERDSMAN: We left the sheep in God's care.
28   SHEPHERD: It would have cost us our jobs if the priests found
29   that out — no shepherd ever leaves his flocks!
30   HERDSMAN: But no shepherd ever heard and saw what we did —
31   and we left to see ... to see.
32   SHEPHERD: The only guide we had were those words: a baby born
33   this night, laid in a manger. The streets were so crowded with
34   people there for the census. How could we ever find the babe?
35   HERDSMAN: No one would speak to us. We were shepherds, and

1   that was the lowest class of people — the ones people poked

2   fun at and locked their doors against and protected their

3   daughters from.

4   SHEPHERD: But I figured we should start with the inns. After all,

5   with the town so bulging with people, the mother of God

6   would have begun there to find a place to have her baby.

7   Maybe one of the innkeepers would remember.

8   HERDSMAN: The very first inn we came to told us what we

9   wanted to know. A Nazarene couple had been there, and she

10   was nearly at her time. They were in the rocky stable. And we

11   ran there to see ... to see.

12   SHEPHERD: We saw Mary and Joseph and that babe, lying in the

13   manger. We gave thanks. We worshiped. We touched.

14   HERDSMAN: And we told them all that we had seen and heard —

15   the great light, the angels, the song. Then we left, telling

16   everyone we saw that we had seen the Son of God in a manger.

17   SHEPHERD: We had seen ... we saw!

18   HERDSMAN: And everyone wondered ...

19   SHEPHERD: Most thought us crazy.

20   HERDSMAN: Some thought us foolish.

21   SHEPHERD: A few wished we were telling the truth.

22   HERDSMAN: But no one really believed.

23   SHEPHERD: After all, we were only shepherds. *(HERDSMAN and*

24   *SHEPHERD exit Stage Right as MARY steps forward again to*

25   *Center Stage.)*

26   MARY: How fitting that those who protected the lamb for the

27   temple sacrifice should be the first ones to see the Lamb of

28   God who takes away the sins of the world! My son came to the

29   rejected ones — to the outcasts — to those society passed by.

30   When these shepherds came in — so excited — so filled with

31   the wonder of my child, I was overcome with joy myself.

32   These were the people my son would love. These were the

33   people my son would save. These were the people who came to

34   see me on my day. A city full of people, and only these outcasts

35   cared enough to see. And this filled my heart, and I kept all

1	these things in my heart. They were precious.
2	We stayed in the stable about a month, and then found a
3	house. It was small, but Joseph was a carpenter, and he added
4	on a room for the baby and opened his carpentry business to
5	support us until we could return home to Nazareth. Some
6	people came to see us. The shepherds had told many people
7	about the angels' song. And later, they all heard about those
8	visitors from faraway lands who gave my son such wonderful
9	gifts. *(The three WISE MEN enter from Stage Left to Center Stage*
10	*as MARY steps back to Upstage Right.)*
11	MELCHIOR: My name is Melchior, one of the three you call the
12	wise men.
13	BALTHAZAR: Although brains were never really your long suit.
14	*(CASPAR laughs.)*
15	MELCHIOR: He's Balthazar ... the wise guy.
16	BALTHAZAR: *(Bowing)* Happy to meet you — and this is Caspar,
17	completing our famous little road show of Gentile wizards.
18	MELCHIOR: Balthazar, behave.
19	CASPAR: We are astronomers.
20	MELCHIOR: Astronomers read the skies and can make
21	prophecies about great world events based on what they see.
22	CASPAR: One night we saw a new star ...
23	BALTHAZAR: ... a bright star ...
24	MELCHIOR: ... more magnificent than any we had ever seen before.
25	CASPAR: Surely this star marked the birth of a king.
26	BALTHAZAR: Ah, but what king?
27	CASPAR: Where in the world was a king born that would so affect
28	the world that even the heavens would proclaim the glory of
29	his birth?
30	BALTHAZAR: We studied and argued and calculated and
31	argued ... oh, did we argue! But finally we agreed. A king was
32	born to the Jews.
33	MELCHIOR: But not just any king.
34	CASPAR: This was the King of kings.
35	BALTHAZAR: And we packed up our camels and set off to see

1   what all the hullabaloo was about.

2   MELCHIOR: Now, we are Gentiles.

3   BALTHAZAR: Not exactly on speaking terms with the Jews. You

4   know: "I wouldn't want my daughter to marry one ..."

5   CASPAR: Balthazar! Let's just say that racially they didn't get

6   along with us any more than we got along with them.

7   BALTHAZAR: OK. Let's just say that.

8   MELCHIOR: But we left — bringing valuables that we could

9   exchange for Jewish money to pay for lodging and food and such.

10 CASPAR: It was a long trip — it took us many months.

11 BALTHAZAR: It was two years if it was a day!

12 MELCHIOR: It was a very long trip, but we finally got there.

13 CASPAR: And we went to the capital city of the Jews to ask where

14   their king would be born.

15 MELCHIOR: The prophets said Bethlehem, and so that's where

16   we went, still following that star.

17 CASPAR: Herod the King wanted us to come back and tell him who

18   the king was so he could worship him too.

19 BALTHAZAR: He didn't want to worship him — he wanted to kill him.

20 MELCHIOR: But we didn't know that then.

21 BALTHAZAR: We learned that in a dream — that was really

22   something. The God of all creation talking to us — three star-

23   gazing migrants.

24 CASPAR: We're getting ahead of ourselves. First, we found the child.

25 MELCHIOR: They were living in a house in Bethlehem, not

26   wanting to return home to Nazareth until the baby was

27   weaned.

28 BALTHAZAR: We fell down.

29 CASPAR: We worshiped.

30 MELCHIOR: We joyously gave him the glory.

31 CASPAR: This was a King.

32 MELCHIOR: This was a Savior.

33 BALTHAZAR: This was God.

34 CASPAR: And I gave him gold — a gift for a king.

35 MELCHIOR: And I gave him frankincense — a gift for a priest.

1   BALTHAZAR: And I gave him myrrh — a gift for one who has to die.
2   MELCHIOR: And then we returned home.
3   BALTHAZAR: ... by another way. *(The three WISE MEN exit Stage*
4   *Right as MARY again steps forward to Center Stage.)*
5   MARY: When these three men came to our door, we were afraid.
6   We have all heard stories about "those kinds of people." But
7   when I saw their faces, I knew they had come from God ...
8   come assuring me that all that Gabriel had promised had
9   come true. And as the rejected from Israel were the first to
10   worship my son, the nations of the world that Israel had
11   rejected were the second to worship him. My son — secretly
12   born Savior to my people was to be worshiped by Jews and
13   Gentiles alike ... all the world! And I kept this joy in my heart.
14   *(If possible, the church choir can begin humming "O Come, All Ye*
15   *Faithful." MARY begins speaking halfway through verse.)*
16   MARY: This is the story of my son's birth. He has come for you.
17   Now everyone can know, and so therefore, I no longer need to
18   keep this just in my heart. Now you too can be filled with the
19   knowledge and the promise and the love in your hearts. Oh
20   come let us adore him!
21
22   CHOIR *(sings chorus to "O Come, All Ye Faithful.")*
23   O come, let us adore him,
24   O come, let us adore him,
25   O come, let us adore him,
26   Christ, the Lord!
27   *(After the verse ends, the choir director indicates that the entire*
28   *congregation should join in for the remaining verses. During the*
29   *congregational singing, MARY and all of the other ACTORS leave*
30   *the stage and, in procession, walk back down the aisle and leave*
31   *the sanctuary.)*

The Twelve Months of Christmas

By Joanne Owens

A church-fellowship supper script
for the Epiphany Season.

Cast of Characters

3 men, 3 women, 4 optional
12 children, singers (any number)

Reader I	**February's Child**
Reader II	**March's Child**
Reader III	**April's Child**
TV Reporter	**May's Child**
Wise Person #1 (a man)	**June's Child**
Wise Person #2 (a woman)	**July's Child**
Wise Person #3 (a man)	**August's Child**
First Woman	**September's Child**
First Man	**October's Child**
Second Woman	**November's Child**
January's Child	**December's Child**

Production Notes

This program could be performed at a church fellowship supper sometime during the Twelve Days of Christmas (December 25-January 6).

Table decorations should include centerpieces representative of all seasons of the year, for example: Valentine's Day, St. Patrick's Day, Easter, July Fourth, Halloween, Thanksgiving, Christmas, etc. It would be effective to use paper plates, cups, and napkins that carry out the theme of the various holidays. Perhaps each table could be decorated to represent a different holiday.

No props are necessary, but the TV Reporter might want to carry a microphone, and the Wise Persons could carry attaché cases.

Musical accompaniment for the tune to "The Twelve Days of Christmas" may be downloaded free of charge from Sheet Music USA at http://www.sheetmusicusa.com/piano/christmas.htm. Note that there are four pages to the song, and each one is in a separate file.

Costumes

Readers, TV Reporter, Wise Persons, Women, and Man wear appropriate street clothes.

The twelve children of the month wear costumes representative of each month. Each child has a wide ribbon across his or her chest with the name of his/her month printed on it in bold letters.

Choose from among the following suggestions, or substitute other appropriate costumes.

January: 1. Snowman costume, 2. Father Time, 3. Baby New Year.
February: 1. Valentine box worn over red leotards and tights, 2. George Washington, 3. Abraham Lincoln.
March: 1. St. Patrick's costume; 2. Irish leprechaun; 3. A box decorated with shamrocks, worn over green tights.
April: 1. A giant Easter egg cut from two pieces of poster board and hung over the child's shoulders in sign fashion; 2. Easter bunny costume; 3. Dressy Easter Sunday outfit, complete with bonnet and Easter basket.
May: 1. Large colorful flowers cut from poster board and worn over the shoulders in sign fashion; 2. A May queen costume, complete with flowers in the hair and basket.
June: 1. A baseball uniform, 2. A wedding gown.
July: 1. Uncle Sam; 2. A red, white, and blue outfit of any kind, worn with an American flag held by the child.
August: 1. Picnic clothes worn by a child carrying an ice chest and picnic basket; 2. Beach clothes, with a large towel and beach ball.

September: 1. A football uniform; 2. A cheerleader uniform.

October: 1. A red, gold, or yellow fall leaf cut from two pieces of poster board and hung over the child's shoulders in sign fashion, 2. A Halloween costume of any kind, 3. A box decorated like a pumpkin and worn over orange tights.

November: 1. A pilgrim costume, 2. An Indian costume.

December: 1. Santa Claus, 2. Gaily-decorated Christmas gift box worn over red or green tights.

CHRISTMAS ALL YEAR LONG

Words & Music by JOANNE OWENS

Christ-mas is more than the crowds in the store. — It's not just a big shop-ping spree. — Christ-mas is more than a fes-tive de-cor. — It's not just a wreath and a tree. — Christ-mas is be-ing to-ge-ther; Christ-mas is fam-i-ly and friends; Christ-mas is lov-ing each ot-her, And

good will that nev-er ends. Christ-mas is more than the par-ties and food. — It's more than the gifts and the toys. — Giv-ing to ot-hers and do-ing some good. — It's shar-ing your love and your joys. Re-mem-ber the rea-son for Christ-mas.—Christ Je-sus has come for each

1	*(READERS I, II and III enter and stand at Stage Left.)*
2	**READER I:** Tonight you will hear a story that has two endings.
3	Listen carefully, for *you* must choose the outcome. *You* will
4	decide how this story ends. You already know the beginning of
5	the story, so I won't repeat it in detail. It's the one about the
6	three wise men who followed the star, seeking the promised
7	Messiah.
8	**READER II:** The Bible doesn't tell us exactly when the Magi
9	arrived to bring their gifts to the Christ child, but tradition
10	says the wise men found the baby Jesus twelve days after
11	Christmas. For centuries, the church has celebrated this
12	event, calling it by various names, including "Epiphany,"
13	"Twelfth Night," "Day of the Kings," and "Little Christmas."
14	**READER III:** But there's another story. It says that after almost
15	two thousand years, wise men again came seeking the Christ
16	child. Highly respected individuals appeared shortly after
17	Christmas in search of Jesus. They weren't kings or
18	astronomers, but they were very prestigious members of
19	society — the experts — the authorities — the super-
20	achievers. As you might guess, these modern-day sages were
21	not just the wise *men,* but they were wise *persons. (The THREE*
22	*WISE PERSONS enter and stand at Stage Right.)*
23	**READER I:** Naturally, as soon as the wise persons' mission was
24	made public, TV news reporters followed their every move.
25	*(TV REPORTER enters and approaches WISE PERSON #1.)*
26	**TV REPORTER:** Pardon me. I understand you're a wise person.
27	Would you please answer a few questions for our television
28	audience? Tell us something about yourself and your
29	background.
30	**WISE PERSON #1:** Of course. I'm a computer scientist. I have an
31	undergraduate degree from Yale, an M.B.A. from Harvard,
32	and a PhD. in computer technology from M.I.T. In my latest
33	project, I used the computer to devise a system to analyze
34	trends in the stock market, and I can now accurately predict
35	the market's actions every day. I am also an astronaut. In my

1   spare time, I am a neurosurgeon.

2 TV REPORTER: Do you have any hobbies?

3 WISE PERSON #1: Yes, for relaxation, I am a Country and
4   Western singer. This past year, I was named to the Country
5   Music Hall of Fame.

6 TV REPORTER: Thank you, sir. Now, let's talk to this very
7   attractive lady. *(To WISE PERSON #2)* Tell us please, what is
8   your profession?

9 WISE PERSON #2: I'm a psychoanalyst with a thriving practice in
10   New York City. I'm also the host of a television talk show that
11   is carried on all three major networks, as well as PBS. I write
12   a nationally syndicated advice column and over a dozen of my
13   books have made the *New York Times* Bestseller List. In my
14   spare time, I am a concert pianist and an Olympic gold medal-
15   winner in figure skating.

16 TV REPORTER: Could you tell us the accomplishment of which
17   you are the proudest?

18 WISE PERSON #2: Well, let's see — there are so many, but I
19   suppose it was when I was selected Miss Universe.

20 TV REPORTER: Now, let's hear from our third visitor. *(To WISE
21   PERSON #3)* Tell us about yourself, sir.

22 WISE PERSON #3: I've always been interested in politics. I've
23   been Secretary of State, Secretary of Defense, and Secretary of
24   the Treasury. I'm a professor of international studies at
25   UCLA, and I'm a member of the President's think tank. I've
26   also been a United States Senator and an Ambassador to three
27   foreign countries. I have been a personal advisor to five
28   presidents. From time to time, I'm a guest soloist with the
29   Metropolitan Opera.

30 TV REPORTER: And how do you spend your leisure hours?

31 WISE PERSON #3: I'm a halfback for the New York Giants
32   football team.

33 TV REPORTER: I understand you three have been involved in a
34   significant search in recent days. I'm told you are looking for
35   the Christ child. Have you been successful in your search?

1 WISE PERSON #1: No, I'm afraid not. No one seems to want to
2   talk to us. *(FIRST WOMAN enters.)* But wait, here comes
3   someone we haven't asked. *(Approaches FIRST WOMAN.)*
4   Pardon me, I'm looking for —
5 FIRST WOMAN: Whatever it is, I can't help you. I don't live here.
6   I've just come to town for a doctor's appointment.
7 WISE PERSON #1: I don't think you understand. I only wanted
8   to —
9 FIRST WOMAN: Listen, I can't talk now. You wouldn't believe
10   how exhausted I am. Every year about this time, I come down
11   with post-Christmas trauma. The holidays are more than I
12   can take. All the parties wear me out, and the shopping and
13   cooking are absolutely too much! Just decorating my house
14   makes my back go out of joint. Christmas is a real pain — the
15   whole thing is completely draining. It'll take me all year to
16   recover from being around my relatives so much during the
17   holidays. All that togetherness makes me a nervous wreck. On
18   top of that, I've spent two miserable days exchanging tacky
19   and ill-fitted gifts. I'm too tired to talk about anything. I'm
20   pooped! *(FIRST WOMAN exits. FIRST MAN enters.)*
21 WISE PERSON #2: Let me try this one. *(Approaches FIRST MAN.)*
22   Sir, could I talk to you about Jesus Christ?
23 FIRST MAN: Oh, no. You must be one of those religious fanatics.
24   Well, don't try to buttonhole me. You probably want a
25   donation, and I'll tell you right now, I can't give you a dime.
26   Christmas has left me so deep in debt, it'll take me all year to
27   become solvent again. My wife gets her hands on the credit
28   card and can't stop spending. The gift-giving is completely out
29   of hand. The kids think they have to buy presents for every
30   teacher and half the students in school. My wife gives
31   something to the mail carrier, the garbage collector, her hair
32   dresser, and anyone else she comes across. And those
33   teenagers of ours — they have to have stereos, computers,
34   skis, and exercise equipment that cost a fortune. Whatever
35   happened to candy canes and oranges? I can't stand all this

1 spending. It'll put me in the poorhouse for sure. A few more
2 Christmases like this one, and I'll be bankrupt. *(FIRST MAN
3 exits.)*
4 WISE PERSON #3: You two aren't making a bit of progress
5   toward finding the Christ child. Let me try. *(SECOND
6   WOMAN enters. WISE PERSON #3 approaches SECOND
7   WOMAN.)* Hello, may I ask a question, please? My friends and
8   I are from out of town, and we are looking for the Christ child.
9   Could you help us?
10 SECOND WOMAN: The Christ child? What's that — one of those
11   religious rock groups? No, I can't help you. I'm not into that
12   sort of thing. And besides, I'm in a hurry to get to the weight
13   loss clinic. I put on fifteen pounds during the holidays, and I
14   simply must do something about it. Oh, but the food was so
15   good! We had cakes, pies, cookies, candy — the works. I ate
16   until I was miserable. Of course, we had turkey and all the
17   trimmings, and ham, too. The homemade bread and
18   casseroles were delicious, but now I can't get into my clothes.
19   I go to this weight loss clinic every year about this time. I
20   figure it's as economical as checking into a spa for a couple of
21   weeks. If I stick to the diet and buy the special supplement
22   that comes with the plan, it costs me about thirty dollars per
23   pound that I lose. That's only four-hundred fifty dollars, so I
24   guess it's worth it. It just wouldn't be Christmas if we weren't
25   gluttons. *(SECOND WOMAN exits.)*
26 READER II: And so the wise persons searched for the Christ child
27   for twelve days with no success. Finally, they gave up. *(Exit
28   WISE PERSONS and TV REPORTER.)*
29 READER III: Do you like that story? Here's another version that
30   you might like better.
31 READER I: Once upon a time there were some people who were
32   truly wise. They looked for the Christ child not only during
33   the twelve days after Christmas, but all year long. For twelve
34   months, they sought to see Jesus. *(JANUARY'S CHILD enters.)*
35 JANUARY'S CHILD: January is a cold month. But the warmth of

1   friendship and love can be felt anytime.

2   READER II: In January, some of these wise persons got to know

3   their neighbors. These people were helpful to each other in a

4   number of ways. They shared Christian concern for one

5   another's problems, and they all took time to show that they

6   cared. They found the love of Christ in the love of good

7   neighbors. *(FEBRUARY'S CHILD enters.)*

8   FEBRUARY'S CHILD: February is the month of valentines and

9   president's birthdays.

10   READER III: February was special for wise persons who found

11   Jesus at Sunday school. Through the well-prepared lessons of

12   a dedicated teacher and the warm love of other class

13   members, they came to know what it means for Christ to be

14   among his people. *(MARCH'S CHILD enters.)*

15   MARCH'S CHILD: The month of March brings St. Patrick's Day

16   and windy weather.

17   READER I: In March, wise persons experienced the presence of

18   Christ in their daily work. They realized that they could serve

19   God by making their own unique contributions to the

20   betterment of the world by carrying out their personal tasks

21   to the best of their abilities. *(APRIL'S CHILD enters.)*

22   APRIL'S CHILD: April brings showers, the Easter bunny, colored

23   eggs, and the celebration of Christ's resurrection.

24   READER II: In April, wise persons shared generously by

25   contributing their time, talents, and tithes to their churches.

26   They came to know the true meaning of the words, "It is

27   better to give than to receive." *(MAY'S CHILD enters.)*

28   MAY'S CHILD: May reminds us of maypoles, baskets of flowers,

29   and springtime.

30   READER III: Wise persons found the Christ child in May as they

31   practiced the power of prayer. As they spoke to God and

32   allowed him to speak to them, they learned that prayer really

33   does change things. *(JUNE'S CHILD enters.)*

34   JUNE'S CHILD: When June arrives, there are baseball games,

35   weddings and no school.

1 READER I: It was a beautiful evening in June when wise persons
2 felt especially close to God watching a magnificent sunset. The
3 glories of the creation made them aware of God's power and
4 love. *(JULY'S CHILD enters.)*
5 JULY'S CHILD: We usually feel patriotic in July when we
6 celebrate Independence Day.
7 READER II: During a Sunday morning worship service in July,
8 wise persons felt the presence of Christ in their lives as they
9 listened to an inspiring and thought-provoking sermon.
10 *(AUGUST'S CHILD enters.)*
11 AUGUST'S CHILD: August is the time for picnics and vacations.
12 READER III: In August, wise persons were brought closer to
13 Christ through serious, diligent Bible study. They learned that
14 Bible study, although never easy, is richly rewarding.
15 *(SEPTEMBER'S CHILD enters.)*
16 SEPTEMBER'S CHILD: In September, school starts, and there
17 are exciting football games.
18 READER I: The joys and growth that come with Christian
19 fellowship were very real to wise persons in September. They
20 saw Christ in the lives of fellow Christians as they participated
21 in various wholesome activities. *(OCTOBER'S CHILD enters.)*
22 OCTOBER'S CHILD: Clear, crisp days come in October. Jack-o-
23 lanterns *(or pumpkins)* are everywhere during the Halloween
24 *(or Autumn)* season.
25 READER II: October brought a new sense of family solidarity to
26 wise persons. They were keenly aware of God's plan for his
27 people to live together in loving families and to come to know
28 his love through those who love one another. *(NOVEMBER'S*
29 *CHILD enters.)*
30 NOVEMBER'S CHILD: Pilgrims, Indians, turkeys, Thanksgiving
31 — all these remind us of November.
32 READER III: In November, wise persons felt Christ's presence as
33 they listened to a beautiful anthem sung by the church choir.
34 Worshiping God through music brought the wise persons closer to
35 Christ. *(DECEMBER'S CHILD enters.)*

1 DECEMBER'S CHILD: December brings holiday decorations,
2 Santa Claus, and familiar carols, as we celebrate the birth of Jesus.
3 READER I: In December, wise persons helped a stranger. They told
4 no one of their good deed, and there was no visible reward for their
5 service. In helping someone in need, the wise persons felt the true
6 spirit of Christmas, and they knew the meaning of the word
7 *Immanuel* — "God with us."
8
9 SONG: "The Twelve Months of Christmas"
10 *(Sung to the tune of "The Twelve Days of Christmas.")*
11   In the first month of Christmas,
12   The Christ child came to me
13   In a friend who was neighborly.
14
15   In the second month of Christmas,
16   The Christ child came to me
17   At Sunday school,
18   And in a friend who was neighborly.
19
20   In the third month of Christmas,
21   The Christ child came to me
22   At Sunday school, While I worked,
23   And in a friend who was neighborly.
24
25   In the fourth month of Christmas,
26   The Christ child came to me
27   While I worked, When I shared,
28   At Sunday school,
29   And in a friend who was neighborly.
30
31   In the fifth month of Christmas,
32   The Christ child came to me
33   As I prayed,
34   While I worked, When I shared,
35   At Sunday school,

1	And in a friend who was neighborly.
2	
3	In the sixth month of Christmas,
4	The Christ child came to me
5	While I watched the sunset,
6	As I prayed,
7	While I worked, When I shared,
8	At Sunday school,
9	And in a friend who was neighborly.
10	
11	In the seventh month of Christmas,
12	The Christ child came to me
13	In the preacher's sermon,
14	While I watched the sunset,
15	As I prayed,
16	While I worked, When I shared,
17	At Sunday school,
18	And in a friend who was neighborly.
19	
20	In the eighth month of Christmas,
21	The Christ child came to me
22	When I read the Bible,
23	In the preacher's sermon,
24	While I watched the sunset,
25	As I prayed,
26	While I worked, When I shared,
27	At Sunday school,
28	And in a friend who was neighborly.
29	
30	In the ninth month of Christmas,
31	The Christ child came to me
32	In Christian fellowship,
33	When I read the Bible,
34	In the preacher's sermon,
35	While I watched the sunset,

1	As I prayed,
2	While I worked, When I shared,
3	At Sunday school,
4	And in a friend who was neighborly.
5	
6	In the tenth month of Christmas,
7	The Christ child came to me
8	Through a loving family,
9	In Christian fellowship,
10	When I read the Bible,
11	In the preacher's sermon,
12	While I watched the sunset,
13	As I prayed,
14	While I worked, When I shared,
15	At Sunday school,
16	And in a friend who was neighborly.
17	
18	In the eleventh month of Christmas,
19	The Christ child came to me
20	In the choir's anthem,
21	Through a loving family,
22	In Christian fellowship,
23	When I read the Bible,
24	In the preacher's sermon,
25	While I watched the sunset,
26	As I prayed,
27	While I worked, When I shared,
28	At Sunday school,
29	And in a friend who was neighborly.
30	
31	In the twelfth month of Christmas,
32	The Christ child came to me
33	When I helped a stranger,
34	In the choir's anthem,
35	Through a loving family,

1	In Christian fellowship,
2	When I read the Bible,
3	In the preacher's sermon,
4	While I watched the sunset,
5	As I prayed,
6	While I worked, When I shared,
7	At Sunday school,
8	And in a friend who was neighborly.
9	
10	READER I: Immanuel — God is with us — all year long. The wise
11	persons in this version of the story experienced the real meaning of
12	Christmas. They knew what it meant for God to dwell among his
13	people. The Christ child was not hidden from them. He was among
14	them not only during the Christmas season, but throughout the year.
15	Which version of the story do you choose? Will the Christ child be
16	hidden from you, or will you have Christmas all year long? Only *you*
17	can decide.
18	
19	SONG: "Christmas All Year Long" *(Solo or group)*
20	Christmas is more than the crowds in the store.
21	It's not just a big shopping spree.
22	Christmas is more than a festive décor;
23	It's not just a wreath and a tree.
24	Christmas is being together;
25	Christmas is family and friends;
26	Christmas is loving each other, and good will that never ends.
27	
28	Christmas is more than the parties and food.
29	It's more than the gifts and the toys.
30	Giving to others and doing some good.
31	It's sharing your love and your joys,
32	Remember the reason for Christmas.
33	Christ Jesus has come for each one.
34	Our Savior is here now among us,
35	The Father's only Son.

1   Immanuel means God is with us,
2   So we'll worship in prayer and in song.
3   With Christ in our hearts and God's love in our lives,
4   We'll have Christmas all year long.

.

About the Playwrights

Brian Bopp (*Christmas Kingdom*) currently resides with his family in scenic Urbandale, Iowa, where he serves as a full-time children's pastor. Rev. Bopp has been involved in dramatic ministry in every aspect, including acting, singing, producing on a shoestring budget, set construction, and writing, with several published dinner theatre plays to his credit. He continues to believe that theatre is one of the most powerful tools there is for truth-telling.

Myrtle Forsten (*Little Fir's Vision*), a retired teacher, lives in Holland, Michigan. She has taught in both Christian and public schools at every level from preschool to high school, but mainly elementary. She has written and directed programs and plays in schools, churches, camps, nursing homes, et al. She also taught workshops for children and adults on how to make and use puppets and developing their talents. She has two daughters and seven grandchildren, some of whom assisted her in Christian programs in the area. She still enjoys creative writing.

Karyl Jane Garner (*Christmas Around the World*) wrote her script in response to a request to direct the annual children's Christmas pageant at her church. She was intrigued with the different rites and traditions celebrating the birth of Jesus and combined these international cultural celebrations with traditional scenes in appropriate age-related roles. Karyl is a registered nurse who has given drug abuse education presentations for elementary school children. She and her husband Bill have two children and four grandchildren.

Kenneth L. Gibble (*Heavenly Committee Plans Christmas*), in his nearly forty years as a pastor, attended more committee meetings than he cares to remember. He lives in Greencastle, Pennsylvania, where he gardens, teaches, and writes poetry.

Lia Goens (*My Son, the Messiah*) is Director of Creative Worship Arts at Church of the Savior in Indianapolis, where she writes and directs drama and clown sketches for worship in addition to choreographing and performing liturgical movement. She facilitates workshops in spiritual journaling and creative worship and is the author of chancel drama and a book, *Praising God Through the Lively Arts*.

Douglas Grudzina [*Jesus Lives! (If We Give Him Half a Chance)*] is also the author of an Easter drama, *As We Survey the Wondrous Cross*, and a Christmas anthem, "Lullaby for Christmas." He is also the author of five novels (unpublished, but he remains ever optimistic). A retired high school English teacher, he writes and edits for Prestwick House, Inc., in Delaware where he lives with his wife Jane and two lovable but psychotic cats.

Pat Hall (*The Nutcracker Story*) spent many years working in puppet theatre, both amateur and professional, followed by several more years of being involved in community theatre, all in Wisconsin. In her retirement, she has mounted slow-moving "productions" with her garden plants — a process which is amazingly like setting a stage and casting a play.

Paul Neale Lessard (*Getting Ready for Christmas*) is a writer, teacher, and musician currently living in Grand Junction, Colorado. He is the author of a book of dramatic sketches, *Sermons Alive!* Paul has over twenty-five years of experience using the arts in worship in both the local church and large event settings. He is also the Director of the Western Colorado College of Adult and Graduate Studies for Colorado Christian University. He has been married to Rebecca for twenty-six years and they have two children.

315

Joanne Owens (*The Twelve Months of Christmas*) is a writer for a national farm magazine. Her past positions include Manager of the Gordon County Chamber of Commerce and Director of Program at her hometown church, Calhoun, Georgia's First United Methodist. She was named Writer of the Year by the North Georgia Writers Association, with a wide range of articles, curriculum materials, and plays, as well as a book, *The Official Sunday School Teachers' Handbook*, to her credit. She has three grown children.

Nancy Amondson-Pitts (*Creatures Christmas*) is currently serving as a missionary in Kenya. She teaches religion at Africa Nazarene University near Nairobi, and also serves as the University's Alumni Association Coordinator. She and her husband Mark have five children. Her interests include spiritual formation, photography, journaling, and hearing people's stories.

Valarie L. Short (*Big Times Day*) — Information unavailable.

Jon McCauley Smith (*Kept in Her Heart*), an ordained minister in the Christian Church (Disciples of Christ), has served as pastor of eight churches and is currently the pastor of First Christian Church in Palo Alto, California. He holds a doctorate degree in Church Revitalization. He is the author of several published plays. His other involvements include ministry to those living with HIV/AIDS, the mentally or physically challenged, the imprisoned, and those dealing with grief. He has four children.

Michael C. Vigilant (*The Story of "Silent Night"*) and his writing partner Gerald Castle have provided lyrics and music for several Contemporary Drama Service works including *Phantom of the Op'ry*, *Greecers*, *The Little Star*, *Befana*, and *Would You Believe ... a Stable?* In total, Mike and Gerald have had approximately fifteen plays and musicals published and/or produced. Mike currently resides in Montgomery, Alabama, where he is the chief operating officer for the Alabama Shakespeare Festival and co-director of the University of Alabama's theatre management program. Mike and his wife, Sandra, have two daughters.

The late **Melvin R. "Mel" White** (*Christmas by Injunction, The Eyes of El Cristo, A Brief History of Christmas Customs, A Christmas Carol, The Fir Tree, Merry Christmas Plus Peace on Earth*) served in the Navy during World War II. He taught at Brooklyn College, the City University of New York for forty-two years, and at several other universities upon "retirement." A lecturer and joke-teller, he appeared in a variety of international locales, from Tokyo to Spain. He also conducted Readers Theatre workshops and directed plays worldwide. Dr. White had seventeen books and 107 plays published.

Daniel Wray (*O Little Town of Bennington*) works in special education administration for the Douglas County (Colorado) School District. He is also an adjunct professor at the University of Colorado at Colorado Springs. He has written two published books of drama (*Service with a Smile* and *More Service with a Smile*), nine plays, an entry in *Chicken Soup for the Soul: Children with Special Needs*, and is co-author of a software program for vocational choice-making. As always, he's run ragged by his teenage daughter and her three energetic brothers.

Arthur L. Zapel (*And the Child Was Born, Here We Come A-Caroling, A Pageant of Love*) has had a lifetime career as a writer/editor of plays, documentaries, and advertising for radio, TV, and film. Fine art painting became the passion of his senior years. His oil paintings are sold in galleries and are exhibited at major art shows in the West. He lives and works in Colorado Springs and Westcliffe, Colorado.

Scripture Permissions

Many of these plays contain quotations from various versions of the Bible. Following is a listing of the *predominant* version used in these scripts. We gratefully acknowledge the following publishers for the use of their respective Scripture versions.

New International Version — *Getting Ready for Christmas, Little Fir's Vision, Christmas Kingdom*
Scripture taken from the HOLY BIBLE, NEW INTERNATIONAL VERSION ®. Copyright © 1973, 1978, 1984 by International Bible Society. Used by permission of Zondervan Publishing House. All rights reserved.
The "NIV" and "New International Version" trademarks are registered in the United States Patent and trademark Office by International Bible Society. Use of either trademark requires the permission of International Bible Society.

Revised Standard Version — *Here We Come A-Caroling*
All Scripture quotations are from the Revised Standard Version, copyright © 1971 by the Division of Christian Education of the National Council of Churches of Christ in the USA. Used by permission.

Today's English Version — *A Pageant of Love*
All Scripture is taken from the Today's English Version — Second Edition Copyright © 1992 by American Bible Society. Used by Permission.

King James Version — *Christmas Around the World, Big Times Day, And the Child Was Born*

Author's Paraphrase — *Jesus Lives! (If We Give Him Half a Chance), Kept in Her Heart*

Order Form

Meriwether Publishing Ltd.
PO Box 7710
Colorado Springs, CO 80933-7710
Phone: 800-937-5297 Fax: 719-594-9916
Website: www.meriwether.com

Please send me the following books:

_____ **More Christmas on Stage #BK-B294**   **$19.95**
           edited by Rhonda Wray
           An anthology of royalty-free Christmas plays

_____ **Christmas on Stage #BK-B153**   **$17.95**
           edited by Theodore O. Zapel
           An anthology of Christmas plays for all ages

_____ **The Drama of Easter #BK-B235**   **$17.95**
           edited by Rhonda Wray
           An anthology of royalty-free Easter plays for all ages

_____ **Costuming the Christmas and Easter Play $12.95**
           #BK-B180
           by Alice M. Staeheli
           How to costume any religious play

_____ **The Human Video Handbook #BK-B289 $15.95**
           by Kimberlee R. Mendoza
           Christian outreach in dramatic movement and music

_____ **Acting Up in Church #BK-B282**   **$15.95**
           by M.K. Boyle
           Humorous sketches for worship services

_____ **'Twas the Night Before #BK-B143**   **$14.95**
           by Rachel Olson and Arthur L. Zapel
           A Christmas picture book for children

**These and other fine Meriwether Publishing books are available at
your local bookstore or direct from the publisher. Prices subject to
change without notice. Check our website or call for current prices.**

Name: _____ e-mail: _____

Organization name: _____

Address: _____

City: _____ State: _____

Zip: _____ Phone: _____

❑ **Check enclosed**

❑ **Visa / MasterCard / Discover / Am. Express #** _____

                                          Expiration
Signature: _____ date: _____ / _____
           (required for credit card orders)

Colorado residents: Please add 3% sales tax.
Shipping: Include $3.95 for the first book and 75¢ for each additional book ordered.

❑ *Please send me a copy of your complete catalog of books and plays.*

Order Form

Meriwether Publishing Ltd.
PO Box 7710
Colorado Springs, CO 80933-7710
Phone: 800-937-5297 Fax: 719-594-9916
Website: www.meriwether.com

Please send me the following books:

_____ **More Christmas on Stage** **#BK-B294**   **$19.95**
edited by **Rhonda Wray**
An anthology of royalty-free Christmas plays

_____ **Christmas on Stage** **#BK-B153**   **$17.95**
edited by **Theodore O. Zapel**
An anthology of Christmas plays for all ages

_____ **The Drama of Easter** **#BK-B235**   **$17.95**
edited by **Rhonda Wray**
An anthology of royalty-free Easter plays for all ages

_____ **Costuming the Christmas and Easter Play**   **$12.95**
#BK-B180
by **Alice M. Staeheli**
How to costume any religious play

_____ **The Human Video Handbook** **#BK-B289**   **$15.95**
by **Kimberlee R. Mendoza**
Christian outreach in dramatic movement and music

_____ **Acting Up in Church** **#BK-B282**   **$15.95**
by **M.K. Boyle**
Humorous sketches for worship services

_____ **'Twas the Night Before** **#BK-B143**   **$14.95**
by **Rachel Olson and Arthur L. Zapel**
A Christmas picture book for children

**These and other fine Meriwether Publishing books are available at
your local bookstore or direct from the publisher. Prices subject to
change without notice. Check our website or call for current prices.**

Name: _____ e-mail: _____

Organization name: _____

Address: _____

City: _____ State: _____

Zip: _____ Phone: _____

❑ **Check enclosed**

❑ **Visa / MasterCard / Discover / Am. Express #** _____

Expiration
Signature: _____ date: _____ / _____
(required for credit card orders)

Colorado residents: Please add 3% sales tax.
Shipping: Include $3.95 for the first book and 75¢ for each additional book ordered.

❑ *Please send me a copy of your complete catalog of books and plays.*

Printed in the United States
221607BV00001B/1/P